PUBLIC THEOLOGY
in the POST-SECULAR AGE

PUBLIC THEOLOGY
in the POST-SECULAR AGE

Lessons Learned from Manchester Cathedral

DOMINIC BUDHI-THORNTON

☙PICKWICK *Publications* • Eugene, Oregon

PUBLIC THEOLOGY IN THE POST-SECULAR AGE
Lessons Learned from Manchester Cathedral

Copyright © 2025 Dominic Budhi-Thornton. All rights reserved. Except for brief quotations in critical publications or reviews, no part of this book may be reproduced in any manner without prior written permission from the publisher. Write: Permissions, Wipf and Stock Publishers, 199 W. 8th Ave., Suite 3, Eugene, OR 97401.

Pickwick Publications
An Imprint of Wipf and Stock Publishers
199 W. 8th Ave., Suite 3
Eugene, OR 97401

www.wipfandstock.com

PAPERBACK ISBN: 979-8-3852-1889-9
HARDCOVER ISBN: 979-8-3852-1890-5
EBOOK ISBN: 979-8-3852-1891-2

Cataloguing-in-Publication data:

Names: Budhi-Thornton, Dominic, author.

Title: Public theology in the post-secular age : lessons learned from Manchester cathedral / Dominic Budhi-Thornton.

Description: Eugene, OR : Pickwick Publications, 2025 | Includes bibliographical references.

Identifiers: ISBN 979-8-3852-1889-9 (paperback) | ISBN 979-8-3852-1890-5 (hardcover) | ISBN 979-8-3852-1891-2 (ebook)

Subjects: LCSH: Public theology. | Political theology. | Postsecularism. | Liberalism (Religion). | Manchester Cathedral (England)—History.

Classification: BT83.63 .B83 2025 (paperback) | BT83.63 (ebook)

VERSION NUMBER 072925

This book is dedicated to the clergy, staff, and congregation at Manchester Cathedral, who continue to encourage and inspire me with their dedication to inclusion and justice.

CONTENTS

Acknowledgments | xi
List of Abbreviations | xiii
Introduction | xv

1 THREE APPROACHES TO RELIGION
  IN THE PUBLIC SPHERE | 1
  Religion and Public Reason: A Diversity of Approaches | 2
  The Rawlsian Approach to Religion in the Public Sphere | 3
  The Habermasian Approach to Religion in the Public Sphere | 7
  The Ricoeurian Approach to Religion in the Public Sphere | 13
  Comparison of the Three Approaches | 17
  Conclusion | 20

2 APPROACHES TO PUBLICNESS IN THE FIELD
  OF PUBLIC THEOLOGY | 22
  The Publicness of Theology | 22
  "Bilingualism" in Public Theology | 26
  Approaches to Translation | 29
  The Post-Liberal Critique of Public Theology | 33
  Ricoeur Between Public Theology and Post-Liberalism | 37
  Whose Public Is It Anyway? | 41
  Other Forms of Publicness | 44
  Conclusion | 49

3 A THEOLOGY OF METHOD AND A METHOD
  OF PUBLIC THEOLOGY | 50
  A Pentecostal Walks into a Cathedral . . . | 50
  Publicness-Ethnographic Approach | 52
  Interrogating the Place and Role of the Researcher | 54
  Data Collection | 57

Data Analysis: Phenomenological Hermeneutics | 64
Conclusion: A Pentecostal Walks into a Cathedral . . . and Becomes an
  Anglican | 68

4 INTERRELIGIOUS DIALOGUE AT MANCHESTER
  CATHEDRAL | 69
  The Interreligious Character of Manchester Cathedral's Public
    Theology | 70
  Understanding the Public Theological Character of Manchester Cathedral's
    Interreligious Activity | 80
  The Limits of a Rawlsian Approach to Interreligious Dialogue and
    Activity | 86
  Scriptural Encounter and Scriptural Reasoning as One Outworking of a
    Ricoeurian Approach to Interreligious Dialogue | 93
  Diversity in Interreligious Engagement | 94
  Conclusion | 95

5 MANCHESTER CATHEDRAL'S PUBLIC THEOLOGY
  OF RACIAL JUSTICE | 97
  Racism and Society, the Church, and the Academy | 97
  Manchester Cathedral's Public Theology of Racial Justice | 104
  Evaluating Manchester Cathedral's Public Theology of Racial Justice | 112
  Conclusion | 122

6 MANCHESTER CATHEDRAL'S PUBLIC THEOLOGY
  OF LGBTQ+ INCLUSION | 123
  Manchester Cathedral's Approach to LGBTQ+ Inclusion | 124
  Critical Evaluation of Manchester Cathedral's Public Theology of LGBTQ+
    Inclusion | 136
  Hearing an Alternative Queer Word: A Queer Public Theological
    Transformation | 144
  Is a Queer Mother Church Possible in the Church of England? | 147
  Conclusion | 151

7 CRITICALLY EVALUATING MANCHESTER CATHEDRAL'S
  PUBLIC THEOLOGY: INCLUSION, IDENTITY, AND LINGUISTIC
  HOSPITALITY | 153
  The Rawlsian Character of Manchester Cathedral's Approach to
    Publicness | 153
  "We Want to Claim Our Humanity as Our First Religion": Human Flourishing and Common Humanity as Public Theological Categories at
    Manchester Cathedral | 155

Human Flourishing and Epistemological Challenges | 159
Between Exclusivists and Inclusivists | 165
Linguistic Hospitality: Between Exclusivism and Inclusivism | 168
The "Other" as Guest and Host | 170
Otherness and Formation: Challenges from the Three Areas of Public Activity | 173
Conclusion | 177

CONCLUSION | 178
Lessons Learned | 178
There are Multiple Approaches to Public Theology | 179
We Must Focus Not Only on What to Say, but How We Are Formed | 181
Theology Doesn't Just Need to Be Translated, It Needs to Be Decolonized | 182
A Final Word | 184

Bibliography | 185

ACKNOWLEDGMENTS

This project would not be possible without the support and kindness of numerous colleagues, friends, and family.

I am extremely grateful to Dean Rogers Govender and the chapter at Manchester Cathedral, who have demonstrated their values and hospitable character in the way they have opened themselves to me and this research. To all the interviewees, thank you for sharing your insights so openly and with enthusiasm.

I am so appreciative of my PhD supervisors, without whom this book would not have been imaginable. Thank you, Professor Peter Scott, Rev. Dr. David Holgate, and Dr. Wren Radford, for your enthusiasm, direction, and encouragement, which have been consistent throughout the entirety of this project.

A special mention to all of my friends and family without whom the completion of this project would not have been possible. In particular, to Jacob and Lauren: thank you for your consistent friendship, encouragement, and love. To Sam and Laura: thank you for always being there (and for the many meals!). To Becki, Stuart, Millie, George, and Ronnie: thank you for making us part of your family and for being a constant source of joy even in my lowest moments. To my Bridge Coffee family: thank you for fueling me with Americanos and laughter. Mum, Dad, Julie, and Dave: thank you for always believing in me.

Finally, to Anna, who, though pursuing their own PhD, has been cheering me along the whole way. Thank you for putting up with my ramblings, challenging me, loving me, and reminding me that I am more than my work. I will always be thankful to you.

LIST OF ABBREVIATIONS

AST	Anglican social theology
BAME	Black, Asian, and minority ethnic
BLM	Black Lives Matter
CHF	Challenging Hate Forum
CofE	Church of England
CMEAC	Committee for Minority Ethnic Anglican Concerns
COP26	Twenty-sixth meeting of the Conference of the Parties
FLTA	*From Lament to Action*
GS	General Synod
IJPT	*International Journal of Public Theology*
JAAR	*Journal of the American Academy of Religion*
LGBTQ+	Lesbian, gay, bisexual, transgender, queer (or questioning), and others
LLF	*Living in Love and Faith*
OFOP	Our Faith Our Planet
SJT	*Scottish Journal of Theology*
UKME/GMH	United Kingdom minority ethnic/global majority heritage

INTRODUCTION

I ARRIVED EARLY AT Manchester Cathedral to attend its six-hundredth anniversary celebration on May 5, 2022. Stewards were still setting up, adjusting flower arrangements, and making sure that the sound equipment was in full working order. I quickly found my seat and observed as numerous people filed in for the next thirty minutes or so. I had met some of the people who had come to celebrate the cathedral's anniversary previously at various events or forums, and others I was seeing for the first time. I listened to the trio of flute, violin, and, piano from Cheetham's School of Music which played through the chatter of the room. Filling in the seats were members of the civic authorities from the city. For example, in attendance were the high sheriff of Greater Manchester and the lord mayor of Manchester, both of whom provided greetings at the service.

I had been conducting my PhD research evaluating Manchester Cathedral's public theology since September 2019. Therefore, for the service I had been asked to briefly read a statement about the cathedral's public work from 1787 until the present day. Quickly flicking through the order of service I found the moment I was supposed to stand at the podium and read. I followed four greetings from representatives of different faiths. There were greetings from the Muslim community, the Hindu community, the Jewish community, and the Sikh community. When it was my turn to read, I walked to the podium and read the title of my segment: "From Thomas Clarkson's Anti-Slavery Address in 1787 to the Challenging Hate Forum: Learning with Others How to Live Christian Social Responsibility." It read:

> On 28 October 1787, Thomas Clarkson gave a speech to a packed audience in Manchester Cathedral, which included fifty Black Africans, that mobilized opposition to the transatlantic slave trade in the city for the first time. Since then, Manchester Cathedral has been active in learning how to work for social justice with people of other faiths and beliefs. The Challenging Hate

Forum convened and led by the dean has been at the forefront of this since 2007. We continue to hold regular events to understand the problems of human trafficking and slavery today. With people of other denominations and living faiths, Our Faith Our Planet works to raise awareness of climate change and teach carbon literacy. Two regular study groups, Scriptural Reasoning and Scriptural Encounter, meet to discuss topics and issues raised by the scriptures of faiths other than our own. Through partnerships with local universities and colleges, we host book launches and lectures, on topics ranging from affordable housing to whether humans can ever love robots. I am a University of Manchester doctoral student, currently in my third year of a collaborative PhD researching the public theology of the cathedral.

David Tracy argues that there are three publics that the public theologian must address. These are the church, the academy, and society.[1] The paragraph that I read at the service demonstrates in a snapshot Manchester Cathedral's public presence and engagement with all three of these publics. Not only that but the cathedral was also packed with members from all three of these areas. As demonstrated from the reading's opening line referencing the sermon given by Thomas Clarkson, Manchester Cathedral has historically played an important role in many significant moments of the city of Manchester's life.[2] But the public profile and impact of the cathedral in the present day have no doubt developed and transformed in significant ways due to the appointment and leadership of Dean Rogers Govender in 2006.

Govender was ordained as a priest in South Africa in 1986 and ministered during the apartheid struggles. What has remained consistent in Govender's ministry from that time until now is an active and energetic passion for justice, inclusion, and peace both within the church and outside of it. Govender is a Black South African with Asian Heritage, who was the first person of color to be appointed as a dean of an English Anglican Cathedral. Govender and his team have developed the cathedral's reputation for being inclusive, accessible, and welcoming to people of all faiths and

1. Tracy, *Analogical Imagination*, 6–8.

2. In 2021, *Manchester Cathedral: A History of the Collegiate Church and Cathedral, 1421 to the Present*, which was edited by Jeremy Gregory, was published. This volume takes a historical approach to many aspects of the cathedral's life including its public engagement. This book, in contrast, focuses only on the period since Dean Rogers Govender was appointed dean of the cathedral. In particular I focus on the activities and engagements of the cathedral from Sept. 2019 until May 2022, which is when I completed my data collection for the project. I reference events and statements from before this time, but there is a primary focus on events and activities that I attended and experienced firsthand.

none. The cathedral team considers the cathedral to be a spiritual hub in the heart of the city, attending to the spiritual needs of the city. This focus has led to the development of various networks with partners from different institutions and organizations who represent diverse worldviews, cultures, and traditions.

However, despite the important role that Manchester Cathedral plays in the region of Greater Manchester, there has not been an in-depth analysis of the public theology informing the cathedral's work in these areas. While the cathedral is active and present in its community, an in-depth theological appreciation of its public ministry has not yet been undertaken. This book is an undertaking in this necessary work.

KEY QUESTIONS AND CONCERNS

Elaine Graham defines public theology as:

> The study of the public relevance of religious thought and practice, normally within the Christian tradition. It is both an academic discipline and ecclesial discourse, in that it seeks to comment and critically reflect from a theological perspective on aspects of public life such as economics, politics, culture and media. Traditionally, public theology sees itself as rooted in religious traditions, but strongly in conversation with secular discourse and public institutions.[3]

While there are numerous definitions of this relatively recently developed field,[4] this definition captures the essence of what all public theologies have in common. Public theologians all agree that there is an inherent publicness within the Christian tradition, which is found most prominently

---

3. Graham, *Between Rock and Hard Place*, 19.

4. Kim states: "Public theology is the result of the growing need for theology to interact with the public issues of contemporary society" (Kim, "Editorial," 2). Similarly, Grey suggests, "Public theology is the quest to contribute to a civil society, particularly by exploring and engaging issues of moral, spiritual, social and philosophical concern in the public debate" ("Princess Theology," 14). But the dominant definition of public theology comes from Harold Breitenberg, where he argues: "Public theology is thus theologically informed public discourse about public issues, addressed to the church, synagogue, mosque, temple, or other religious body, as well as the larger public or publics, argued in ways that can be evaluated and judged by publicly available warrants and criteria. Similarly, a public theologian is someone who—from the perspective of a particular religion—analyses, discusses, or proposes solutions for issues, conditions, and questions that are of concern and import to those within his or her religious tradition, as well as to the general public, and does so in ways that can be understood and evaluated by, and to possibly be persuasive to, society at large" ("To Tell the Truth," 65).

in the impetus to work for justice, love, and the common good for all our neighbors. However, public theology, while recognizing the publicness of Christian theology generally, seeks to effectively operate within the challenges of the post-secular situation which characterizes the place of religion within contemporary Western societies. Post-secularity describes the present situation in which the church and wider society are caught between two experiences: secularism and the new visibility of religion.[5] For Jürgen Habermas, this does not mean the insignificance of religion, nor does it indicate the potential for religions to dominate the public sphere. Rather, the new visibility of religion requires a new understanding of the significance of religion within democratic societies.[6] As Graham reminds us, "The 'post' in 'post-secularity' does not mean 'not secular', but names the instability of the label secular".[7]

The complex, post-secular situation of religion within Western societies is one of the contexts in which religious public institutions like cathedrals are currently ministering. And it is within this post-secular situation that public theology finds its particular interest, as it seeks to explore theologically what role religion can play within society in an age where "God is one option among many."[8]

However, it is not simply post-secularity that Manchester Cathedral must navigate, but also the realities of pluralism. In many ways, public theology and philosophies of publicness seek to understand how diverse people groups can interact with one another constructively as citizens of democratic societies. In this context, "religion" and "secular" cannot be understood as stable categories that public theologians must navigate. Rather each of these contains within them countless worldviews and traditions. Thus, one of the key concerns of this project is not only about discerning how Manchester Cathedral can make religion relevant to a secular sphere, but how it fosters publicness in the context of diversity and pluralism.

---

5. Graham, *Between Rock and Hard Place*, 3.
6. Habermas, *Between Naturalism and Religion*, 5–8.
7. Graham, *Apologetics Without Apology*, 38.
8. Taylor, *Secular Age*, 2. In an article I explore how Manchester Cathedral's use of space for commercial activities embodies post-secularity and how it attempts to foster an open and inclusive posture that gives a sense of ownership to the diverse groups who enter its doors (Budhi-Thornton, "Harvey Nichols Fashion Shows").

FORMATION AND PRACTICE IN THE PUBLIC SPHERE

The majority of public theology is conducted with a view to what should be *said* in public and how that speech should be conducted. As a result, many of the models of public theology that are represented in the field are concerned with discourse and debate. However, in this book, while acknowledging the importance of discourse, seeks to understand not so much what should be *said* in the public sphere, but how we, both the religious and the nonreligious, are being shaped and formed as ethical beings in the public sphere.

Central to my analysis in this book is a seeking to understand how particular ethical visions are formed, and how to engage others in their different perspectives, which are often the result of complex formative influences, including religion. As a result, one of my key contributions to the field of public theology is to focus on the theme of formation and what implications this theme has regarding engaging the public sphere. This book challenges those of us seeking to be public to ask, "Who are we becoming, and how are we becoming it?"

I approach formation not only as something resulting from discourse but also from the practices of communities. Therefore, I am contributing to a minority approach within public theology that seeks to understand publicness as a practice. As I have argued above, public theology tends to produce and analyze written or spoken discourse about particular social issues to contribute to public debates. Thus, definitions of public theology often assume that the public sphere is primarily a space of debate about social issues. As a result, discourse becomes the primary mode through which those within the field understand the nature of public theology.

However, in this book, I develop a methodological approach which I term a "publicness-ethnographic approach." This approach combines the concerns and insights of public theology with some methodological practices and approaches of practical and ethnographic theology. This is because, as I shall demonstrate in this book, over the course of my participation in the life of Manchester Cathedral, I recognized that the cathedral's *practices* outside the realm of spoken or written discourse were as important, if not more important, for understanding its public theology. Therefore, even just by the nature of my methodological approach, I am resisting primary understandings of publicness in the field of public theology. I am thus in agreement with Judith Butler, who notes:

> It matters that bodies assemble.... Embodied actions of various kinds signify in ways that are, strictly speaking, neither discursive nor prediscursive. In other words, forms of assembly already signify prior to, and apart from, any particular demands

they make. Silent gatherings, including vigils or funerals, often signify in excess of any particular written or vocalized account of what they are about.[9]

As a result, public theology cannot be understood to concern only what is spoken in Manchester Cathedral or by those who represent the cathedral. It also matters what practices take place in Manchester Cathedral, what symbols are present, how art is utilized, and how bodies are organized within the space. Therefore, my discussions of the public theology of Manchester Cathedral are not simply analysis of its discourse about certain topics and how effective or accurate I consider its discourse to be. Rather, I interpret various moments of performance, practice, and speech as forming ethical and social visions and indicating held notions of publicness and theology.[10]

Therefore, it is important to make clear that I am approaching public theology as a practice. Understood in this way, public theology informs the cathedral's public practice, and in turn, the public practice shapes the cathedral's public theology. As a result, through approaching the public theology of the cathedral in this way, I am analyzing the practices of the cathedral as they relate to each area of engagement and seek to understand what implications this has concerning its theological understanding of its public role.

READING AN INSTITUTION

But what am I talking about when I talk about "Manchester Cathedral" in this book? On one level the words "Manchester Cathedral" denote a particular building, with a particular history in a particular location. Thus, one could be forgiven for thinking that this project is about the public theology

---

9. Butler, *Performative Theory of Assembly*, 8.

10. My focus on vision as a public and ethical category first began when reading Hauerwas, where he argues that Christian ethics should focus on the nature and moral determination of the self, rather than adopting a situation ethical approach. He writes, "We are as we come to see and as that seeing becomes enduring in our intentionality. We do not come to see however just by looking but by training our vision through the metaphors and symbols that constitute our central convictions" (*Vision and Virtue*, 2). Hauerwas's focus on the formation of vision in relation to ethics is what I have found most helpful in his work and in the thinking of those in the post-liberal tradition. However, despite beginning with Hauerwas, I ultimately depart from much of his ethical perspective and those of post-liberal tradition because of their too-narrow understanding of the church as being the only source of ethical formation for Christians. Instead, I follow a more Ricoeurian approach to formation that allows for multiple, overlapping sources of formation and a more generous account of identity and relationality. I expand more on this in chs. 1 and 2.

of the building of the cathedral, i.e., exploring the theology that the building through its structure, artwork, memorials, engravings, etc., communicates. While there are moments where the cathedral building comes into focus during my analysis, it is not the central focus.

When I discuss the public theology of Manchester Cathedral, I am analyzing several things at once. I am analyzing the articulated public theology of the clergy, staff, and chapter that were working at the cathedral during the period of data collection. I am also analyzing the public practices and activities which take place within the cathedral walls. Further, I examine some events and activities conducted by representatives of the cathedral. For example, Scriptural Reasoning and Scriptural Encounter groups often take place outside the cathedral, yet it is an important part of the cathedral's life because, before he retired from the role of canon for theology and mission, Canon David Holgate regularly participated in it as a representative of the cathedral. Therefore, when I use the language of "the cathedral," or "Manchester Cathedral," it is often a shorthand for the institution, but particularly relating to the team at the cathedral, its activities, and the practices that give the cathedral its particular public character. If I am speaking about the cathedral building specifically, I will indicate this.

MY ANALYSIS OF THREE AREAS OF PUBLIC ENGAGEMENT

Manchester Cathedral is engaged in multiple areas of public life and contributes to a variety of discussions that concern public life in partnership with other organizations. The cathedral engages with many different social issues including climate change, poverty, the challenges of mental health, knife crime, and medicine, among many others. Because of the scope of Manchester Cathedral's influence and work I chose to focus on the three main areas: interreligious dialogue, racial justice, and LGBTQ+ inclusion. This is because the significant overlaps between the cathedral's approach to all three demonstrate overlapping characteristics of its public theology that underpins its approaches to other social issues. However, I will give some further reasons for each of the areas of engagement that I have chosen and the concerns that each raise in the context of public theology.

I chose to develop a case study on the cathedral's approach to interreligious dialogue because "interreligious" names not only a type of activity at Manchester Cathedral but is the character that much of its activity adopts. Because interreligious networking and dialogue are an important part of the cathedral's life and public work, Manchester Cathedral offers insights into how the public realm can be navigated not only with secular worldviews and perspectives but in the context of religious pluralism. However, the cathedral's interreligious networking raises key questions about how the contribution of diverse perspectives on ethics, the good, and identity could and should be conducted in public.

The cathedral's public theology of racial justice became a central aspect of my analysis for two key reasons. First, this was a topic that repeatedly arose in interviews as an important part of the cathedral's work, especially work conducted by the dean. Govender has worked both with the Church of England and with Manchester City Council in areas of racial discrimination and hate crime, meaning that this topic is a very important one in the life of the cathedral. Second, the murder of George Floyd in the USA and the subsequent Black Lives Matter protests that took place across the world in 2020 put racial justice at the forefront of public discourse during the time that I was gathering data for my PhD. The analysis of the chapter raises key questions about how the cathedral approaches ethical topics and the limits of certain approaches to complex socio-ethical issues.

The importance of focusing on LGBTQ+ inclusion at Manchester Cathedral became apparent to me during the course of writing for three reasons. The first is that the cathedral's affirmation of LGBTQ+ people was highlighted to me several times in the first round of interviews I conducted with cathedral staff and chapter members as a key marker of the cathedral's distinctiveness and inclusive nature.[11] The second is that the Church of England (CofE) published the *Living in Love and Faith* (*LLF*) book and resources during the data collection period of this project. The cathedral, through the work of Canon David Holgate and the cathedral curate at the time Steven Hilton,[12] was involved in a process of working with others from the diocese to encourage churches to participate in the *LLF* process. Thus, because the conversation of LGBTQ+ inclusion is a live issue within the CofE presently, and the cathedral is involved in that conversation it struck me as also, in part, demonstrating aspects of the public theology of the cathedral as it relates to the public of the wider church.

The third reason is that, as I will argue in chapter 6, one of the most publicly visible and symbolic actions that Manchester Cathedral performs is raising the pride flag on its roof annually during Pride Week. As I conducted

---

11. As I shall demonstrate, inclusion is a primary lens through which the cathedral understands its public work.

12. It is important to note that Canon David Holgate began his role as subdean and canon for theology and mission at Manchester Cathedral in Nov. 2014 and retired in May 2022. Steven Hilton started his curacy position in June 2019 and finished in June 2022.

my research, I recognized that this particular topic raises questions about how "wild" public spheres may be engaged, particularly by those institutions with relative power, such as Manchester Cathedral. A central question in this analysis is whether the public value of inclusion is sufficient to resist homogenization in the public sphere.

THE STRUCTURE OF THIS BOOK

Chapters 1 and 2 offer a mapping of public theology. In chapter 1, I outline the three approaches to religion in the public sphere. I explicate these approaches with three key thinkers: John Rawls, Jürgen Habermas, and Paul Ricoeur. While public theologians are not necessarily drawing on the works of these three thinkers, I argue that each of these thinkers' theories about religion and publicness characterizes three broad approaches to publicness that public theologians often adopt.

In chapter 2 I develop a more in-depth analysis of the field of public theology, describing its development, distinguishing marks, and some criticisms from other strands of theology, namely post-liberal theology. I attempt to show how the broad field of public theology is diverse in part because of public theologians' various adherence to different approaches of publicness, such as the approaches outlined in chapter 1. As will be clear in this chapter, the dialogical mark of public theology is at the center of the field's various critiques from a variety of other theologians. I will thus explore what public theologians mean by the concept of "bilingualism" and why concepts such as "translation" are critiqued by some outside of the field of public theology.

In chapter 3 I outline my methodology to demonstrate how I am conducting the evaluative process. As I will show, methods are theological, and theology is governed by method. I develop my method both within the field of public theology and practical theology. Because this research is a study of an institution "on the ground" I draw on ethnographic theory in my approach to gathering and analyzing data. However, I also combine the hermeneutical theory of Paul Ricoeur with these ethnographic approaches to expound the various aspects of interpretation that are in play in my analysis of the cathedral. The methodology chapter demonstrates the complexity of the interpretation of a community and how I have tried to navigate this complexity in an intersubjective manner.

Following this, I begin my analysis and evaluation of three areas of engagement which are important in the public activity of Manchester Cathedral. In chapter 4, I analyze the cathedral's public interreligious character.

Interreligious dialogue has been an integral part of the cathedral's character under the leadership of Dean Rogers Govender. In this chapter, I outline some activities that adopt this interreligious character and explore some of the explanations and theologies that were given during recorded interviews about interreligious dialogue at the cathedral. I use the approaches to publicness developed in chapters 1 and 2 to understand how interreligious dialogue functions at the cathedral and what role explicit religious symbolism and discourse play in interreligious settings and events. I then draw on the work of interreligious theorists and theologians to evaluate this approach to interreligious publicness. Central to my analysis in this chapter are questions about how the cathedral understands the nature of religion and how it subsequently navigates and explores its own distinctive religious identity and the religious identities of those it seeks to engage in dialogue.

Chapter 5 focuses on the cathedral's public theology of racial justice. Racial justice is a prime concern of the current cathedral team, particularly in addressing the causes of and solutions to racially based hate crimes. In this chapter, I analyze a wide variety of data concerning this topic at the cathedral. I then use key black and womanist theologians to test and evaluate the approach to publicness that is adopted in relation to this topic. In conversation with these thinkers, I consider how racism is defined at Manchester Cathedral and the role that theology currently plays and could potentially play regarding racial justice.

In chapter 6 I analyze and evaluate the cathedral's public theology of LGBTQ+ inclusion. I begin by analyzing the cathedral's activity and public speech acts that relate to this topic within the wider context of LGBTQ+ inclusion in the Church of England. I then demonstrate the public theological approach that the cathedral adopts in relation to this topic. Drawing on the perspectives of queer theorists and theologians I demonstrate the tensions that arise when an ethic of inclusion is central to the cathedral's approach to the LGBTQ+ community.

In chapter 7, I explore some unifying themes and concerns across the cathedrals public work. I argue that the concepts of common humanity and human flourishing are central concepts that operate as unifying principles across the cathedral's diverse range of public work. I, therefore, interrogate these notions, drawing on critiques of post-liberal theologians, and their concerns about Christian distinctiveness. I also draw on some of the issues raised about identity and interpretation throughout the previous three chapters.

I then conclude this book by highlighting some of the key lessons that can be learned from Manchester Cathedral. I take Manchester Cathedral as both a model institution, that has much to teach others who seek to be public with their faith. These lessons, as I will show, demonstrate what is possible to achieve in the public realm, what role and space religion can play in public, and what developments may need to be considered to address an ever changing and shifting postmodern and post-secular culture.

1

THREE APPROACHES TO RELIGION IN THE PUBLIC SPHERE

It is not shocking to say that questions of whether theology can or should enter the public sphere are subject to a variety of viewpoints. These range from those who seek religion's dominant return as the leading force in public matters, to those who encourage the complete eradication of religion from the public sphere. Answers to the question of *ought* religion enter the public sphere and *how* should it enter the public sphere often depend on each other. And yet the possible range of answers to these questions are not always sufficiently analyzed by public theologians despite them being central to their aims and objectives.

Therefore, in this chapter I outline three sophisticated differing accounts of religion's potential publicness. These contributions are given by John Rawls, Jürgen Habermas, and Paul Ricoeur. By attending to each of these thinkers, I will demonstrate how "publicness" and the publicness of religion in particular can be interpreted in a variety of ways. Each of these thinkers has a differing answer in relation to the *ought* and the *how* of religion in the public sphere. These approaches will be important in my analysis of Manchester Cathedral's public theology, as they offer a framework for understanding how different notions of publicness shape the public discourse and practice of religious institutions on the ground. I will first offer my reasoning for using these approaches as a primary lens in my interpretation of the public theology of the cathedral. I will then outline each thinker's approaches to this topic and then offer a comparison of all three approaches.

RELIGION AND PUBLIC REASON: A DIVERSITY OF APPROACHES

In *Religion and Public Reason*, Maureen Junker-Kenny outlines the contributions of these thinkers to demonstrate a range of understandings of the relationship between religion and public reason. Junker-Kenny seeks to address the key question of whether religion is public reason's opposite because public reason tends to insist on universal and generalizable criteria over any particular claims and judgments.[1] However, central to her analysis in addressing this question, she demonstrates that there are diverse understandings of what can count as "reasonable" and thus what publicness entails.

Therefore, Junker-Kenny analyzes the work of the public philosophers John Rawls, Jürgen Habermas, and Paul Ricoeur to demonstrate a variety of approaches to public reason and the way that religions are considered to be able to enter into the public sphere. She argues that "theological ethics is impoverished when it does not engage with the paradigmatic approaches represented by these three thinkers."[2] She aims to outline and compare these approaches so that the reader may see various options and frameworks for ways theology can engage in the public sphere.[3] As Harold Breitenberg argues:

> Public theology is thus theologically informed public discourse about public issues, addressed to the church, synagogue, mosque, temple, or other religious bodies, as well as the larger public or publics, argued in ways that can be evaluated and judged by publicly available warrants or criteria.[4]

However, as my analysis will demonstrate, determining what does or does not count as "publicly available warrants and criteria," is a crucial question and yet one often under-addressed by public theologians. Therefore, following Junker-Kenny, I have analyzed these three thinkers to understand how their approaches have implications in the field of public theology. In the following chapter, I will show how these approaches are present in different ways within the field of public theology. Ultimately, this chapter will demonstrate that there is much to be considered in understanding what it means to be "public" for Manchester Cathedral and other religious groups and individuals who seek to be public facing.

1. Junker-Kenny, *Religion and Public Reason*, 1.
2. Junker-Kenny, *Religion and Public Reason*, 2.
3. Junker-Kenny, *Religion and Public Reason*, 3.
4. Breitenberg, "To Tell the Truth," 65.

THE RAWLSIAN APPROACH TO RELIGION IN THE PUBLIC SPHERE

Forrester argues that after World War Two political thinkers viewed all "theory" as totalitarian and dangerous. "So 'theory' was abandoned for a time until it was revived by Rawls's *Theory of Justice*, which took people by surprise."[5] Rawls argues that because all ideological formulations that sought to guide society through policy were viewed with suspicion, utilitarian ethics dominated the public sphere.[6] He suggested that the utilitarian ethic simply defined the good in terms of satisfaction.[7] The problem that Rawls sees with utilitarian politics is that there is no theoretical reason why a great cost to a few members of society would not justify the satisfaction of the many. In this way, policies can be introduced that are of great cost to a few without their consent, to benefit many.[8]

For Rawls, this is a dangerous system when it is not guided by a first moral principle because the system cannot distinguish effectively between various persons.[9] Thus Rawls's theory of justice attempted to resist utilitarian approaches to politics.[10] Rawls's political philosophy, therefore, aimed to find a moral theory of justice that all parties within a democratic society would find foundational for shared political discourse.

A key element of his theory of justice was the "veil of ignorance" thought experiment, which sought to "nullify specific contingencies which put men at odds and tempt them to exploit social and natural circumstances to their own advantage."[11] The thought experiment requires participants, who are policymakers, to imagine they are to be born into their current society, but they do not know what specific location, economic class, or social stratification they will be born into. The goal is that the participant must decide on specific resources and opportunities to be made available to all groups and members of society so that the individual would be pleased to be born into any social stratum. Rawls states:

> All social primary goods—liberty and opportunity, income and wealth, and the bases of self-respect—are to be distributed

---

5. Forrester, *Christian Justice*, 25.
6. Rawls, *Theory of Justice*, 19.
7. Rawls, *Theory of Justice*, 22.
8. Rawls, *Theory of Justice*, 23.
9. Rawls, *Theory of Justice*, 23–24.
10. Rawls, *Theory of Justice*, 22.
11. Rawls, *Theory of Justice*, 118; see 118–23 for fuller discussion.

equally unless an unequal distribution of any or all of these goods is to the disadvantage of the least favored.[12]

Rawls thus seeks to construct a theory of justice that is accessible to all, and that makes it possible for the participants making political decisions to do so without regard for their own self-interest, and indeed think in favor of the less favored. Rawls termed this theory "justice as fairness." This becomes central in his later work, *Political Liberalism*, as Rawls attempts to find an answer to the question "How is it possible for there to exist over time a just and stable society of free and equal citizens who remain profoundly divided by reasonable religious, philosophical and moral doctrines?"[13] In attempting to develop this political ethics one of the problems that Rawls is trying to address is the task of doing political ethics in the context of reasonable pluralism.[14] He does not want to abandon the ethical task but also recognizes that there are competing definitions of ethics and the good in society, including diverse religious groups. Instead, he offers a moral first principle that all reasonable people will act in accordance with. He states:

> The principles of justice for the basic structure of society are the object of the original agreement. They are the principles that free and rational persons concerned to further their own interests would accept in an initial position of equality as defining the fundamental terms of their association. These principles are to regulate all further agreements: they specify the kinds of social cooperation that can be entered into and the forms of government that can be established. This way of regarding the principle of justice I shall call justice as fairness.[15]

It is on this basis that an original agreement can be found among rational persons that Rawls rejects the need and possibility of constructive metaphysical arguments being given in the public sphere. Metaphysical claims are not neutral and therefore not accessible to all involved in a particular discussion or debate. Religions are, therefore, part of what Rawls terms "background cultures." The background culture, for Rawls, is the space where citizens can debate and form opinions, but it is not the realm of political decision-making. This realm of political decision-making, and

---

12. Rawls, *Theory of Justice*, 303.
13. Rawls, *Political Liberalism*, 47.
14. Rawls, *Political Liberalism*, 4. See Junker-Kenny, *Religion and Public Reason*, 23. Rawls will later define reason as that which conforms to the basic theory of justice he has given in the previous book.
15. Rawls, *Political Liberalism*, 10.

not the background cultures, is the public sphere in Rawls's theory.[16] The background culture, which Rawls categorizes as "non-public," may form the opinion or reason of an individual or group, but this cannot be the basis of the argument made in public.[17]

For Rawls, religion can contribute to the opinion and formation of the individual citizen's self-realization, but it cannot contribute arguments to the public/political realm with metaphysical foundations and terms. Rather, religious communities are provided with a proviso:

> Reasonable doctrines may be introduced in public at any time, provided that in due course public reasons, given by a reasonable political conception, are presented sufficient to support whatever the comprehensive doctrines are introduced to support.[18]

In other words, religious individuals can introduce comprehensive doctrines in support of the political conception being sought, which is governed by the basic theory of justice. But it is crucial to understand what Rawls takes to be "reasonable" in this framework. Rawls outlines three features he thinks all reasonable doctrines have:

1. Exercise in theoretical reason: seeking the complementary values across religions' philosophical and moral aspects of human life.

2. General beliefs about human nature and the way political and social institutions generally work and how this relates to the first principle of justice.

3. The doctrines are not necessarily fixed but belong to some form of tradition.[19]

For Rawls, for a doctrine to be considered reasonable, and therefore public, it must conform to the theory of justice. He argues, "Only a political conception of justice that all citizens might be reasonably expected to endorse can serve as a basis of public reason and justification."[20] Of concern for Rawls is that he sees the potential for religions to dominate one

---

16. Rawls, *Political Liberalism*, 220. See also Junker-Kenny, *Religion and Public Reason*, 64.

17. Rawls, *Political Liberalism*, 220. Of course, as Junker-Kenny argues, it is not clear that Rawls's conception of justice as fairness is neutral at all. Instead, the theory rests upon elements from undiagnosed metaphysical thinking (*Religion and Public Reason*, 28).

18. Rawls, *Political Liberalism*, li–lii.

19. Rawls, *Political Liberalism*, 59.

20. Rawls, *Political Liberalism*, 137.

another through coercive means. He suggests that it is possible to reach an overlapping consensus within the context of pluralism only by bypassing those doctrines that are particular to differing religious traditions and focusing instead on conceptions of the just that are reasonable, communicable, and therefore universal. For Rawls, peace between the religions was only made possible through "the peaceful practice of toleration in liberal institutions."[21]

Underlying his conception of the relationship between religion and reason is the assumption that religious views, while being distinct enough to cause violence and war if not governed by liberal tolerance, will certainly overlap in certain areas, as well as with nonreligious views. Junker-Kenny notes that this is an assumption Rawls makes which he does not provide a philosophical justification for, other than the assumption of the universal accessibility of his theory of justice.[22]

However, even though he admits there may be overlaps, he does not believe that different truth claims arising from different comprehensive doctrines can communicate with one another, and thus he proposes that "in public reason, comprehensive doctrines of truth or right be replaced by an idea of the politically reasonable addressed to citizens as citizens."[23] It is important to note, Rawls does not think that political liberalism can replace religion and provide the equivalent of religious ethics. Instead, he is constructing a very specific understanding of the public sphere and privateness, where the public sphere is understood as a political sphere where the principles of justice are established structurally to ensure that all citizens have equal opportunity to pursue their own *private* vision of the good and flourishing life. Religion in this instance falls into the realm of the private, though religious individuals may contribute to the public realm if they aim to help establish a just society on the grounds of political liberalism and the publicly held notion of justice as fairness.

In summary, a Rawlsian approach to religion in the public sphere treats religion primarily as a private and potentially motivational factor in the lives of citizens entering the public sphere. However, religious, or theological discourse is only able to contribute explicitly in a public setting if it is offering support to the establishment of shared public values such as justice

---

21. Rawls, *Political Liberalism*, xxvii. His claim rests on an interpretation of the wars of religion in the sixteenth century. He argues that war is the inevitable result of religions engaging with one another without the structures of liberalism to govern them and produce the virtues of toleration.

22. Junker-Kenny, *Religion and Public Reason*, 51.

23. Rawls, *Political Liberalism*, 132. See also Junker-Kenny, *Religion and Public Reason*, 62–63.

as fairness. As we will see in the following chapter, Rawlsian approaches to public theology seek shared values to find ground for an overlapping consensus.

THE HABERMASIAN APPROACH TO RELIGION IN THE PUBLIC SPHERE

Jürgen Habermas is arguably the most influential political philosopher in the field of public theology of the three that I am analyzing.[24] This is because his understanding of what the public sphere is, how it functions, and how religion can enter it has been foundational for theologians to understand how their arguments can "go public." Habermas's understanding of how the public sphere emerged in Enlightened society has been particularly important for theologians seeking to understand the potential place of religion in the public sphere.

The Emergence of the Public Sphere

In *The Structural Transformation of the Public Sphere*, Habermas attempts to map the history of the development of the public sphere that emerged out of the medieval period and through the Enlightenment. He suggests that a structural division between the private and public realms can be seen in the Greco-Roman ancient societies that separated the *oikos* from the *polis*.[25] There was a distinction between what responsibilities and power one may have had in the *oikos* and that of the *polis*. In contrast, he argues there was no real sense of a public realm that could exist separately from the private realm in the feudal society of the High Middle Ages.

However, two main events and social situations created the environment for the genesis of the bourgeois public sphere and a firmer structural separation between public and private: the Reformation and the emergence of trade capitalism. Habermas argues that before the Reformation individual rationality had to be protected from going public. Individual rationality necessitates the power of the individual to challenge the structures of the monarchy. Thus "reason had to remain within the private and secret chambers of princes and monarchies, and reason's light was revealed in stages."[26]

---

24. Graham, *Between Rock and Hard Place*, 18. She argues that Habermas's understanding of the public sphere and public reason is highly significant for public theology.
25. Habermas, *Structural Transformation*, 35.
26. Habermas, *Structural Transformation*, 35.

In his view, it was the authority of the Catholic Church across Europe that gave spiritual dimensions to the necessity of the population leaving the state largely unchallenged, trusting the state to be the purveyor of reason.[27] For Habermas, the foundation was set for the Enlightenment when the Reformers challenged the spiritual authority of the Catholic Church over the state because the power of the monarchy and structural powers were also implicitly challenged.[28]

Habermas also regards the increase of international trade as one of the key factors that formed the bourgeois public sphere. He suggests that as international trade increased there was an increasing need to have accurate information about other nations overseas. He states that the public sphere emerged "almost simultaneously with the origin of stock markets, postal services and the press institutionalized regular contacts and regular communication."[29] However, the information was only available to information insiders, as neither tradespeople nor those producing and communicating the information had a vested interest in making the information widely available to the general public. However, this realm of communication "in which the publicity of representation held sway" was not threatened until the new domain of the public sphere emerged with the widely available published word towards the end of the seventeenth century.[30]

For Habermas, as society progressed from the high Middle Ages through the Enlightenment and into the modern day, the public sphere emerged. Rationality became increasingly available for the individual citizen to be able to contribute to issues of concern in society. This level of private-public rationality demonstrated the problematic elements of structures of power in society that had not previously been called into question.[31]

Habermas understands the public sphere to be a space of open debate between ordinary citizens, which is free from coercive control from the state and other powerful institutions.[32] The sphere found its origins, according to Habermas, in the "world of letters" where the general population in the eighteenth century had increased access to the newspapers. At this time discussions about society, foreign events, tax laws, etc. took place in coffee houses and other public spaces in bourgeois society. While this space was

---

27. Habermas, *Structural Transformation*, 11–16.
28. Habermas, *Structural Transformation*, 11.
29. Habermas, *Structural Transformation*, 16.
30. Habermas, *Structural Transformation*, 16.
31. Habermas, *Structural Transformation*, 36.
32. Junker-Kenny, *Religion and Public Reason*, 113.

both exclusive in terms of class and gender,[33] it marks the beginnings of private individuals coming together to discuss matters of public interest that in the past would have been solely the business of the state. Individuals were no longer simply subjects, but through the dissemination of information through letters and newspapers, necessitated by the foundational role of capitalism in society, individuals were now becoming a reasoning public.[34]

For Habermas, the bourgeois public realm functioned to ensure universal norms were secured for individuals. He states:

> The bourgeois public's critical public debate took place in principle without regard to all pre-existing social and political rank and in accord with universal rules. These rules, because they remained strictly external to the individuals as such, secured space for the development of these individuals' interiority by literary means. These rules, because universally valid, secured a space for the individuated person; because they were objective, they secured a space for what was most subjective; because they were abstract, for what was most concrete.[35]

As a result, the focus of bourgeois society was to neutralize power, so that, in theory, the status, wealth, and political power of an individual did not dominate and force those with less status, power, and money to conform. Rather:

> The ideals of the political public sphere which granted participation rights regardless of status and privilege, could, in the eyes of the bourgeoisie, only be realized through cleansing privilege, constraint and public interference from the sphere of civil society, and through the development of a constitutional framework based on freedom of contract and laissez-faire trade policies.[36]

For Habermas, the public sphere only works when it is free from the control of a powerful individual or group, and the debates and discourse are open to all people because what is aimed for is a universalizable consensus on issues concerning society.[37] However, this does not necessarily entail the

---

33. Habermas, *Structural Transformation*, 33.

34. Habermas, *Structural Transformation*, 15.

35. Habermas, *Structural Transformation*, 54. Quoted in Goode, *Jürgen Habermas*, 8.

36. Goode, *Jürgen Habermas*, 9. See also Habermas, *Structural Transformation*, 73–79.

37. Goode, *Jürgen Habermas*, 9; Habermas, *Structural Transformation*, 53, 141. Habermas is skeptical about whether such an ideal is achievable because information that the public has access to through mass media is not necessarily neutral but can be co-opted by the state by using news outlets as platforms for their own agenda, which manipulates the general public into a particular way of thinking (*Structural*

removal of the religious voice from the public realm for Habermas. Hence, he disputes Rawls's conception of religion as only being able to offer "tacit support to a society oriented towards justice"[38] and sees religious traditions as fundamental to democratic deliberation. But this was not always the case.

Habermas's Shifting Approach to Public Religion

In another of her books, *Habermas and Theology*, Junker-Kenny points out that Habermas's thought about religious engagement in the public sphere has gone through three main phases:

1. Supersession by communicative reason
2. Abstemious coexistence (between religion and reason)
3. Genuine cooperation in the task of sustaining the normative project of a universal modernity in the face of its pathologies[39]

In the first phase, his 1981 book *The Theory of Communicative Action* portrays religion as something that can be superseded by communicative action. Communicative action rests on the presupposition that when one person speaks to another both the speaker and hearer have a common reference point to make the language intelligible. There is an objective world that is true for both parties, and the objectivity of the world demonstrates "that it is given to us as: 'The same for everyone.'"[40] While Habermas openly states that he cannot answer questions about the presence or existence of God or questions about meaning, there is still a common moral point of view, the evidence of which is seen in common language.[41]

Habermas does qualify this by suggesting that the proposed truth from the speaker may need to be *justified* but the justification can take place on the assumption that the speaker and hearer are both oriented towards the truth.[42] The differing truths of both the speaker and author are united in both conversation partners' belief that their truth is equally true for the other. It is the orientation towards the truth (the universal truth) that can be the bridge between different life worlds.[43] Therefore, Habermas moves away

---

Transformation, 236).
    38. Junker-Kenny, *Religion and Public Reason*, 102.
    39. Junker-Kenny, *Habermas and Theology*, 3.
    40. Habermas, *Between Naturalism and Religion*, 30–31.
    41. Junker-Kenny, *Habermas and Theology*, 17.
    42. Habermas, *Between Naturalism and Religion*, 366.
    43. Habermas, *Between Naturalism and Religion*, 36.

from "the veil of ignorance" strategy, which sought to hide all the differences of participants, in favor of reconstructing plurality while simultaneously being able to recognize the other, through language.

However, Habermas acknowledges later on in his career that religious dialogue in the public sphere ought not be eliminated by communicative reason (as he thought in his second phase)[44] but that religion is a valuable resource for moral insight in the public sphere (third phase). As Junker-Kenny explains, for Habermas the exclusion of religion's public use of its own reasons would be harmful to the democratic process and its citizens.[45] Instead, Habermas argues that religious language contains moral resources that wider secular society vitally needs, because instrumental reason, which is the main mechanism of democratic deliberation in Habermas's view, lacks sufficient moral content.[46] Habermas maintains that religion's role is to keep alive the public's sensitivities to our past failures and sufferings as a society and culture for the political to maintain moral contents.[47]

Yet, having similar concerns to Rawls concern about the public potential for religious violence and domination, Habermas distinguishes between two types of public spheres: the strong public and the weak public. For Habermas, religious arguments should be given in the weak publics of opinion formation but should not be used in the strong political sphere where policymaking happens. He thinks the weak public sphere is prior to the political and should inform the political (strong public), but at this point, the religious contents should be translated, either by the religious voice or the secular listener.[48] Thus, Habermas disagrees with Rawls that religious

---

44. This is a recognition, not of the value of religion in the public sphere, but that religion cannot be eliminated from the public sphere without compromising democracy, which is part of the universal modernity he searches for. Habermas's perception of the value of religious contributions came in the later phase (Junker-Kenny, *Habermas and Theology*, 13–17).

45. Junker-Kenny, *Religion and Public Reason*, 166.

46. Habermas, *Between Naturalism and Religion*, 6. Graham notes that one of Habermas's central concerns is of the challenge of the hegemony of the global market. She suggests, "It is the morality of the global market, plus its apparent inability to save itself from imminent collapse, that leads him to turn to religious values as one potential source of alternative global values" (*Between Rock and Hard Place*, 89).

47. Habermas, *Between Naturalism and Religion*, 6.

48. Habermas, *Between Naturalism and Religion*, 140. It is important to note that for Habermas the distinction between "strong" and "weak" publics is not a matter of hierarchy or importance, as both rely on an interdependent relationship with one another. Rather, the strength and weakness are determined by the language rules governing each as the strong public must maintain universality, though it is impacted by the subjective influences of weak publics where there are less rules governing discourse. See Ward, "Rekindling 'Radical Democratic Embers,'" 832.

content has no immediate public value, but agrees that for religious content to be influential in the strong public sphere of politics, it should be translated into publicly accessible terms, so that those outside of the community can be convinced by their arguments.[49] He further argues that secularists need to resist the tendency to evaluate all things based on pure instrumental reason because:

> When one describes how a person has done something that he didn't mean to do and also shouldn't have done, then that person is not being described as natural science would describe one of its objects. This is because, in the description of persons, there is a silent moment of pre-scientific self-conception of what it is to be a subject capable of language and behavior. When we describe a phenomenon such as a person's behavior, we know for example that we're describing something not as a natural process, but as something that can be justified if necessary. Behind this is an image of personhood, persons who can hold each other accountable, who at home and away are involved in normatively regulated interactions and who encounter one another in a universe of public fundamentals.[50]

In sum, Habermas sees religion as being able to contribute to questions of morality and ethics because secular discourse has not yet produced a replacement for religious discourse that can provide the same kind of moral energy. However, because of his emphasis on language, religion's publicness is determined primarily by speech acts/argumentation because the weak public entails a space in which private citizens gather to talk and argue to influence the strong public of politics collectively. Habermasian approaches to public theology, then, recognize that religious stories and symbols contain moral content that secular discourses cannot provide, but that these must in the end be translated in some way to be deemed relevant and convincing in the context of public debate. I will expand on this approach to public theology further in chapter 2.

---

49. Junker-Kenny, *Religion and Public Reason*, 121–22; Habermas *Between Naturalism and Religion*, 245–46.

50. Habermas, *Future of Human Nature*, 107.

THE RICOEURIAN APPROACH TO RELIGION IN THE PUBLIC SPHERE

The French philosopher Paul Ricoeur wrote extensively on a range of topics, including ethics, politics, theology, and linguistic theory. However, one uniting factor in his work is his phenomenological approach to the subject. His philosophy resists the Cartesian notion that being takes place purely in the consciousness of the individual and rather insists that being is the relationships and interactions of the self with the outside world which are often elements out of the control of the agent.[51] Thus, one of his central concerns is how ethical agents are formed to act within the world. For Ricoeur, paradoxically the subject must interpret the world to navigate it, yet the way they interpret the world is being shaped by the world around the agent. Thus, hermeneutics plays a central role in Ricoeur's philosophy, which earns him the description of being a hermeneutical philosopher.

Ricoeur's phenomenological hermeneutics largely centers on questions about the formation of the subject as he explores epistemology, ontology, and ethics, which all have implications for how the relationships between the publics, politics, and religions should be understood. For Ricoeur, the ethics of an agent cannot be divorced from the culture that the agent is formed in and how the agent interprets the world.[52] As such, Ricoeur is not simply concerned with finding a universal social ethic that can provide the basis of unity in pluralist societies, but is concerned with how a variety of narratives, symbols, and practices form individual and communal visions to interpret their own lives and the world around them.[53]

Both Martin Heidegger and Hans-Georg Gadamer influenced Ricoeur's understanding that hermeneutics is not an event that takes place only when an individual or group sits down to interpret a piece of written or spoken text. Rather, he affirms that we are hermeneutical all the way down.[54] What this means is that we are always interpreting our lives, not

---

51. Junker-Kenny, *Religion and Public Reason*, 186.
52. Ricoeur, *Hermeneutics and Human Sciences*, 143.
53. Stiver, *Ricoeur and Theology*, 9.
54. Stiver, *Ricoeur and Theology*, 9. It is important to note that for Ricoeur there are key shared characteristics between interpreting texts and quasi-texts (actions and events). As Karl Simms describes Ricoeur's hermeneutical emphasis: "Ricoeur's philosophy is simultaneously a philosophy of life and a philosophy of reading. It is this which enables it to be universally applicable: whatever discipline we are in, be it history, psychoanalysis, literary criticism or whatever, that discipline is constructed through texts, and those texts each in different ways conceal their true meaning that hermeneutics reveals—the meaning of life. By extension, life itself can be 'read,' or interpreted, and that interpretation itself reveals life to be a narrative. Our ethical aim is, according

as neutral bystanders with objective standards of interpretation, but ones who are culturally and relationally conditioned. For Ricoeur, the subjective ways we interpret the world around is not a feature of human reality that can be bypassed in public ethics for something more objective. Rather these subjectivities are what must be thoroughly engaged in public. By placing hermeneutics at the foundation of knowledge, Ricoeur resists the Enlightenment notion that objective certainty can be realized and therefore resists objectivist approaches to ethics.[55]

For Ricoeur, ethics cannot be elaborated as a neutral endeavor of individuals operating separately from cultures, relationships and the narratives that have formed their vision of the world. As such, public rationality cannot be something as understood outside the formative practices, cultures and discourses represented within the public sphere. Rather, the plurality of cultures testifies to the plurality of rationalities. For Ricoeur, the particularity of culture derives its strength from its particular symbols, narratives, and myths. As Junker-Kenny states:

> By anchoring concrete agency in the productive power of imagination, ethics as a well-directed expression of striving is not given a foundational but constituted status. There is a level prior to the will that evokes action.[56]

Ricoeur, following Aristotle, argues that humans are oriented towards a particular vision of the good, which is prior to ethics. For Ricoeur, "Desire precedes law, and intention precedes the norm."[57] The desires, and visions of the good, however, are embedded within a tradition: "Narratives, rules, ritual forms, and symbols both mediate *and* mold the way the understanding of the good life takes shape."[58] Ricoeur calls these "ultimate frameworks of legitimation." These frameworks provide the setting in which ethical life can be formed. Key to understanding Ricoeur's thought here is that ethics are not abstract, or universally ingrained in the consciousness of every human. Rather they are formed within a tradition, or traditions, whether secular or religious, that the individual does not choose.[59] As such, "we must admit we are always situated in such a way that our consciousness does not

to Ricoeur, to make the story of our life a good story" (*Paul Ricoeur*, 2).

55. Stiver, *Ricoeur and Theology*, 11.

56. Junker-Kenny, *Religion and Public Reason*, 192.

57. Moyaert, *In Response to Religious Other*, 81.

58. Moyaert, *In Response to Religious Other*, 81; emphasis in original. See also Ricoeur, *Oneself as Another*, 172.

59. Moyaert, *In Response to Religious Other*, 81–82; Changeux and Ricoeur, *What Makes Us Think*, 276.

have the freedom to bring itself face to face with the ethical framework that orients us."[60]

Within this perspective, one cannot assume that diverse cultures will automatically subscribe to a universal concept of justice that all must strive toward, as in Rawls. Instead, the philosopher or theologian would be concerned to ask how cultures are formed to understand just practices and relationships and how these differ from other communities' and agents' understandings of justice. Are the concepts of justice at play formed by symbols, stories, or myths? To give an example specifically related to Christian ethics, the Bible would not be seen as a collection of texts offering normative commands for the ethical life, but symbols and stories that open a new imaginative world that will form the reader's understanding of what the good life looks like, which will then form subsequent ethics.[61]

The question is then raised of whether and how those formed in different cultures and traditions can converse and work together in the public sphere. This question is also the primary concern of both Rawls and Habermas, and indeed of those identifying as public theologians. Both Rawls and Habermas depend on some notion of a universal ethic being discoverable, though each in their own way as seen above. The aiming towards universal principles or language in Rawls and Habermas for them provides the basis of shared interaction in the context of pluralism and diversity in the public sphere. Ricoeur on the other hand approaches the possibility of universal ethics somewhat tentatively. He does not deny the possibility of a universal ethic or norm but thinks that an emphasis on particularity must be prior to predetermining a universal ethic. Ricoeur affirms the project of democracy but wants to resist some modernist tendencies towards homogenization, where particularity is not considered an important factor in ethics.[62]

Rather, Ricoeur affirms the "inchoative universals." What this means is that particularity does not preclude access to universality, but rather each culture harbors its own potential universalism which must be drawn out through conversation. For Ricoeur, the process of inchoative universalism becoming accepted and applied universally is a long one, involving dialogue, argument, friendships, actions of hospitality, both literally and metaphorically and the unfolding of history.[63] Ricoeur "does not dismiss the notion of the universal, but he claims that only in a long discussion between cultures

---

60. Moyaert, *In Response to Religious Other*, 82. See also Ricoeur, *Political and Social Essays*, 252.

61. Junker-Kenny, *Religion and Public Reason*, 192.

62. Junker-Kenny, *Religion and Public Reason*, 193.

63. Ricoeur, *Oneself as Another*, 290.

and religions can claims surface that truly deserve to be called universals."[64] Or as Boyd Blundell puts it: "Argumentation is not the nemesis of convention, but rather a necessary detour that convictions must pass through in order to be considered convictions."[65]

In this way, Ricoeur values the contribution of religion to democratic societies precisely because of their differences. Perhaps it is not overstating things to suggest that the Ricoeurian type differs from the Rawlsian and Habermasian types because the uniqueness, difference, and space of disagreement provide the most promising opportunities for discovering the pluralism of foundations that govern democracy and determine its future.[66] In contrast to Rawls and Habermas, Ricoeur's philosophy resists predetermining what contribution these groups will make to a democratic society but sees the exploration of the diversity of ethical frameworks and visions as crucial for the joint enterprise of creating democracy.[67] But, for Ricoeur, this does not do so at the expense of pluralism, with one religious group dominating the others, but rather it affirms pluralism and sees pluralism as a positive aspect of democracy, rather than a challenge to be overcome.[68] For Ricoeur, unlike Habermas and Rawls, the emphasis is placed on

> judgement or "practical wisdom" where universal principles and the respect for singularity have to be mediated and concrete solutions to conflicts worked out. It is here that cultural and religious resources for public reason come into play.[69]

Therefore, key to a Ricoeurian approach to publicness is to facilitate ways in which ethics are formed in the context of cultural particularity. By exploring these formational elements present within a community, rather than bracketing or bypassing them, in a Ricoeurian approach there is the possibility of sharing wisdom and values from the context of particularity in the public sphere.

---

64. Moyaert, *In Response to Religious Other*, 86.
65. Blundell, *Paul Ricoeur*, 123. Cited in Moyaert, *In Response to Religious Other*, 87.
66. Junker-Kenny, *Religion and Public Reason*, 229.
67. Junker-Kenny, *Religion and Public Reason*, 229–30.
68. Junker-Kenny, *Religion and Public Reason*, 230.
69. Junker-Kenny, *Religion and Public Reason*, 285.

COMPARISON OF THE THREE APPROACHES
Differing Views on the Nature of the Public Sphere

Having elaborated on these three different approaches, it is important to compare them more explicitly. First, the three thinkers' approaches to religion in the public sphere demonstrate diverse understandings of the public sphere's nature. For Rawls, the public sphere is the place of policymaking, which requires neutral political rhetoric, not value-based religious rhetoric. Religions can, therefore, translate their concepts into terms that every reasonable person holding to a theory of justice and political liberalism can accept. For Habermas, the public sphere is a space prior to the space of policymaking, which is the realm of the state. The public's purpose is to influence the state so that the state can implement policies that represent the will of the people. Religion can enter the public space in several forms, but must ultimately be translated, either by a religious person, or a nonreligious person to create a unified view of what policy should be implemented. For Habermas, religions must remain a part of public debates to ensure the moral dimensions of any issue at hand are kept in focus by a public whose ethical worldview is increasingly technocratic. This seems to be the dominant approach to academic public theology.

Ricoeur's hermeneutical approach would suggest that the task of building a common life together in a democratic society, which is ultimately Rawls's and Habermas's concern, cannot be done without citizens engaging with one another in their difference, and seeking to understand their differences. For Ricoeur, the ethical life, which impacts political life, is formed first by worldview, narratives, and symbols that give individuals and communities meaning. Therefore, in the Ricoeurian approach, publicness cannot be reduced to moments where ethical issues are at the front and center of a discussion, but in any moment where different citizens gather for the shared task of meaning making. One way of understanding this approach in comparison to Rawls and Habermas is that in their perspectives, the key question for religions entering the public sphere is "How can I best contribute to this discussion of a public issue in convincing ways?" The Ricoeurian approach, however, asks instead "How are we becoming and being formed as ethical agents in our diverse contexts?" Framing the discussion in this way challenges theologians to explore the public dimensions of formation of individuals and communities.

Thus, the focus on formation in Ricoeur's approach, according to Stiver, overcomes the traditional split between theory and praxis. In Ricoeur's hermeneutical arch, the end is action, because for Ricoeur "comprehension cannot be separated from the practices that undergird it and may best be realized in practice."[70] Ricoeur's approach to publicness then joins the turn towards practices in theology. Stiver states that "Ricoeur does not provide a system for doing theology, but a framework in which theology can be pursued in its multiplicity."[71] In the same vein, I would argue that Ricoeur does not provide a system for publicness and public theology, but a framework in which publicness and public theology can be pursued in their multiplicity because formation happens through multiple influences and practices. It is this multiplicity which best characterizes a Ricoeurian approach to publicness.

Thus, because Ricoeur's hermeneutical phenomenology questions strong demarcations between the public and private, this approach demonstrates the potential publicness of the practices of Manchester Cathedral, in that publicness is not being reduced only to statements in the context of public debates. If publicness is reduced only to speech (as Rawls and Habermas affirm), there would be significant limits as to what could be evaluated at the cathedral. However, questioning and testing the division between discourse and practice enables us to analyze the praxis of the cathedral. Ricoeur has therefore been crucial for developing the ways that I analyze the public theological practices of Manchester Cathedral.[72]

The Universal and the Particular

The second comparative difference between the thinkers that I would like to highlight is that Ricoeur challenges the presumption that difference is to be avoided to make progress in the public sphere, a challenge more detrimental to the Rawlsian approach. For Rawls, the public sphere needs to be neutral and governed by universal principles. For Habermas, the public sphere is combined of wild publics of debate, conversation, and opinion formation, but ultimately to translate into a neutral and universal policy. For Ricoeur, both paths tend towards homogenization, without rigorous appreciation for both the complexity of the human self and the value of difference.

For Habermas and Rawls, finding common ground or overlapping consensus is the aim. For Ricoeur, aims cannot be set prior to engagement, because the first aim in any public sphere is a common understanding of our differences, out of which we may, or may not, find a consensus. Thus, with a Ricoeurian approach, we have good reason to be suspicious of

---

70. Stiver, *Ricoeur and Theology*, 25.

71. Stiver, *Ricoeur and Theology*, 35.

72. I describe this approach more thoroughly in ch. 3.

theologies which tend towards finding universal norms or ethics as the goal of theological engagement, because of this tendency towards homogenization. However, this is not a rule that can be applied to every instance where an appeal to universality or neutral common ground is made, of course, but more of an awareness or suspicion to question further when appeals to neutrality and universality are made, by both religious and nonreligious people.

A way of putting this in an explicitly public theological way, public theology aims to find publicly valid warrants and criteria to offer theological reflection in society,[73] but we have to ask, "Whose publicly valid warrants and criteria?" Again, leading from the last conclusion, the three thinkers demonstrate a variety of understanding of what could be meant by the signifier "publicly valid claims." For Rawls, claims are only valid if they conform to the rules of justice set out in his theory, which he thinks are the natural result of political liberalism functioning well. Habermas sees religion as offering public warrants and criteria if they are given the chance to be heard uncritically by secular society in as much as they appeal to common morality. Ricoeur calls into question approaches which require having a predetermined understanding of what should be considered publicly valid, as this would assume we know more about the other than we do. To place predetermined boundaries on the discussions in question is to again function in a homogeneous way which will lead to the diluting of distinct religious identities. With Ricoeur, I argue that what might be considered to be publicly reasonable in society may be called into question by both religious and nonreligious citizens.

Varieties of Publics

Both of the Rawlsian and Habermasian perspectives depend on describing the public sphere as essentially singular. Even where Habermas in his later work describes the existence of wild/weak public spheres, these are ultimately still understood and interpreted in relation to the strong public sphere, which he argues the weak public spheres should be aiming to influence and contribute to. However, as Fraser argues:

> This narrative, then, like the bourgeois conception itself, is informed by an underlying evaluative assumption, namely, that the institutional confinement of public life to a single, overarching public sphere is a positive and desirable state of affairs,

---

73. Breitenberg, "To Tell the Truth," 65.

whereas the proliferation of a multiplicity of publics represents a departure from, rather than an advance toward, democracy.[74]

In my view, Ricoeur's approach to publicness allows for wild, subaltern counter publics to be able to speak their own language, perspective, and visions without there being a requirement to aim towards a larger whole.[75] While the Ricoeurian approach does not lead to the conclusion that subaltern publics can never communicate with any other kind of public, it does allow for there to be a self-sufficiency of wild publics that do not require them to be absorbed into a larger public. Instead, Ricoeur's approach provides a potential framework for a conflicted, contested, and argumentative interaction between different publics, through which new interpretations and visions could be discovered. As Fraser suggests:

> Insofar as these counter publics emerge in response to exclusions within dominant publics, they help expand discursive space. In principle, assumptions that were previously exempt from contestation will now have to be publicly argued out. In general, the proliferation of subaltern counter-publics means a widening of discursive contestation, and that is a good thing in stratified societies.[76]

CONCLUSION

In this chapter, I have outlined three diverse theories of religion's potential publicness. John Rawls's theory is one in which religion's publicness is determined by religious individuals' ability to translate their concepts into the language of justice, which provides an overlapping consensus among diverse people groups. Jürgen Habermas's theory does not want to bracket distinctive religious markers and perspectives but does understand the need

---

74. Fraser, "Rethinking the Public Sphere," 66.

75. In his important work *Subaltern Public Theology* Raj Patta frames public theology in this way: "Public theology is not only concerned of doing its theology in public but is called to do its theology of public and often called to do its theology against the dominant public, from sites of excluded public" (8). Patta, using this framing, interrogates public theology from the site of Indian subaltern communities.

76. Fraser, "Rethinking the Public Sphere," 67. In relation to the primary aims of this thesis, the question of how Manchester Cathedral relates to different conceptions of publicness and different publics is central. Does Manchester Cathedral aim to absorb wild publics, such as the LGBTQ+ community, into a larger whole in the name of inclusion? Or does it act as a host to various weak, subaltern publics? If so, how does it host such interaction, and what is the cathedral aiming for through its hosting?

to translate their concepts through a process of demythologization for them to be influential in the strong public sphere of policymaking. Paul Ricoeur's theory, however, is a hermeneutical theory that emphasizes religions and cultures as possessing unique visions of interpretation of meaning, the good and therefore the ethical. For Ricoeur publicness entails shared exploration of these visions, narratives, and symbols even if such exploration may lead to conflict.

By using these three thinkers as representatives of three distinct approaches to religious engagement in the public sphere I have developed lenses through which to interpret and question how public theologians employ terms such as "religion," "ethics," "translation," "reason," "public sphere," "relevance," and others. By attending to these three thinkers, we are better able to understand how some of these words function in a theologian's sentence and what presumptions might underpin those statements. In the following chapter, I demonstrate how public theology as a field is diverse in terms of what understandings of publicness are present in their work and what their assumptions about the *how* and *why* of religion entering the public sphere. As we shall see, by attending to these three thinkers, we can better understand what differences are present in the works of public theologians.

2

APPROACHES TO PUBLICNESS IN THE FIELD OF PUBLIC THEOLOGY

In chapter 1 I have argued that there are several approaches to the public sphere and understanding religion's purpose and methods for entering the public sphere. These are highlighted by the diversity seen in the three philosophers I have analyzed: John Rawls, Jürgen Habermas, and Paul Ricoeur. In this chapter I want to use that analysis to understand the field of public theology. If public theology is concerned with religion and theology entering the public sphere, what purpose do theologians give to this project? What methods are employed and what are the potential problems and opportunities in the post-secular city arise when theologians seek to be public? In particular I will show how the theme of translation dominates discussions in public theology, but that the question of formation should equally be regarded by public theologians.

THE PUBLICNESS OF THEOLOGY

While diverse understandings of the field of public theology have been offered by various scholars, an accurate and broad definition is offered by Elaine Graham, who states: "Public theology is the study of the public relevance of religious thought and practice."[1] The term was originally used by Martin Marty in an essay exploring the public theological dimensions of the theology of Reinhold Niebuhr. Marty sought to identify a tradition within theology that was not simply concerned with individual pietism and

---

1. Graham, *Apologetics Without Apology*, 71.

conversion (as in many evangelical traditions at the time) and could provide the basis for social activism and comment to hold organizations and institutions to account in their shaping of public life.[2] This understanding of public theology emerges in the North American context where public theology seeks to influence public life for the sake of the flourishing of all, while respecting the separation of church and state.[3]

Public theology may be challenged because by designating some theologies as "public," this appears to suggest that some theologies are "private."[4] However, as Hak Joon Lee argues, public theology arose in the North American context specifically to resist the privatization of religion and the domination of secularism in the public sphere.[5] For Lee, public theology exists not to confirm particular demarcations between the sacred and the secular, or public and private, but to highlight the religious dimensions of many elements concerning public life. In this way, public theology attempts to resist strong demarcations between the public and private in the public sphere.

Lee argues that public theology arose in the North American context to respond to the challenges of immigration, pluralism, and secularism, which were perceived to be leading the American public to be losing its "spiritual anchor."[6] However, though influenced by North American public theology, European public theology operates in the context of established religious institutions. As Malcolm Brown argues, at least in the context of Scotland and England, the establishment context means that there is an understanding that the established church and the state are in theory working together, aiming for the flourishing of all people within society. For Brown, this establishment relationship means that the church has already turned away from a purely introspective approach to the Christian faith.[7]

South Africa is also an important center in the field as its public theology is continually developed in the postapartheid period. Many public theologians in other geographical contexts draw on the work of pastors and theologians during the apartheid struggle as model examples of public

---

2. Marty, "Two Kinds of Civil Religion"; Graham, *Between Rock and Hard Place*, 73–74.

3. Graham, *Between Rock and Hard Place*, 116.

4. Graham argues that this is one of the key challenges to public theology in the postmodern era. Many binaries that became commonplace in the modern era, such as public and private, secular and sacred, masculine and feminine, are being dissolved in the postmodern period. See Graham, *Between Rock and Hard Place*, 69.

5. H. Lee, "Public Theology," 45.

6. H. Lee, "Public Theology," 46. See also McElroy, *American Public Theology*, 15.

7. Brown, "Establishment," 331.

theology in practice. A common example that is sometimes used by scholars is "The Kairos Document" produced by pastors and theologians in South Africa under the Nationalist Apartheid Regime when a national emergency was declared.[8] Graham, Day and Kim, and Kjetil Fretheim show this document as containing key aspects of theological engagement with the public sphere.[9] For example, Fretheim upholds the social analysis that shapes the theology of the document as exemplary of the kind of social analysis needed when engaging issues of public concern.[10] Graham highlights the prophetic character of the document as exemplary of a public theology oriented towards justice. She cites a paragraph in the document that says:

> The Church should challenge, inspire, and motivate people. It has a message of the cross that inspires us to make sacrifices for justice and liberation. It has a message of hope that challenges us to wake up and to act with hope and confidence. The Church must preach this message not only in words and sermons and statements but also through its actions, programs, campaigns, and divine services.[11]

In addition to the North American, European, and South African locations of public theology, many theologians identifying their work as public theology are contributing from other parts of Africa, Asia, Latin America, Australia, and New Zealand. Each of these social locations gives rise to distinct approaches to public theology.[12] And the social locations in which public theology is performed or written shape the theology, because public theology often operates in an "incarnational" manner, meaning that theology is not being done in the abstract, but in concrete communities.

Sebastian Kim and Katie Day draw on Dietrich Bonhoeffer and his emphasis on theology being done in the concrete rather than in the abstract. As they argue, this incarnational approach to theology dissolve's potential polarities between sacred/secular, public/private, church/world, and Christ/culture. Instead, the reality is "much more interactive," as Christ can be known only in the concrete.[13] For Day and Kim, this means that public theology is not focused on evangelizing "sinful societies" or focusing on

---

8. Graham, *Between Rock and Hard Place*, 72.

9. Graham, *Between Rock and Hard Place*, 72. See also Fretheim, *Interruption and Imagination*, 74–76; K. Day and Kim, "Introduction," vii–viii.

10. Fretheim, *Interruption and Imagination*, 74–86.

11. National Initiative for Reconciliation, "Kairos Document" 5.6. Cited in Graham, *Between Rock and Hard Place*, 72.

12. Graham, *Between Rock and Hard Place*, 75.

13. K. Day and Kim, "Introduction," x.

individual salvation. Instead, the project is focused on seeking God's intentions for all creation, which they express through the term "the common good."[14]

For Elaine Graham and Duncan Forrester, the incarnational mark of public theology is seen in the public theologian's concern for "the welfare of the city" (Jer 29:7) rather than the growth and expansion of the church or other religious institutions.[15] They both argue that part of the distinctive approach of public theology is that its interest lies in the mutual flourishing of all members of a given society, not simply those who belong to Christian institutions.

As a result of this emphasis on the "welfare of the city," public theology functions, in part, as an alternative to biblicism. When I use the term *biblicism*, I am using it to designate a particular religio-ethical methodology where a "plain meaning" of Scripture is searched for as the sole authority and voice on a particular ethical issue. For those who enter the public sphere with a biblicist approach, Scripture is seen as all sufficient for both understanding ethical issues and for communicating in public. For the public theologian, this approach is simply untenable and necessarily leads to sectarian withdrawal with a "Christ against culture" posture towards the wider social world for there is no need to enter into dialogue. For the public theologian:

> Simply muttering among ourselves (or worse, shouting from our soapboxes) that contemporary social practices violate the standards presented to us by the Christian tradition will serve only to relegate Christianity to an increasingly powerless position on the margins of society. Rather, we must "translate" our Christian "doctrines" into a language that the secular listener (and the religious other) can understand so that we can meet them halfway.[16]

From this quote, we are introduced to a central theme in public theology: translation. In the following sections I will elaborate how I see this notion of translation being present in public theology and the diverse approaches to translation in public theology.

---

14. K. Day and Kim, "Introduction," xi.

15. Forrester, "Scope of Public Theology," 6; Graham, *Between Rock and Hard Place*, 28.

16. Blundell, *Paul Ricoeur*, 23.

"BILINGUALISM" IN PUBLIC THEOLOGY

For Day and Kim, public theology is necessarily dialogical. They suggest, "True dialogue incorporates several facets critical to the production and reproduction of public theology: self-critique, transparency, accountability, and the construction of authority."[17] For these facets to be applied within public theology, "bilingualism" is needed for the theological contribution to be understandable by the particular public being addressed.[18] Defining the bilingual nature of public theology, Elaine Graham argues:

> Public theology speaks of itself as "bilingual" in drawing from the resources of its own tradition while listening to and *being comprehensible* by non-theological disciplines.... The aim is engagement, and public theology tries to practice what it preaches in conducting its research dialogically and in public, through colloquia, consultation, and dialogue with policymakers and activists.[19]

A key phrase in this paragraph is "being comprehensible by non-theological disciplines." Interdisciplinarity has developed in public theology, Day and Kim argue, as there has been an increasing recognition that to be able to effectively communicate with a variety of publics the public theologian must draw on a wide range of disciplines. One example they use to demonstrate this is the case of theological responses to climate change. They argue that for public theologians to effectively contribute in the public realm to these issues is that they must be well-versed in the most recent scientific data.[20] Dirk J. Smit argues that this is the one aspect of public theology that unites all public theology. He suggests that when one looks through the topics addressed in *The International Journal of Public Theology* (*IJPT*) there seems to be no uniting factor in terms of theology. The only uniting factor for Smit is that the public theologians are well informed on the issues they address. And thus, the interdisciplinary method is the most distinguishing aspect of public theology.[21]

Scott Paeth in his book *Exodus Church and Civil Society* argues that Jürgen Moltmann offered an effective threefold model of how a public theology should be conducted in an interdisciplinary fashion.[22] The first step is

---

17. K. Day and Kim, "Introduction," xiv.
18. K. Day and Kim, "Introduction," xiv.
19. Graham, *Between Rock and Hard Place*, 99–100; emphasis added.
20. K. Day and Kim, "Introduction," xiii.
21. D. Smit, "Does It Matter," 80.
22. Paeth, *Exodus Church and Civil Society*, 8–9. Though Moltmann is most

analysis. Analysis involves asking the question "What is going on?" by using resources across different disciplines. The next step is interpretation. Using the resources and data gathered from the analysis the Christian theologian must interpret this data from a Christian perspective. For Moltmann, this means interpreting the data through the lens of the crucified messiah who suffers for the marginalized. The third step in this model is to offer a constructive response considering the first two stages for the public(s) involved in this situation.[23] For Moltmann, dialogue is used to best know what theological tools, language, and praxis should be used in each situation.

This interdisciplinary method is also comparable to the middle axiom approach often adopted by Anglican public theologians influenced by William Temple and the subsequent Temple tradition. While Anglican social theology[24] is as diverse and broad as the Church of England itself, it can be recognized that, at least until recent years, there was a dominant approach to engagement with the public sphere. This approach is called the *middle axiom* approach. The phrase "middle axiom" was coined by J. H. Oldham in 1937. He states:

> It is not the function of the clergy to tell the laity how to act in public affairs, but rather to confront them with the Christian demand and to encourage them to discover its application for themselves. Hence, as between purely general statements of the ethical demands of the gospel and the decisions that must be made in concrete situations, there is need for what may be described as middle axioms.[25]

Therefore, the middle axiom approach is a way for Christians to engage in ethical issues and practice, without relegating decision-making to a kind of proof texting, but instead taking seriously the context and situation one finds themselves in to know how to respond. The Bible, in this sense,

---

commonly associated with political theology, in his later work the terms "public theology" and "political theology" are used somewhat interchangeably. Paeth argues that Moltmann's use of the term "political" in political theology is broader than simply "concerning state action" and instead connotes much of what is of interest to North American public theologians. Thus, in his later work, he adopted the language of public theology to describe his own understanding of the church's relationship to the world. See Moltmann, *God for Secular Society*, 5.

23. Paeth, *Exodus Church and Civil Society*, 63–67.

24. The identifier "Anglican social theology" is, in my view, interchangeable with "Anglican public theology" as these are concerned with the same issues of how the Anglican Church can contribute to public life in the context of post-Christendom, secularized, pluralist societies. See Brown, "Case for Anglican Social," 9–27.

25. Oldham, "Function of the Church," 193–94. Cited in McCann, "Middle Axioms," 75–76.

does not provide universal, timeless ethical norms, but a way of being in the world that is more about ethical form than content.

The middle axiom approach is fundamentally about dialogue. Learning as much about the context and situation by learning from the various disciplines and listening to a wide range of voices in the discussion to find common ground for public consensus. But the middle axiom approach is not simply about finding ways of speaking that are relevant to other members of a social order in which the church wishes to engage. It is, moreover, a means for the church to identify ways in which their speech and practice must be modified and revised, if necessary, to contribute effectively to the social realm.[26] This is reflective of a key aspect of Anglican theology generally, as Bretherton states:

> It is not hyperbolic to say that Anglicanism, from its very origins, has been a pathway into imagining what it means to be modern, but one that does not require rupture with or disavowal of the past criterion for being modern. Indeed, an emphasis on tradition and history is one of the hallmarks of Anglican theology.[27]

One striking aspect of public theology is its analysis of the various "publics" into which a theologian may speak. Day and Kim argue that it would be a mistake to imagine that publicness is monolithic. Instead, they argue that a key mark of public theology is for public theologians to identify and reflect on the nature of the public sphere(s).[28] David Tracy is attributed with being the first theologian to emphasize the importance of identifying a variety of publics that the theologian must address. He argues there are multiple publics that the public theologian addresses, even if these publics overlap in some way. According to Tracy the three publics that the public theologian addresses are: church, academy, and society.[29] For Tracy, each of these publics has its own sets of criteria and warrants that the public theologian must adhere to if they are to make a constructive contribution to that public arena. This is important to our question of translation, because, according to Tracy, differing publics contain different languages and rules of reasoning into which theology needs to be translated.[30]

---

26. McCann, "Middle Axioms," 87.

27. Bretherton, *Christ and Common Life*, 188. Of course, this is partly significant for Manchester Cathedral because it is an Anglican institution. Part of my discussion in later chapters will be about how Manchester Cathedral's public theology is connected to the tradition of Anglican public theology.

28. K. Day and Kim, "Introduction," xi.

29. Tracy, *Analogical Imagination*, 7.

30. Importantly, Kristin Heyer critiques Tracy's work for rarely addressing the

Since Tracy's outlining of the three publics, other public theologians have offered their own variations of the various publics that the theologian should aim to speak to. Max Stackhouse, for example, accepts Tracy's three but adds an "economic" public as a fourth.[31] Kim has the three publics Tracy proposed but added three more: the state, media, and the market.[32] While it is possible to debate the usefulness of such attempts to identify how many different publics the public theologian could speak to,[33] it is important to emphasize that these authors are doing so to identify what language and modes of reasoning should be used for particular audiences. In this perspective, the theologian needs to participate in a public discussion according to the language, processes, criteria, and social rules of the public they are addressing to have influence.

But there needs to be an analysis of what approaches the public theologian may take to translation, because translation requires methodological and philosophical decisions based on assumption about *how* the Christian "language" is conceived, and what the alternative "secular" language actually entails. This is where the philosophical approaches to publicness outlined in chapter 1 can help in demonstrating how different approaches to publicness and translation are operant within the field.

APPROACHES TO TRANSLATION

Each of the philosophers and their corresponding approaches interprets the potential of religious comprehensibility differently, and thus there are different approaches to translation and bilingualism in the field of public theology. In my view, a Rawlsian approach to the dialogical mark of public theology assumes that there are principles that provide an overlapping consensus that diverse groups have in common that theology should be able to

---

public of the church, despite him naming this as one of the three publics a theologian must address. As a result, she argues that his "conversations" are limited to the academy as he does not address questions about the institutional implications of his conversation model ("How Does Theology Go Public," 322).

31. Stackhouse, "Public Theology and Ethical Judgment." It is important to note, however, that for Tracy, "economy" would fit within the broad public of "society." Tracy's three publics are broad sectors that cover all potential audiences while also recognizing that there are specific demarcations to be made within each public.

32. Kim, *Theology in Public Sphere*, 13.

33. Linell Cady, for example, has criticized how public theologians have exerted a lot of energy on this task without spending time on more interesting questions, such as the role secularism plays in debates about the publicness of religious reasoning. See Cady, "Public Theology and Postsecular Turn," 310.

translate their concepts into. If the end, for theology, is the establishment of justice in society, for example, theology can be adapted and translated to achieve those ends.

In this way, theology need not play a discernible role in the public dimensions of the interaction. Because the establishment of justice is the perceived end of public theology in this approach, and justice is assumed, in this model, to be a universal concept, theology does not have to be part of the means of justice's establishment in public. The theologian may be motivated by the Christian tradition in this model, but the tradition does not need to form a part of the content for establishing justice. Instead, certain collective values provide the moral content that theology may offer tacit support to. For example, Júlio Zabatiero argues:

> Theology must position itself as a constructor of a discourse carrying principles and universal . . . values of freedom, selflessness, and justice; values that are clearly espoused in the Gospel. . . . These values, however, are not only present in the Gospel, but in many other religions and also in non-religious ethics. . . . The challenge here for theology is to learn how to find other knowledge and interpret it and translate it for a public language for justice.[34]

As can be seen in this quote, Zabatiero understands the public theological task to elucidate and offer support to universal values already shared in the public sphere. In this way, universal values are the focus of public theology, and the public theologian's task is to translate their own resources into these terms.

Another example of the Rawlsian approach can be seen in the appeal to human rights as an already theological category. In his essay "Can Natural Law Still Address Civil Society?" Terence Kennedy argues that to use the language of rights is already to be articulating a natural theology in a language that civil society can understand. For Kennedy, and other theologians who primarily appeal to rights as a dominant moral discourse, rights language is the primary mode of moral discourse that provides the ground for dialogue with the "other" and the means of collective decisions on issues of justice.[35]

For this approach, the language of values and universal principles is a sufficient shared language between the religious and the secular. The theologian adopting this approach will assume an understanding of love and justice which they are religiously motivated to see established in society,

---

34. Zabatiero, "Public Character of Theology," 66.
35. Atherton, *Public Theology for Changing Times*, 11.

but don't think that religions have exclusive claims on, or interpretations of, these concepts. Put within a Christological frame, Christ provides the motivation to act rationally or justly but does not necessarily inform the content of how rationality or justice is understood.[36] Thus, in this Rawlsian approach, the public theologian articulates their positions from the definitions and concepts of justice given by the public they are addressing.

The Habermasian approach offers a different understanding of dialogue from the Rawlsian approach. The Habermasian model maintains the potential for religious discourse to contribute something that the secular cannot generate on its own terms. As I explained in the previous chapter, the Habermasian approach views religious discourse as a potential corrective to the domination of instrumental reason in the public sphere.[37] As we have seen, for Habermas, there is a universal moral truth that all are oriented towards, but this is articulated from different perspectives and insights. It is the unique religious perspective that can provide a valuable moral contribution to the public realm when it is allowed to articulate its views.[38] Public theologians adopting the Habermasian approach consider their religious tradition to offer moral insights that other perspectives, such as the secular, do not have. What differentiates the Rawlsian approach from the Habermasian approach is that religious traditions and stories and symbols are seen as expendable and background in the Rawlsian model.

In the Habermasian approach, religious stories and symbols contain moral contents that secular rationality cannot provide. To relegate religion and theology to the field of private motivation, moral discourse is reduced to instrumental reason, which as we have seen Habermas wants to resist for fear that such reasoning is in the end morally deficient. Religion and secular are in equal dialogue, for a time at least. But in the end, the religious view must be translated into secular terms, through the process of dialogue. Tracy similarly argues that in our post-Enlightenment world, it is important for theologians to demythologize the Christian texts to demonstrate to secular society Christianity's relevant meanings. Tracy affirms the universal character of theology because people are driven by universal existential questions.

For Tracy the classics contain and disclose answers to these questions, making them universal texts. He suggests that the Christian theologian does not have a responsibility to claim something as true based on tradition, i.e.,

---

36. Milbank, *Theology and Social Theory*, 231. This is a summary of Milbank's criticism of the theology of Karl Rahner, who as Martinez has argued is influential on the public theology of David Tracy, and by extension on public theology as a whole). Martinez, *Confronting Mystery of God*, 184–200).

37. Graham, *Between Rock and Hard Place*, 94–95.

38. Habermas, *Between Naturalism and Religion*, 65.

natural impossibilities such as the incarnation, resurrection, miracles, etc. because the theologian has a commitment to the scientific knowledge of their colleagues in philosophy, the sciences, and social sciences.

But this doesn't mean that the limit meanings of those aspects of the Christian "myths" are irrelevant. Tracy describes myths (which include metaphors and narratives) as "intending adequate representations of basic beliefs," i.e., as "first narrative representations of ourselves holding certain basic beliefs."[39] For Tracy, the problem with the classical theistic interpretation of the Christian tradition is that the theologians have literalized myths. In a similar vein, Habermas argues:

> Assuming this anthropocentric foundation, rational hermeneutics must reject many articles of faith, such as the resurrection of the body, for example, as historical embellishments.[40]

This demythologizing approach to translation is, in my view, an extension of Kant's project in *Religion Within the Boundaries of Pure Reason*. Kant writes:

> We most assuredly will not class the last grounds of morality along with the holy mysteries; for the whole theory of ethics is publicly communicable, although the suprasensible causality lying at the bottom of moral conduct is neither known or given. That alone, therefore, which may be an object of the possible, but incommunicable knowledge, will we regard as possessing the dread of character of the Sacro-sanct.[41]

For Kant, metaphysical claims about God and questions of the historical reliability of biblical narratives are unimportant, because the aim of the Christian faith to him is to produce and encourage moral behavior that every reasonable person would accept as moral. Ethics then for Kant is the grounds for Christianity's publicness.

Some theologians however maintain the need for translation but do not assume this entails the demythologizing of Christianity. For example, Elaine Graham aims to distinguish her apologetic framework from, as Heather Walton puts it, the "sloppy assumption that there is . . . something inherently progressive in theological discourse per se when coherently and rationally expressed, which usually means avoiding references to God in any form that could be recognized by the untrained reader."[42] She thinks

---

39. Tracy, *Blessed Rage for Order*, 162.
40. Habermas, *Between Naturalism and Religion*, 215.
41. Kant, *Religion Within the Boundaries*, 184.
42. Walton, "You Have to Say," 25. Cited in Graham, *Between Rock and Hard Place*, 158.

that public theology must hold in tension faithfulness to its tradition and the realities and complexities of the contexts the public theology speaks to.

She draws on the critiques of radical orthodox and post-liberal theologians such as William Cavanaugh and John Milbank, arguing that public theologians do operate from the confession that Jesus Christ is the Word of God to the world. She wants to hold to a Christocentric soteriology, but she argues some form of translation must take place to communicate that Word to the public sphere.[43] Graham seeks to move away from an understanding of public theology that can marginalize specific Christian doctrines to be more fitting within a secularist ideology. Instead, she aims to develop an approach to publicness that does not require such marginalization and in turn draws more explicitly on the rich resources of the Christian tradition. As we can see from the tensions seen between Tracy's and Graham's approaches. The problem arises that translation into a secular discourse potentially

> blurs the unique and specific flavor of Christian witness and in some cases, particular religious concerns seem difficult to translate into a universal language, which indicates how translation is not an innocent activity. . . . In the attempt to please its audience public theology risks losing authenticity, credibility, and its recognizable character.[44]

Thus, the dialogical, bilingual mark of public theology, especially the notion of translation, is at the center of public theology's aims, methods, and its contestation. Therefore, it is important to further take into account the critiques of this aspect of the fields emphasis that further demonstrate how the field has come to be understood by its critics. Post-liberal theologians are among the most ardent critics of public theology, and so to them we now turn.

THE POST-LIBERAL CRITIQUE OF PUBLIC THEOLOGY

One of the main streams of theology that critiques public theology quite heavily is the "post-liberal tradition." Maureen Junker-Kenny describes the post-liberal approach to theology as following the theologies of George Lindbeck and Hans Frei, who argue that "theology is about the internal grammar of the Christian faith, which is to be explained primarily for its followers, and not in relation to the other traditions or to the light of reason."[45]

---

43. Graham, *Between Rock and Hard Place*, 204.
44. Fretheim, *Interruption and Imagination*, 130.
45. Junker-Kenny, *Approaches to Theological Ethics*, 93.

This definition, of course, provides a stark contrast between public theology and post-liberal theology, in that public theology often seeks to translate the "internal grammar of the Christian faith" into terms accessible and relevant to publics outside of the church.

Lindbeck's approach to theology argues for a clear distinction between the Christian language and other languages because for him language is not simply a sign pointing to a shared reality. He critiques what he calls an "expressivist" approach to theology, in which it is assumed that different cultures and communities experience the same thing but simply use different language to describe that experience. Instead, he argues that the language used by the community itself shapes the experience.[46] Thus, the theology and practice of the church can only come from within itself and only based on the shared language that individuals must adopt to participate. As Tracy argues, the only method of communication in this system is confessional, as opposed to dialogical.[47]

Post-liberals argue that only the church can fulfil the concept of a community that is joined together by shared convictions. For example, Stanley Hauerwas argues that the world outside of the Christian community lacks any epistemological foundation on which to base its ethical and moral claims because those outside the church are governed by liberal individualism which he sees as characteristic of Enlightenment rationality. For Hauerwas, "In a world without foundations, all we have is the church."[48] Gary Comstock critiques this post-liberal, cultural-linguistic model because it perpetuates a theological and ecclesial closedness, in that it is sustained and formed by its own inner convictions that cannot be challenged by any other forms of reason found outside of the Christian church.[49] However, Hauerwas contends that despite this kind of critique, this is not a problem for Christian theologians, because, in his view, the primary Christian call to be witnesses does not depend on any notions of shared intelligibility.[50] Its

---

46. Lindbeck, *Nature of Doctrine*, 2–3.

47. Tracy, "Lindbeck's New Program," 465–66.

48. This is the subtitle of Hauerwas, "Church's One Foundation." As Samuel Wells argues, Hauerwas is part of the tradition of post-liberalism established by Lindbeck and Frei. One uniting factor among their theologies, for example, is the influence of Karl Barth. However, Hauerwas broadens the grammatical emphasis of Lindbeck and Frei to recognize the tradition and history of the community of faith as important for understanding the development of the Christian language. This moves Hauerwas away from the arguably more static view of Christian grammar being derived from Scripture alone as argued by Frei and Lindbeck. See Wells, "Stanley Hauerwas' Theological Ethics," 433–34.

49. Comstock, "Types of Narrative Theology," 699.

50. Hauerwas et al., *Wisdom of the Cross*, 33.

role within the world is simply to discover and be faithful to its own internal shared convictions, which those outside might seek to imitate.[51] Within this framework, there are clear boundaries and distinctions made between the "church" and "the world" and these boundaries are created and sustained through language.

Post-liberal theology, then, seeks to challenge the church to live up to its calling to be an alternative polis in the world speaking its own language. Further, post-liberal theology tends to understand the "language of the church" through the liturgy. The liturgy becomes the place in which Christians learn the grammar of their faith. One example of this can be seen in James K. A. Smith's evangelical public theology. Smith argues that political theology and public theology have mistakenly assumed a spatial account of politics, wherein the church can move into the space of civil society to speak to the state, which has an obligation to listen to the voice of its citizens. Smith argues that this fails to grasp how society has become the ruling force in the world and that society is structured and governed by economic markets. According to Smith, the market molds the desires of citizens who demand publicity, usually in the form of "monetizing their Instagram feeds."[52] For Smith, the church is an alternative polis, which should be shaped by different forces, namely through liturgical practices.[53] Because the desires of the church are formed through the eschatological hope revealed in Christ, the church is able to speak an alternate word in the world about what it may mean to be human.[54]

Similarly, William Cavanaugh argues in favor of what he calls ecclesial ethics:

> "Ecclesial ethics" is an unapologetically theological approach to ethics, one in which an attempt is made to apply the Gospel to political and economic realities. Jesus' command to love one's enemies, for example, is not restricted to private relationships, but is taken seriously as a basis for Christian action in public. This approach is ecclesial in that the church is seen as a sacrament of Christ to the world, whose job is to speak the word of God that is not simply reducible to common sense or natural law principles.[55]

---

51. Junker-Kenny, *Approaches to Theological Ethics*, 93–94.
52. J. Smith, *Awaiting the King*, 12.
53. J. Smith, *Awaiting the King*, 13.
54. See J. Smith, *Desiring the Kingdom*, for his full account.
55. Cavanaugh, "Ecclesial Ethics," 502.

Cavanaugh goes on to give the example of Christian opposition to war, where he argues that the process of opposing war cannot simply be Christians quoting Jesus's command to love one's enemies to the public sphere. Instead, Christians can oppose war by both refusing to participate in war and building peace communities. Such practice, he argues, fulfils the true nature of the church's politics, which does not receive its power from the state, and offers itself as a sacrament to the world.[56]

Thus, one way of characterizing this ecclesial, post-liberal approach is that it largely emphasizes the distinctiveness of the church as its main purpose and service in the world. It therefore focuses on how that distinctiveness is formed through the distinctive confession of the death and resurrection of Jesus Christ and the distinctive practices that embody that confession, such as the liturgy and Eucharist. Smith, therefore, following Oliver O'Donovan, argues that the crucifixion and resurrection of Christ must surely be the basis of any Christian ethic, including public ethics.[57] Therefore, Smith complains that much of public theology draws so much on contemporary social convention and moral vision that many public theologies could operate perfectly well if the resurrection had never happened.[58]

However, this critique of public theology is not exclusive to post-liberal theologians. Practical feminist theologian Heather Walton writes that she has an "ambivalence bordering on antipathy" towards public theology.[59] One of her key criticisms of the field is that it often depends on

> the liberal hope that there is something inherently progressive in theological discourse per se when coherently and rationally expressed—which usually means avoiding references to God in any form that could be recognized by the untrained reader.[60]

It seems therefore that there is a tension in public theology, as revealed by these critiques of the field, between striving for public relevance and theologians maintaining the distinctive elements of their traditions. For the public theologian, the main purpose of public theology is to positively impact a

---

56. Cavanaugh, "Ecclesial Ethics," 518–19.

57. J. Smith, "Beyond Creation and Natural Law." Smith draws on O'Donovan, *Resurrection and Moral Order*.

58. J. Smith, "Beyond Creation and Natural Law."

59. Walton, *Writing Methods*, 149.

60. Walton, *Writing Methods*, 153. Similarly, Luke Bretherton resists describing his work as "public theology" and opts instead for describing his work as a "theology of public life." He argues public theology relies on theologians conforming to the biases of secular societies, seen most visibly in the demythologizing of Christian doctrine and Scripture, to achieve public relevance (*Christ and Common Life*, 33).

given society, or public, towards a shared democratic decision about a particular topic. It is partly concerned with how the speech and practice of the church can contribute to the welfare of the city, rather than the churches own growth or health. On the other hand, for the post-liberal theologian, the validity of a particular theology is not determined by its reception by "the world." Rather, theology exists primarily to serve the formation of the church in its common life, established as it is by the Eucharist and the gospel narrative that is told and performed through liturgical practice. From their perspective, it is only through these that the church can truly serve the world.[61]

However, as Kristin Heyer argues there is greater complementarity between post-liberalism (as represented by Lindbeck) and public theology (as represented by Tracy) than is often acknowledged. In her view, the impasse between these two approaches is in their different views of what it means to "go public."[62] The public theologian's desire to translate the Christian tradition's symbols into wider categories, she argues, is contrasted by Lindbeck's perspective that the symbols should function to redescribe reality.[63] However, she argues that it is each model's incompleteness that leads her to perceive these as complementary. She argues that Lindbeck's focus on the singularity and distinctiveness of Christ leads him to miss the presence of the Spirit in the world, outside the church. On the other hand, Tracy's (and by extension public theology's) emphasis on creation and grace comes at the expense of the singularity of Jesus Christ.[64] In my view, the Ricoeurian approach to public theology provides the possibility of drawing on the strengths of both these approaches, while also avoiding the pitfalls of the exclusive approaches to each of them.

RICOEUR BETWEEN PUBLIC THEOLOGY AND POST-LIBERALISM

Marianne Moyaert argues that Ricoeur has more in common with the post-liberal theologians concerning interreligious and cross-cultural dialogues because he is suspicious of the reductionist tendencies present in attempts of inclusivism and pluralism that do not take cultural distinction seriously and assume that all cultures and religions are articulating the same principles

---

61. Junker-Kenney, *Approaches to Theological Ethics*, 116–18.
62. Heyer, "How Does Theology Go Public," 308.
63. Heyer, "How Does Theology Go Public," 314–15.
64. Heyer, "How Does Theology Go Public," 321.

in different ways.⁶⁵ Ricoeur's emphasis on the formation of ethical agents overlaps with the post-liberal concerns of the formation of the Christian community as the body of Christ.

On the other hand, he departs from post-liberalism represented by Lindbeck because he thinks that their understanding of Christian identity and relationality is too reductionist. For Ricoeur, religions don't operate within the firm boundaries that are often imagined by post-liberals influenced by Lindbeck. Instead, the boundaries are much more porous and overlapping, so it is difficult for Ricoeur to think of a single religion as being equivalent to a single language.⁶⁶ Instead, Ricoeur imagines a religious map in terms of an

> intersection of influences radiating out from the centers, the sources that are defined by their creativity and capacity to influence and generate sources of response within others. It is thus through this phenomenon of an intersection of effects of illumination forming dense networks that the notion of the inter-religious would be defined, in opposition to the notion of boundary.⁶⁷

Therefore, while the post-liberal theologians emphasize Christian speech and habits as the primary, or only, source of formation for Christians, Ricoeur demonstrates that all people are formed by multiple sources which often overlap. Therefore, important to understanding this aspect of Ricoeur's thought is to explore further his understanding of identity and how identity is formed. Ricoeur distinguishes two poles of an individuals identity: an *idem* identity, meaning "the same," and an *ipse* identity, meaning "oneself." The idem identity refers to that which is unchanging in the individual, across time and experience. The ipse identity is that which develops over time and through experience. For Ricoeur, selves are to be understood in terms of ipse, because the idem identity is too fixed and unchanging to be a properly human self. While Ricoeur recognizes that there may be unchanging characteristics in a person, for example, biology and language, the human self, because of its relation to time, develops and changes.⁶⁸ This reality makes it difficult to recognize what is constant in the human.

For Ricoeur, there is a dialectical relationship between these two poles of identity in a person, which can be made sense of through the narrative identity, which is formed through the self's interpretation of itself. For

---

65. Moyaert, *In Response to Religious Other*, 133.
66. Moyaert, *In Response to Religious Other*, 134–35.
67. Ricoeur, "Cultures." Cited in Moyaert, *In Response to Religious Other*, 137.
68. Ricoeur, *Oneself as Another*, 121–22; Moyaert, *Fragile Identities*, 250.

Ricoeur, this narrative identity doesn't neglect or exclude the idem aspect of a person but is rather the necessary process by which the two identities interact. The way the narrative of the self is told will change over time and through experiences. As Ricoeur writes, "We are always in the process of revising the text, the narrative of our lives. In this sense, we may construct several narratives about ourselves, told from several points of view."[69]

For Ricoeur, this means that there cannot be a closed-off narrative self, as we often learn to tell stories and narratives through listening to and reading other narratives. In a sense, this emphasis on the narrative self opens an individual up to the impact of another, because their identity is not fixed and unchanging, but is open to alternative stories to ones already known and told by the individual.

This perspective then neither assumes identity as absolutely fixed nor as completely arbitrary. The implication, therefore, is that the cultural-linguistic model depends too much on seeing Christian identity through an idem lens, i.e., Christian identity is imagined as being fixed and essentially uniform. On the other hand, those perhaps like Rawls might treat the religious identities of individuals as less foundational than other identity markers, as religious people are presumed to be able to bracket their distinctive religious beliefs, and not take account of how their religious narratives impact and shape their visions and therefore their identities.

Such a notion resists the mistake of thinking that there could ever be a Christianity or reading of Scripture that exists outside of the influence of particular cultures. As Miroslav Volf argues:

> We can look at our culture through the lenses of religious texts only as we look at these texts through the lenses of our culture. The notion of inhabiting the biblical story is hermeneutically naïve because it presupposes that those who are faced with the biblical story can be completely "dis-lodged" from their extratextual dwelling places and "re-settled" into intratextual homes.[70]

Further, as Ricoeur argues, Christianity itself has historically been impacted by several sources including Greek, Roman, and Islamic, to name a few. So, the "pure" religion imagined by the post-liberals that can be understood to be separate from the world is produced within and in conversation with the world. While Ricoeur would suggest that the particularity of the Christian vision means that ethical questions and experiences are received by

---

69. Ricoeur, *Oneself as Another*, 309. Cited in Moyaert, *Fragile Identities*, 245.

70. Volf, "Theology, Meaning, and Power," 103. Cited in Heyer, "How Does Theology Go Public," 315.

Christians in a particular way, this does not preclude the possibility of being impacted by and influenced by alternate visions. In this way he writes:

> Yes, I believe it is possible to understand those different from me by means of sympathy and imagination, just as I understand a character in a novel or at the theatre or a real friend who is different from me. Moreover, I understand without repeating, portray without reliving, make myself different while remaining myself. To be a man is to be capable of this projection into another center of perspective.[71]

The key for Ricoeur then, is that because we are not fixed in our identities, we must remind ourselves that we are strange even to ourselves, and in a sense, other to ourselves, because we, even as Christians, cannot at this moment say who we will be in the future. This openness to our own strangeness makes it possible to be open to the stranger.

Ricoeur, therefore, argues for practices of "linguistic hospitality" that rests on the presumption that there is an extent to which we can understand one another, just as we can understand the perspective of a character in a novel who is from a different social and cultural situation than our own.[72] He thus, similarly to many public theologians, envisages the notion of translation as a key metaphor for the interaction of diverse people groups. However, he acknowledges that such translation cannot be predetermined by a set of rules or principles. Rather language and translation possess an inherent weakness that can only be negotiated through relationships and continued dialogue.[73] In a sense, the task of translation cannot come to an end, because we are always in process of discovering the other, and ourselves as a result.

Bilingualism then isn't a term that necessarily constitutes a Ricoeurian approach to translation, as there are multiple languages and cultures in play even within the context of the "Christian" language(s). To neglect this reality is to nourish "numerous linguistic ethnocentrisms, and more seriously, numerous pretensions to the same cultural hegemony."[74] This weakness is translation's value for Ricoeur because it forces the speaker and hearer to learn what needs to be adapted or left behind based on their ongoing friendship-dialogue and to see other languages and cultures as a source of nourishment and critique. Further, each language is understood to be formational for the agent speaking it but also is formed by the wider culture

---

71. Ricoeur, "Universal Civilization and National Cultures," 282.
72. Ricoeur, *On Translation*, 23–24.
73. Ricoeur, *On Translation*, 8, 31.
74. Ricoeur, *On Translation*, 4. Cited in Moyaert, "Ricoeur and the Wager," 176.

that the agent is participating in. Therefore, questions of translation cannot happen outside of questions of ethical and cultural formation.

This analysis is significant for this project because it draws out questions about how Manchester Cathedral interprets its public role, and how it understands its role regarding those with different identities and cultures. In a sense, a Ricoeurian approach to public theology means that my critical evaluation of the cathedral will concern questions about how the cathedral understands other cultures, religions, and perspectives, and the role that formation plays in their public theology. However, the Ricoeurian approach requires that there be an acceptance and awareness of self-identity for the cathedral to know who and how they are becoming. It is within this framework of public theology that the strengths of both sides of the public and post-liberal theologies can be drawn on.

WHOSE PUBLIC IS IT ANYWAY?

It is important to notice the fact that much discussion about religion's publicness largely concerns questions about religion and secularism and how religion can contribute to public debate in contexts that are "not Christian." However, when this becomes the emphasis, we fail to also consider how the public sphere has been constructed to elevate certain voices and to marginalize others. When the only questions we have are about "how to be convincing" and to translate into common publicly accessible terms, we fail to also recognize that publicness entails constructions of power. However, public theologians have by and large not taken these issues into account.

In an important essay, Esther McIntosh writes:

> Clearly, matters of race, gender, and sexual equality are highly significant areas of engagement for public theology. Both biblical material and the theological interpretation of it are used on both sides of the debate: by campaigners in favor of greater equality and those arguing against it. Therefore, as key areas of debate and tension in which church and society struggle to reach agreement, there is a need for public theologians to make their voice heard. However, there are few theologians engaged with issues of race, gender and sexual equality who refer to themselves as "public theologians" or to their work as "public theology."[75]

---

75. McIntosh, "I Met God," 301–2.

McIntosh suggests that a large part of the neglect of the topic of sexuality, gender, and race in public theology is because of the field's dependence on a Habermasian construction of the public sphere, a construction which she describes as "exclusionary."[76] Habermas conceived of a public sphere that was in theory open to all, but through aiming at a single overarching public sphere (perhaps we could say, an inclusive public sphere), Habermas had to conceive of a public sphere that bracketed out various social inequalities to unite the different social classes.[77] Habermas noted that women were typically excluded from the public sphere when it first formed in bourgeois society. However, as Nancy Fraser points out, this is to adopt a particular notion of publicness that is gendered. Nancy Fraser states: "The view that women were excluded from the public sphere [is] ideological; it rests on a class and gender-biased notion of publicity, one which accepts at face value the bourgeois public's claim to be *the* public."[78] She further argues that the actual speech that was deemed public was constructed with masculine gender constructs, such as rational thought not too encumbered with strong emotions. Feminist historiography has demonstrated that though women were denied "official access to the political sphere" they developed their own modes and forms of publicness.[79]

Further, in his recording of the history of the development of the bourgeois public sphere, Habermas fails to note the exclusionary nature of the public sphere, because he tries to demonstrate that the public sphere was an inclusive enterprise that everyone had access to in theory. The problem is:

> this network of clubs and associations, philanthropic, civic, professional, and cultural—was anything but accessible to everyone. On the contrary, it was the arena, the training ground, and eventually the power base of a stratum of bourgeois men, who were coming to see themselves as a "universal class" and preparing to assert their fitness to govern.[80]

The question is whether Habermas is right to attribute these flaws as accidental to the formation of the public sphere, or whether these exclusions are constitutive of its nature. Fraser argues the latter, suggesting serious revision is needed in our conception of the public sphere. She argues that aiming towards one overarching public sphere that seeks to unite a whole range of

---

76. McIntosh, "I Met God," 303.
77. Fraser, "Rethinking the Public Sphere," 65.
78. Fraser, "Rethinking the Public Sphere," 61; emphasis in original.
79. Goode, *Jürgen Habermas*, 32. See also Fraser, "Rethinking the Public Sphere," 61.
80. Fraser, "Rethinking the Public Sphere," 60.

social classes by bracketing out various inequalities in society, rather than eliminating them, cannot achieve what it sets out to do, but will only lead to further inequalities because only dominant forms of reason are taken to be reasonable.[81] Instead, she argues that we should not see minority publics that resist and challenge dominant publics as a departure from democracy, but an advancement of it. This leads to theories of multiple public spheres and the necessity of their representation in contrast to theories of publicness that depend on conceiving of a single unifying public sphere which will only lead to homogenization.[82]

Habermas, in accepting and responding to this criticism, distinguishes between two types of publics: the weak public and the strong public. The weak public is the space of opinion formation, which can be used to influence the state and policy, which is the strong public. It is important to note that for Habermas the distinction between "strong" and "weak" publics is not a matter of hierarchy or importance, as both rely on an interdependent relationship with one another. Rather, the strength and weakness are determined by the language rules governing each as the strong public must maintain universality, though it is impacted by the subjective influences of weak publics where there are fewer rules governing discourse.[83]

The weak publics are characterized as anarchistic and wild by Habermas, and their purpose is to demonstrate to the strong public and competing weak publics where the problems in society can be addressed. For Habermas, there is still an overarching public sphere, because both the weak/wild and strong publics are interdependently aiming together towards emancipation. Thus, he can include those marginalized groups in the common quest for publicness in society without relinquishing his concept of an overarching public sphere.[84]

Despite Habermas reforming some of his theories in response to these criticisms, public theologians following Habermas's understanding of the nature of the public sphere have often spent more time on questions about which public to address, rather than addressing the potentially exclusionary natures of those publics.[85]

81. Fraser, "Rethinking the Public Sphere," 65.

82. Fraser, "Rethinking the Public Sphere," 65.

83. Ward, "Rekindling 'Radical Democratic Embers,'" 831–32.

84. Mansbridge, "Long Life," 111; Habermas, *Between Facts and Norms*, 304–5. Habermas specifically references Fraser's criticisms here when he discusses this concept of weak and strong publics.

85. I would further argue that Tracy's three publics are not inherently homogenous but could be if they are utilized in such a way to absorb differences and minority perspectives in the public spheres.

As a result, public theology as a field has largely neglected the topics of racism, gender equality, and LGBTQ+ inclusion and theology. In this way, he makes a similar error to John Rawls who imagines that by entering into the veil of ignorance participants can both detach themselves from their own social status and imagine life through the eyes of a person from another social status. Significantly, from my reading of *A Theory of Justice* the concept of "justice as fairness" seems to apply explicitly to issues of economic distribution and opportunity. As a result, power as a complex social issue that is a significant aspect of conversations about race and gender, for example, is not addressed by Rawls.

By assuming a conception of the public sphere as neutral, probably with the hope that following this assumption theology can find a space in the public sphere, public theology has avoided confronting the power dynamics present in the public sphere.[86] The issue of power and authority has not been drawn out by public theologians in a consistent manner.[87] One of the problems with this is that issues of race, gender, and LGBTQ+ inclusion are often marginalized, as these conversations largely concern issues of power. Yet these are significant topics in both the church and wider society. Central to my own understanding is the conviction that public theologians must be engaged with diverse theological traditions such as queer, black, postcolonial, and feminist theorists, to interrogate their potentially exclusionary presumptions about the nature of publicness.

OTHER FORMS OF PUBLICNESS
Art and Classics

The exploration of art is a medium that provides the potential for joint meaning making among diverse peoples. As Nicola Slee argues:

> Church sponsorship of the arts is, we might say, one very ancient example of public theology that seeks to create spaces for the interaction of culture and religion in which both may be challenged, enriched, and broadened. . . . Church buildings themselves are spaces in which the arts live and thrive and mingle, and they are significant public spaces in which

---

86. The exception to this is often the analysis of the power of secularism, which potentially marginalizes the religious voice itself. My argument is that if the issues of power relate only to religious voices influencing wider society, and thus gaining more power, the potentially exclusionary nature of the public sphere will be adopted by religious individuals and theologians, rather than challenged.

87. McIntosh, "I Met God," 303–4.

conversation around the art can take place and analysis of the values enshrined in the works of art can be encouraged and in which the divide between insider and outsider can be blurred.[88]

Similarly, David Tracy suggests that "classics" cross boundaries between different communities because they explore universal questions of human meaning and experience. For Tracy, one of the concerns of public theology, as we saw in the Habermasian approach, is that the public sphere may be vanishing (if it has not already vanished) because it is often only governed by technocratic rationality. Martinez describes this focus of Tracy's work, stating:

> If reason has become purely instrumental, then technocratic problem-solving has taken over moral-practical reasoning and the public realm has been reduced to a simply technical domain. Questions about principles, ends, and values have been, therefore, pushed into the private sphere.[89]

Tracy's public theology seeks to recover these central questions of human existence, namely of meaning, ends and goods in the public realm, and creating spaces of conversation to asses and understand various interpretations and meanings. Thus, one of Tracy's criticisms of Jürgen Habermas is that Habermas does not regard goods or a vision of the good life as being possible to argue rationally in the public realm, and therefore thinks that public discourse should be reduced to the discussion of "right" instead. As such, Habermas's method is purely dialogical and argument based, meaning that the public sphere is primarily characterized as an arena of debate.[90] For Tracy, this is one aspect of public interaction, but he seeks to include and defend other notions of "rationality" in the public realm. Therefore, Tracy's theological method is not simply about translating theological concepts into the terms set by secular society for the sake of contributing to a debate. It is also the joint investigation and interpretation of the classics for the discovery of shared meanings.[91] For Tracy, the definition of a classic relates to the excess of meaning found in a piece of historical work, whether that be Scripture, literature, art, or music. For Tracy:

> A classic is a phenomenon whose very excess and permanence of meaning resist definitive interpretation. The classics of art, reason, and religion are phenomena whose truth value is

---

88. Slee, "Speaking with the Dialects," 25.
89. Martinez, *Confronting Mystery of God*, 170.
90. Tracy, "Hope for Public Realm," 599.
91. Tracy, "Hope for Public Realm," 601.

dependent on their disclosive and transformative possibilities for their interpreters. This means that the concrete classics of art, reason, and religion are likely to manifest disclosive and transformative meaning and truth in a manner that is not reducible to an argument.[92]

For the Christian, whether theologian or not, the primary classic engaged with is Scripture. However, for Tracy, Scripture can be designated as a classic because the Scripture and the religion represented by Scripture bear ultimate, universal truth claims. As such they are open to interpretation by everybody, whether a part of that religious community or not because there are within the classic's universal existential problems and questions which all humans engage with.[93] For Tracy then, the significance of Scripture is not simply its ability to provide moral dimensions to issues of common concern, but in its ability to connect with deep questions of meaning, the good, purpose, and other existential questions.

This corresponds with the incarnational mark of public theology in that the classics become concrete conversation partners among diverse groups of people on a shared quest for meaning. However, since Tracy's turn to the classic, others have argued for a broader understanding of what could count as a classic. One example is Stephen Roberts's article, which argues that Lady Gaga's album *Born This Way* should be understood as a classic as it contains a surplus of meaning for a wide public. He argues that Gaga's social vision of diversity and the celebration of queerness, coupled with her religious imagery and reflections in the album, earns her the title of public theologian.[94]

Another example would be David Bentley Hart's review of Quentin Tarantino's film *Once Upon a Time in Hollywood*, published in *The New York Times*.[95] The article argues that Tarantino's movies often possess a vision of cosmic justice that fits within the Christian vision of the eschaton, of all things being made right. Hart uses this pop culture classic as a way of searching for the meanings to both non-Christians and Christians alike. Thus, cultural artifacts provide a way for theologians to explore with different people questions of meaning, purpose, goodness, and beauty that are

---

92. Tracy, "Hope for Public Realm," 599.

93. For Tracy, according to Martinez, "theology is best understood as philosophical reflection upon both the meanings disclosed in our common human experience and the meanings disclosed in the primary texts of the Christian tradition" (Martinez, *Confronting Mystery of God*, 188).

94. Roberts, "Beyond the Classic."

95. Hart, "Quentin Tarantino's Cosmic Justice."

not independent of questions of morality and ethics but frame understandings of human identity and relationality. In this way, engaging classics, both ancient and contemporary, adopts Ricoeurian perspectives on what form of rationality and publicness religion can adopt.

New Apologetics

One of the key characteristics of a Ricoeurian approach to publicness is its insistence that the public sphere is not merely a place of discourse and dialogue, but a place of action and practice. Public theology is not simply expressed in publications such as academic journals and books but is performed. Public theology engages with matters of public concern and these concerns relate to forms of activism that also engage with these issues.[96] In this way, public theology should go beyond the mode of discourse and be understood and interrogated in through the lens of practice and practical theology. Day and Kim point to theologians such as Dietrich Bonhoeffer, Martin Luther King Jr., Rosemary Radford Ruether, and Oscar Romero to demonstrate the connections between discourse-based theological reflection and the necessary practice of theology through social justice.[97]

With a focus on performative theological dimensions of Christian communities, Elaine Graham has argued that Christian public theology should be a form of "new apologetics."[98] For Graham, apologetics has largely come to be understood as a form of philosophical defense of certain propositions of the Christian faith with the hope that this will provide some rationality and reason for an individual to consider joining the faith. For example, as Os Guinness states:

> Apologetics is pre-evangelism, which is communication that clarifies what is obscuring or obstructing the good news. . . . [It] is the necessary foreword or preface wherever there is indifference or complacency or resistance or hostility. It is the

---

96. K. Day and Kim, "Introduction," xvii.
97. K. Day and Kim, "Introduction," xvii.
98. Graham, *Apologetics Without Apology*. It is important to note that by "performed," Day and Kim seem to be signifying a broad understanding that theology must be "actioned" in some way. It does not seem to me that they are drawing on a theory of "performativity" such as is found in the work of Graham. The difference is that Day and Kim seem to maintain that all theology must have some sort of practical outworking, namely through social activism, whereas Graham argues that the practice itself is theological and seeks to find ways of exploring the theological dimensions of the "disclosive practices" of a community (Graham, *Transforming Practice*, 166).

intellectual, moral, spiritual bush-clearing operation that is the preparation for the gospel to come in.[99]

Graham offers an alternative form of apologetics to characterize the public theological task. Part of the problem she sees with this dominant form of apologetics is that it uncritically adopts the epistemology of modernity that "understands the individual as a rational, autonomous, choosing subject who is independent of context, cultural tradition, or embodied contingency."[100] Further, this kind of apologetic task presents Christianity as a set of propositional truths to intellectually assent to, instead of a way of being a disciple of the Teacher.[101]

Elaine Graham argues that the new apologetic asserts:

> That the truth claims of Christianity, and indeed apologetic exposition of that truth, cannot be pursued independent of our apprehension, as embodied human beings, of qualities of beauty and goodness.[102]

For Graham, therefore, new apologetics takes public theology out of purely discourse-based arguments. The appreciation for beauty and goodness and the church's role in presenting beauty and goodness to the world takes public theology simply out of the realm of discourse and into the realm of practice and art. This is because, as Andrew Davidson suggests:

> The apologist may labor to show that the Christian theological vision is *true*, but that will fall flat unless he or she has an equal confidence that it is supremely *attractive* and *engaging*.[103]

For Graham, apologetics in this form needs to be taught to the laity, so public theology is not restricted to a few highly educated elites. Rather the laity can see, not how to convince nonbelievers of Christianity's truth claims through propositional argument but demonstrate Christianity's beauty and goodness through concrete practices.[104] For the new apologist, the task is to demonstrate that wonder and meaning find their zenith in God and that

---

99. This is a quote from a lecture given by Guinness, "Biblical Basis for Apologetics," s.vv. "Apologetics in the New Testament." This section of his talk is cited in Newitt, "New Directions," 422; and Graham, *Between Rock and Hard Place*, 98.

100. Graham, *Apologetics Without Apology*, 102.

101. Graham, *Apologetics Without Apology*, 105.

102. Graham, *Apologetics Without Apology*, 109. See Davidson, *Imaginative Apologetics*.

103. Davison, *Imaginative Apologetics*, xxvi. Quoted in Graham, *Apologetics Without Apology*, 110; emphasis added by Graham.

104. Graham, *Apologetics Without Apology*, 133.

in God our deepest desires are fulfilled. Theology's relevance to the public in this approach, then, is to demonstrate how the practices, as well as the teachings, of faith can speak to peoples enduring quest for wonder and meaning.[105]

I highlight these examples of what a Ricoeurian publicness might look like in order to show forms of publicness that go beyond "debate." In the Ricoeurian model, deep listening and hospitality are central to publicness.

CONCLUSION

In this chapter, I have demonstrated the diversity and contested areas that are key to understanding public theology. Public theology depends on certain philosophical and theological presumptions that are not always interrogated by public theologians. The diversity of approaches shown in chapter 1 help frame the debates I have highlighted in this chapter. As we delve into the life of Manchester Cathedral and explore its public theology, these frameworks and debates will be shown to have important, living significance, and the analysis in these chapters will shed further light on these debates. However, before we can explore the cathedral's public theology, my own methodology and approach must be interrogated. This is the subject of the next chapter, as I describe and try to explain my own approach to interrogating the public theology of a living religious community.

---

105. Graham, *Apologetics Without Apology*, 125.

3

A THEOLOGY OF METHOD AND A METHOD OF PUBLIC THEOLOGY

A PENTECOSTAL WALKS INTO A CATHEDRAL...

THIS SOUNDS LIKE THE beginning of a joke. When I spoke at a cathedral in the south of England to talk about my research, I broke the ice by saying, "Before I begin, I have a confession to make: I am not an Anglican...I am a Pentecostal." Even I was surprised with how much laughter filled the room. I was even more surprised when somebody shouted "hallelujah" in a cheeky imitation of a megachurch pastor. If there was one thing I was painfully aware of when I began researching Manchester Cathedral's public theology, it was the humor of me conducting this research. I am part of the fourth generation of Assemblies of God UK Pentecostals in my family. When I left school to go to university, I attended the AOG Bible college in the UK with the hopes of being an AOG minister. This form of Pentecostalism was the bread and butter of my Christian faith, practice, and theology from childhood right through to my early twenties.

Yet, the joke gets funnier, because this Pentecostal walks into a cathedral having just taken on the task of evaluating its public theology. Talk about a punch line. The particular brand of Pentecostalism that I was familiar with didn't have much of a desire for its members to pursue academic theology. But in my own faith journey I was being drawn to care deeply about the injustices and structural inequalities in the world. I was searching for a form of faith that was passionate, committed to social justice and love of neighbor, and also liturgical. I was being drawn to deeper, older traditions than the one I was raised in. I needed a theology that could make sense of the version of faith I have felt the Spirit drawing me towards.[1]

And so, when the opportunity arose for me to study the public theology of Manchester Cathedral I seized it with both hands, even though I had never stepped foot in this particular cathedral. Here I was, a young man struggling with faith and the church, offered the opportunity to study in depth a tradition and institution unlike any I had spent any significant amounts of time in.

Now, the reader may be wondering what the purpose of this moment of self-reflection and biography is in relation to the question at hand. As I have demonstrated in the previous chapters, some of the key themes that emerge within the field concern hermeneutics and interpretation, translation, identity, and the power dynamics involved in both speaking and listening. These themes, moreover, are also significant in methodological approaches to both data collection and analysis. As Kathryn Tanner argues: "Methodological questions in theology are never finally independent, however, of more substantive theological commitments."[2] As this chapter will show, it is only with an awareness of where the researcher is located within the research that a truthful, honest, and fair "reading" of particular faith communities can take place. It is important that I am a Pentecostal on this venture because I am taking this with me into both the data collection and the analysis. And I have highlighted only one aspect of my life. It also matters that I am male, straight, and brown skinned and have experienced poverty, while always having a roof over my head. It matters that I am married, and that I am privileged to be working full-time in a job that I thoroughly enjoy. There are many things I am bringing to this work, things I am conscious of, and much more that I am not. But it all matters, because it shapes my developing identity and personhood, both of which are crucial aspects of interpretation.

---

1. I want to make clear; I am not saying that Pentecostalism as I experienced it was all bad. My Pentecostal upbringing inspired my love of God, Scripture, and the church, and convinced me early on that God is actually alive and present in the world. Neither is my particular experience of Pentecostalism definitive of Pentecostals as a whole. For example, Lewin shows how Pentecostalism rooted in its origins at Azusa Street necessarily fights for justice and inclusion because the church cannot govern who the Spirit calls and fills, as shown in Acts 10 (*Filled with the Spirit*). Yet, though I am still a Pentecostal, I recognized that other traditions within the church had much to teach me about my faith. For more on the liturgical practices of Pentecostals historically and present, see Green, *Toward a Pentecostal Theology*.

2. Tanner, *Theories of Culture*, 63.

In this book I am trying to explore what the continuing role of religious institutions and communities may be in post-secular contemporary societies, and I am using Manchester Cathedral as a case study for exploring those questions and possibilities. However, drawing out the theology of any living community and extrapolating relevant insights for other communities require an analysis of *how* such data is being collected and interpreted. Therefore, in this chapter, by drawing on research from fields outside of public theology I show how interpretation of practices and discourse may take place to understand the public theology of a specific community. It is in seeking this *how* that I turn to practical theology and ethnographic research methods in order to develop what I call a "publicness-ethnographic approach."

PUBLICNESS-ETHNOGRAPHIC APPROACH

The approach to public theology in this book contributes to a small but growing body of literature in public theology that adopts a public-practical approach to public theology. Public theology has often been understood to be a field whose aim is to primarily contribute to arenas of public debate. Thus, much of the work understood to be public theology concerns the production and articulation of discourse. In contrast, I not only understand public theology to be a form of discourse and debate but also understand public theology to be practiced.[3]

Therefore, drawing on the work and insights of practical theologians to develop methodological frameworks to interpret the cathedral's practices are of crucial importance. In particular, I have developed a particular ethnographic approach to researching the public theology of a community. I have called this a publicness-ethnographic approach, because of my distinct emphasis on publicness and public theology. *Ethnography* can be understood broadly as:

3. Elaine Graham is one public theologian who also categorizes her work as pastoral theology and practical theology. She argues that the task before theologians is to turn to theories that place practice at their heart to do postmodern ethics and politics. This is because "with no external or absolute prescriptive values, judgements concerning the finality of any particular truth-claims are rendered problematic. What is needed is a critical theory of pastoral action by which reliable and verifiable norms can be established from within the reflexivity of *praxis* and community" (*Transforming Practice*, 141–42; emphasis in original). However, much of public theology has operated with modernist presumptions about the universality of certain values and principles, which in turn provide the basis of publicness as I have argued in ch. 2. Therefore, I still consider the turn to praxis within communities as a minority tradition within public theology, but one that must be developed.

> A process of attentive study of, and learning from, people—their words, practices, traditions, experiences, memories, insights—in particular times and places to understand how they make meaning (cultural, religious, ethical) and what they can teach us about reality, truth, beauty, moral responsibility, relationships and the divine, etc. The aim is to understand what God, human relationships, and the world look like from their perspective—to take them seriously as a source of wisdom and to de-center our own assumptions and evaluations.[4]

While ethnography is a methodology developed first within the social sciences, there has been a turn to the combining of this social scientific approach and theological reflection in recent years. Ethnographic research methods have enabled researchers across a variety of disciplines to engage the particular and subjective experiences and articulations of different communities, rather than assuming normative, objective, and universalizing approaches to research. Intellectual movements such as postmodernism and post-colonialism have meant that acceptable sources in Christian theology have expanded and there has been an increased demand for theologians to be accountable to those outside the academy, particularly those on the margins.[5]

Thus, practical theology seeks to interpret the embodied activity of individuals and communities, in ways that resist treating texts, such as Scripture, as the only valuable sources of theology. In this vein, Mary McClintock Fulkerson argues that the dominant textual approach to Christian theological reflection treats human experience, and social and political realities as secondary issues, which textual theology can comment upon, having first constructed a robust systematic theology. As such, she argues that this textual tradition has no way of reading spaces, material realities and practices which fall outside of the boundaries of normalcy generated by textual theologies. Instead, she argues that ethnography is required to engage the lived, messy complex realities of existence, which she argues should be the purpose of all theological reflection.[6]

As Jennifer McBride argues, practices of ethnography provide a way of developing a dynamic interaction between the revelation of the written word and the revelation of the Word made flesh.[7] For McBride, public theology must be the result of deep engagement with the immediate "this-worldly"

---

4. Scharen and Vigen, "What Is Ethnography," 16.
5. Scharen and Vigen, "Ethnographic Turn," 28.
6. Fulkerson, "Ethnography in Theology," 118.
7. McBride, "Public Discipleship," 209–10.

reality of a particular community. She argues that the ethnographic turn in theology is a way of generating dynamic interactions between scholars, activists, pastors, lay people and others in mutually beneficial ways. She demonstrates that her work in the "Lived Theology" project has shaped her own theology, and those she has worked with have testified to how her subsequent theological reflections helped them to understand their own work and develop it.[8]

While there is an acknowledgment that this turn has implications for public theology, there have, however, not been many who have adopted this approach among those who understand their work to be public theology. Mark Cartledge has demonstrated that there had been only five articles published in *IJPT* between 2007 and 2016 that used any empirical research methods to gather primary data.[9] Following his method of reading the abstracts of articles from the journal I found a further seven articles engaged in ethnographic methods. This demonstrates a slight improvement since the publication of Cartledge's article, but not a significant one.[10]

This book is an attempt to draw upon the life of a living community, in order to see how public theology is being practiced and performed in the public sphere, and one of the hopes is that this research in turn shapes public theology itself. But the question must be asked with the role and place of the researcher. Is the researcher intended to be a scientific independent observer, or a member of the community itself and what impact does the researcher have on the *findings*? It is with these questions that I have found the work of Courtney Goto most helpful.

INTERROGATING THE PLACE AND ROLE OF THE RESEARCHER

Courtney Goto's work interrogating the place and role of the researcher in analyzing various faith contexts has been highly influential in my own methodological considerations. Goto in her book *Taking on Practical*

---

8. McBride, "Public Discipleship," 211–13.

9. Cartledge, "Public Theology and Empirical Research." The five articles were K. Day, "Construction of Public Theology"; T. Winkler, "Super-Sizing Community Development Initiatives"; Landman, "Public Theology for Intimate Spaces"; Fulton and Wood, "Interfaith Community Organizing"; Marshall, "Churches Unusual."

10. The articles are: Wepener and Pieterse, "Angry Preaching"; S. Lee, "Living Out"; Boer et al., "Legal Euthanasia in Pastoral Practice"; Cronshaw, "Exploring Local Church Praxis"; B. Day et al., "Scholarly Circles"; Viftrup and Grabowski, "Third Space"; K. Winkler, "Provocations of Contact Zones."

Theology aims to deconstruct objectivist approaches to practical theology, in which the theologian is treated as the primary "knower" who can find the universal meanings behind the particularities of an individual or community.[11] Goto presents three main approaches that practical theologians relate to, discern, understand, and analyze faith contexts, to advocate for more intersubjective approaches to practical theology. I will outline each of these now, as all three of these approaches have been operative in my interpretation of the data.

Critical Objectivity

The first is the *critical objective* approach, in which the faith context is studied from a distance and analyzed using standard frames of analysis to "illumine" that context.[12] In this model, predetermined categories are applied to the faith community being analyzed. In some ways, I adopt the critical objective approach in the way that I situate some of the cathedral's speech and activity within the frameworks of the public approaches that I have described in chapters 1 and 2. The reason that I adopted this approach is that the field of public theology itself is responding to certain traits, trends, and cultural developments. To adopt the word "public" as a defining characteristic of theology requires prior decisions, whether implicit or explicit, about what is considered public, private, and decisions about which theologies should or should not be considered public theologies. In my view, these presumptions are not always brought to the surface and interrogated, and a reader of public theology is left to determine for themselves what is deemed "relevant" or "accessible" to a general public, without recourse to how these evaluative criteria have been developed by the writer.

Another reason I take this approach is to demonstrate the multiple ways that the word "publicness" and "relevance" can be developed and understood, and why different theories about these words develop socially and politically. As I argued in chapters 1 and 2, I contend that decisions being made about the word "public" and what being public entails, shapes the theology that is communicated by the theologian. As such, notions of publicness must be interrogated. In a sense, this is characteristic of the critical objective approach that Goto outlines because Manchester Cathedral does not interpret their work in the terms of "Rawlsian publicness," "Habermasian publicness," or "Ricoeurian publicness" that I have constructed. I have,

---

11. Goto, *Taking on Practical Theology*, 27. Goto argues that such an approach ultimately erases the subject, her social location, and her community.

12. Goto, *Taking on Practical Theology*, 94.

in the form of the critical objective approach, developed models and categories of analysis outside of the cathedral's self-understanding to interpret it.[13]

Critical Subjectivity

The second approach that Goto outlines is the *critical subjective* approach in which the researcher discovers the categories of analysis from participating in the research setting and allows those categories to arise from the data. The researcher attempts for a time to leave their presumptions behind, perhaps through the practice of reflexivity. However, Goto notes that this is often practiced in a way to separate the author's biases and prejudices to, they hope, interpret more clearly the context which they are studying.[14] As I engaged with the cathedral team and various activities, I have tried to allow the cathedral's own choices of language to govern the direction of the analysis. For example, as my research progressed it was clear that the language of inclusion, diversity, peace, welcome, and justice were key terms in which the cathedral interprets its own ministry. As such, it is these kinds of values that I have sought to interrogate with the approaches to publicness that I develop, while allowing those models themselves to be tested by the practices and speech of the cathedral team. In some ways then, the analysis adopts the critical subjective approach, as I seek to test the cathedral's public theology in the terms of its own language and self-understanding.

---

13. When I first began developing my methodology, I found the theological action research model described by Cameron et al. to be helpful (*Talking about God in Practice*). I found the way that the authors distinguished between the espoused theology of a religious community and the "operant" theology of a religious community to be a helpful way of understanding how theology can be embedded within practice and not just discourse. However, as Goto argues, though the TAR method adopts some intersubjective methods in that the researchers emphasize conversation, the four voices approach means that insiders are working with "an analytic framework which outsiders determine" (*Taking on Practical Theology*, 175). Further, as Goto argues:

> With so much focus on the "text" of a faith community's practices, it would be easy to miss what has been erased, sublimated, or forgotten, attending primarily to what is present to conscious awareness. Without qualifying Graham's claim that action research cultivates attentiveness among researchers, one could unwittingly indulge in self-congratulatory ignorance. (177)

14. Goto, *Taking on Practical Theology*, 95–96.

Critical Intersubjectivity

The third approach, which she advocates for throughout the book, is the *critical intersubjective* approach. In this approach all those involved in the research process practice reflexivity throughout all stages of the research. However, the purpose is not simply to bracket the presumptions and biases of the researcher from the interpretation of the community. Rather, the researcher keeps these in view to be accountable for the way that the knowledge is produced, and the subjects are interpreted. Goto writes: "Research that is sensitive to intersubjectivity incorporates practices to help ensure that the academic(s) do not set the research agenda alone. They are not the sole or ultimate arbiters, interpreters, and editors of what a practice, situation, or problem means or what the outcomes of research are. Instead, the research process is designed so that local stakeholders help to determine research questions and what counts as real and true for them."[15]

The research for this book has adopted intersubjectivity by keeping the research open to key players at the cathedral. I was supervised by the canon of theology and mission, David Holgate, who could provide much needed context and insight to the various interpretations I was developing. I was continually brought into meetings, and discussions where I could test my ideas, and receive feedback and insights from members of the cathedral team, and in some cases to revise my initial interpretation. This opening of research and keeping people informed and involved in the research process are important aspects of intersubjective approaches to ethnographic research.

DATA COLLECTION[16]

Primary Observation

There are four main sources of data that I analyzed to interpret Manchester Cathedral's public theology. These are observations of meetings and events; analysis of public data; recorded interviews; and the recording of field notes. The publicness-ethnographic approach is methodologically relevant to both the collection of data from these sources and my interpretation of that data.

One of the main ways I collected data was by attending certain public events. Over the course of my time studying the cathedral, I attended (and sometimes participated in) events which relate to the aspects of the

---

15. Goto, *Taking on Practical Theology*, 100.

16. I began this project in Sept. 2019 and finished my formal data collection period in May 2022.

cathedral's public theology that I chose to analyze. These events were both in person and online, especially because of restrictions due to the COVID-19 pandemic. I attended these events as an observer and sometimes as a participant (and in the case of the Thomas Clarkson Day, I was invited to be on the organizing committee for that day). The events that I attended also helped me to formulate questions that I wanted to explore deeper with interview participants.[17]

I also participated in the worship life of the cathedral by becoming a regular congregant member for around five months, which took place over the Lenten and Easter periods of 2022. Even though Sunday worship is not a central aspect of my research and analysis, I wanted to experience as much of the cathedral's life as I could to develop a deeper relationship with the cathedral and understand better the ways that its regular liturgical life intersected with the cathedral's wider public work.

Public Data

The second source for data analysis has been articles, statements, public videos, sermons, and other sources of public articulation from the cathedral clergy. For example, I use statements from the cathedral website, or videos that the cathedral has posted as sources of information which I consider to be valuable in demonstrating its public theology. These are important because they demonstrate how the cathedral, under the period of Govender's leadership, has responded to significant events in society. As the cathedral curate at the time, Steven Hilton said to me in an interview, "If I was to analyze the public theology of the cathedral, I would want to look at our literature and the things we put out into the world." Because Manchester Cathedral is such an active and publicly present institution there are plenty of online sources recording various events, statements, sermons, speeches, as well as various news articles either celebrating or critiquing the cathedral's work.

---

17. While Dean Rogers Govender also allowed me to sit in on private meetings, such as chapter and clergy meetings, and planning meetings for certain events, this was on the basis that I did not record or use any of the interactions within those meetings as part of my research. The purpose was more to help me understand the character of the cathedral and some of the organizational structures and tensions.

Recorded Interviews

I think the most important part of the data collection for this project was the recorded interviews that I conducted. Therefore, I will take a little more time to highlight various decisions I made for this part of the collection process was conducting recorded interviews. I wanted to interview each member of the clergy and some members of the chapter who aren't part of the clergy. In the early stages of the research, I had originally designed some questionnaires for congregants and visitors to describe their perception and experiences of Manchester Cathedral and had intended to conduct interviews with some of the cathedral's key partners and other stakeholders. However, in the process of conducting the research I decided to only recruit participants from the cathedral team for interviews. This is for two main reasons. The first was that because of the COVID-19 pandemic and subsequent lockdowns there was significant impact on how much access I had to the congregation and other stakeholders.

However, the other reason I decided to recruit participants only from the cathedral team is because I understood after conducting initial interviews that the cathedral team's self-understanding provided the most helpful details for understanding its public theology. While it would be interesting, in future, to explore how people engage with Manchester Cathedral and its public activities, for this project I argue that the cathedral team's self-understanding of its public activity and theology provided a sufficient data set to evaluate the cathedral's public theology.

One key example where this affected what I chose to research and how I chose to evaluate the cathedral's public theology is in relation to how the congregation is located by the cathedral team. In interviews conducted with the team at Manchester Cathedral it is clear to me that the congregation is not considered by the team to be a central audience or actor in its public theology. When I asked questions about public engagement and motives, rarely was the cathedral congregation brought into discussion. While the limits of this approach to cathedral congregations from a public theological perspective would be interesting for further research,[18] I decided to follow the team's own emphases and understanding of its public theology. This is because the cathedral's public theology is often performed with the cathedral team, particularly Dean Govender, being the central actors, as I will

---

18. See Graham, *Apologetics Without Apology*; Parker, "Public Convergence," for further discussion on the importance of congregations for public theology.

demonstrate in subsequent chapters.[19] However, it is worth noting that several of the interviewees are also regular congregation members.

In total, I conducted fifteen interviews with twelve different people. I adopted a semi-structured interview approach because I recognized that each person may have their own interpretive emphasis of the public activity of the cathedral that I had not anticipated. I tried, while maintaining a structure, to follow the natural flow of the interview. For example, sometimes a participant would tell me a story about an event or conversation they had that was significant to them, and I would ask them to try and articulate why that conversation or story was significant.

I started each interview by asking the participant to describe their role at the cathedral and how long they had been in that role. I then asked about why they wanted to be part of the cathedral's life. I then had several questions that related to their view of the value of Manchester Cathedral in a secular society like Manchester, and how they understand the cathedral as both a Christian space and a public space.

While I had a particular order for these questions, I would often skip certain questions, or move to another question that might follow from the participant's answer to a previous question. In this way, I tried to naturally follow the flow of the participant's own interest in the cathedral, especially because each participant had their level of involvement in different areas of the cathedral's life. One question that I finished with for every participant, which said: "It is no secret that cathedrals across this country struggle annually to keep their doors open due to financial demands. If Manchester Cathedral was to suffer the unfortunate fate of having to close its doors as a cathedral, what would be lost for the city of Manchester?"

I asked this to try and draw out what the participants would be most sad to see end if the cathedral were to close, which is helpful in discovering what area of the cathedral's life was most valuable to them. The interview guide was designed for the first round of interviews. The first round largely

---

19. The cathedral's public theology is shaped by the hierarchy of leadership at the cathedral. As the dean of the cathedral, Govender is the central actor of the cathedral's public work. The cathedral curate at the time, Steven Hilton, discussed this aspect of the cathedral's public theology, saying: "The dean is the senior clergy person in the diocese. He is the head of the cathedral, under the bishop who is the visitor . . . Unsurprisingly at Manchester, the cathedral takes on his passions and influences. His agenda for inclusion and his experiences of apartheid in South Africa have a massive impact on what we do. His sense that the gospel is one of inclusion, equality, and accessibility is reflected at the cathedral." Hilton said further on, "We understand as members of the clergy that in the dean's approach the ministry that we have is a part of his ministry." Therefore, I draw heavily on the interviews with Govender and the team in this thesis. While I draw on the other interviewees, I analyze the clergy's interviews more so because their self-perception is that they are the key actors of the public theology of the cathedral.

concerned questions about the tension between having a distinctive Christian identity and being an inclusive cathedral, which is public. Through these interviews, I came to understand the various points of common language and values between participants and common stories which emerged through the interviews. Further, the interviews in the first round helped me to identify racial justice, interreligious dialogue, and LGBTQ+ inclusion as key public areas of engagement that the cathedral is engaged.

Thus, I conducted a second round of interviews to engage deeper questions about the three topics. I interviewed Govender for a final time on the topics of racial justice, interreligious dialogue, and LGBTQ+ inclusion specifically. I also had an interview with Holgate on his own to discuss the *Living in Love and Faith* (*LLF*) process and his interpretation and connection with the material. I then had a subsequent interview with Holgate exploring his involvement with the interfaith Scriptural Encounter and Scriptural Reasoning groups. Finally, I conducted an interview with Steven Hilton and Holgate together as they were both working on the *LLF* process for a period during my data collection stage. In my first interview with Canon Marcia Wall, we talked extensively about interreligious worship at the cathedral, and I felt as though I had gathered key information from my first and only interview with her on this topic.

Through the transcribing, rereading, and interpretation of the interviews, the interviews become the primary text I am engaged with throughout this book as you will see. However, one final source of data is not from the cathedral itself, but from my own experience of the cathedral. These are "field notes."

Field Notes: A Practice of Reflexivity

One of the major contributions that ethnographic methods have made to theology is a greater awareness of the role of the researcher in gathering, organizing, interpreting, and articulating data. Clifford contends:

> Ethnography is actively situated between powerful systems of meaning. It poses its questions at the boundaries of civilizations, cultures, classes, races, and genders. Ethnography decodes and recodes, telling the grounds of collective order and diversity, inclusion, and exclusion. It describes innovation and structuration and is itself part of these processes.[20]

---

20. Clifford and Marcus, *Writing Culture*, 2–3.

When I first began the project, I had the mistaken notion that my role was to be a kind of independent observer of Manchester Cathedral, producing an objective, scientific reading of the cathedral's public theology. However, as time has gone on and my understanding of the process of evaluating the public theology of the cathedral has developed through practicing that analysis it has become clearer to me how involved I am in the process of analysis and articulation. I am not independent of the cathedral, as if I could stand above, and comment on it without recognizing that my understandings of the cathedral's public theology are interpretations. Therefore, throughout the project, there were moments of self-reflection and reflexivity. As Heather Walton argues: "Reflexivity in this frame refers to the interrogative processes that enable us to understand all our meaning-making, even in the most abstract spheres, as relational, provisional, embodied and located."[21]

Scharen and Vigen argue further that reflexivity is also about adopting a posture of humility to approach research participants as people to be learned from, not simply studied. As such reflexive practice is about being aware of how the researcher's assumptions and expectations are possibly being challenged by the data being collected from research participants and being candid about these results.[22] Further, Walton offers several questions that researchers may ask of themselves in this process. These include:

> How does my personal history generate presuppositions that influence my approach to this topic? How does my gender/class/ethnicity/sexual identity/cultural location influence my understanding? Where do my allegiances lie and how do my commitments guide my approach to inquiry? What can my body and my emotional responses contribute to generating the knowledge I seek?[23]

One of the ways that I tried to develop and maintain a self-reflexive posture throughout the duration of this project, and to ask the kinds of questions above, was through the writing and analysis of my own field notes. Emerson et al. argue that field notes are:

> writings produced in or in close proximity to "the field." Proximity means that field-notes are written more or less

---

21. Walton, *Writing Methods*, xi.
22. Scharen and Vigen, "What Is Ethnography," 18.
23. Walton, *Writing Methods*, xii.

contemporaneously with the events, experiences, and interactions they describe and recount.[24]

My field notes were taken in the context of recording interviews and making notes on my initial reactions to the interviews afterwards. They also include notes I took during events or meetings that I attended and write-ups of descriptions and issues that arose during those events, which I would usually write the same day or the following day. To engage in self-reflexive practice, I regularly wrote in a research journal. Mary Moschella explains:

> Ethnography requires the researcher to reflect regularly upon his or her interactions with research participants. Through this practice—known as reflexivity—the ethnographer examines his or her personal impressions and responses to experiential encounters and records these reflections in rigorous journal notations. These notes become part of the database that is then scrutinized and analyzed. The self-reflections of the researcher help elucidate the interpretive dimensions of every phase of the ethnographic process.[25]

In the research journal, I wrote entries about the interviews I had, my feelings, and key parts of the interview that I thought was significant. These notes also include initial highlighted versions of the transcripts with notes made in the margins. I also recorded entries after attending events at the cathedral, writing about what I thought was significant, how I felt, or interesting conversations I had with others at the meeting or event. For example, after my first recorded interview with Dean Rogers Govender, I wrote:

> Govender sees the cathedral's networks and partners as the central aspect of the cathedral's public theology. He emphasizes his role in representing the brand of the cathedral in key environments, and particularly in relation to key players in the city. The language of being a "brand" is not one I have thought about because this is not a theme found in public theology. I need to think deeper about what this "brand" approach to the cathedral's public image means to them theologically.

This regular practice helped me to understand how my own thinking has developed, and what my assumptions and values were during the

---

24. Emerson et al., "Participant Observation and Fieldnotes," 355. Walford expands this definition suggesting that field notes "are broadly understood to be the written notes about what a researcher observed, wanted to remember, and think about more while in the field" ("Writing Ethnographic Field Notes," 118).

25. Moschella, "Ethnography," 225.

research process. The opening of this chapter describing my own faith journey was the result of this journaling practice and reading over these notes once the project had finished. As a result, on some level, the field notes are part of the overall "text" that I am analyzing at Manchester Cathedral.[26]

Having highlighted how the data has been gathered, we must now understand how the data can be interpreted in this publicness-ethnographic methodology.

DATA ANALYSIS: PHENOMENOLOGICAL HERMENEUTICS[27]

In a similar vein to the Ricoeurian perspective that "people are hermeneutical all the way down," this project is hermeneutical throughout.[28] This is because, at its heart, ethnographic research and writing are ultimately about translation and interpretation. As a researcher I must communicate events and experiences, both my own and others, so that others may understand and interpret them. But my reactions and responses to the texts of the interviews, events, and public data are also key aspects to my interpretation of these. As Ricoeur argues, "Interpretation is the hinge between language and lived experience."[29]

---

26. I recognize there is a debate to how much use field notes can provide to a fieldworker's analysis is debated. For example, Van Maanen argues that the researchers' developed understanding of the field they operate in goes far beyond what a researcher could develop in notes. The understanding, he argues, may be "symbolized" by field notes, but the intellectual activity to reach understanding goes far beyond them. However, because field notes are a practice of condensing lived experience into more "concise, stylized, re-examinable written accounts," the records of these are important, for the researcher to be able to critically analyze *how* they condense these complex lived experiences into words (*Tales of the Field*, 17–18). As I will demonstrate in the next section, field notes are not necessarily a central part of the overall text, but they are nonetheless an important part of it. See Emerson et al., "Participant Observation and Fieldnotes," 364. It is also worth noting at this point that though I explored the language of "brand" after this interview, it didn't yield much in my thinking about the cathedral's public theology and is therefore not addressed in this thesis.

27. There are numerous examples of ethnographic researchers who have adopted Ricoeur's phenomenological hermeneutical framework for interpreting primary data. I draw on some of these examples here, but see especially Simonÿ et al., "Ricoeur-Inspired Approach"; Geanellos, "Exploring Ricoeur's Hermeneutic Theory"; Garcia, "On Paul Ricoeur."

28. Dan Stiver argues this is a central understanding of Ricoeur's phenomenological hermeneutics, which he developed drawing on the perspectives of Martin Heidegger and Hans-Georg Gadamer (*Ricoeur and Theology*, 9). See also Ricoeur, *From Text to Action*, 63.

29. Ricoeur, "Problem of Double Meaning," 66.

However, this hermeneutical emphasis does not mean, of course, that my analysis is reduced to that which is "originally" textual, i.e., interviews and public speeches, etc. Rather, as Ricoeur demonstrates in *From Text to Action* his theory of hermeneutics also includes "quasi-texts" (actions). For Ricoeur, all actions can be narrated, either by the actor or an observer and thus through narration there is a textual interpretation of action.[30] This accounts for the "phenomenological" part of "phenomenological hermeneutics" as it is about the relationship between experience, interpretation, and the subject. Thus, my narration of various events and activities in my field notes, which I have discussed above, became a key part of interpreting the cathedral. In this way, I am the primary author of the interpretation of these observations.

In the case of interviews, the research participant is a key author in what is to be understood as a thoroughly collaborative process. They are producing a text through their responses to my questions as they reflect on their experiences at the cathedral. As Ricoeur says, "Because we are in a world, because we are affected by situations and because we orient ourselves comprehensively in those situations, we have something to say, we have experience to bring to language."[31] However, as the interviewer, I am shaping the discourse through my questioning and responses in the interviews, which is a key shaping aspect of the text which becomes key to my analysis. However, this raises the question of who becomes the main interpreter of these texts. Does the interviewee's intention become the primary interpretive criteria? Or if I prioritize my own interpretation, do I risk becoming the "scientific observer" by adopting the objective approach outlined by Goto?

Key to these questions is outlining how Ricoeur understood the relation between the text and the author. For Ricoeur, the meaning and interpretation of a text do not lie simply in the author's intention. Rather, a text becomes autonomous because the language of a text is inherited by both the author and the reader, meaning that the text cannot belong to either the author or the reader, absolutely.[32] While the interviewee's intention is more accessible to me than with other texts, in that I can ask the participant what they meant when they said X, Ricoeur's hermeneutical framework means that there is a plurality of meanings because language itself is polysemic.[33]

30. Ricoeur, *From Text to Action*, xiii. See also Frey, "Preface," viii.

31. Ricoeur, *Interpretation Theory*, 20. Cited in Simonÿ et al., "Ricoeur-Inspired Approach," 2.

32. Ricoeur, *Hermeneutics and Human Sciences*, 62.

33. Ricoeur, *Hermeneutics and Human Sciences*, 44. Ricoeur seems to make a distinction between oral discourse and writing. He argues that oral discourse is a dialogue in which the author and reader communicate and clarify with one another. For Ricoeur,

One example which illustrates this point is how the participants (as one author of the interview texts) of the various interviews produced those "texts" in isolation from the other participants/authors. Each participant answered the questions based on their own experience and insight but did not have access to how others had or would answer those same questions. Thus, while each author may have had their own intentions in their answers, which are still significant, the meaning of the texts cannot be reduced to the author's intention, because the author could not shape their intention in relation to other texts. Because I have access to all the texts and make connections between each of them, my interpretation of the interviews goes beyond the individual author's intention of each.

Given that, as I am arguing with Ricoeur, the text neither belongs absolutely to the author nor the reader, how should the texts that make up the overall text of analysis be interpreted? It is here that I have found Simonÿ et al's appropriation of Ricoeur's hermeneutical framework to be an excellent model for applying the framework to ethnographic work. The authors draw on Ricoeur's three-part hermeneutical approach to analyze both the transcripts of the interviews they conducted and their field notes.[34] For Ricoeur, there are three stages in the hermeneutical arch that he proposes. The stages are overlapping and somewhat repeated, meaning that they do not necessarily follow sequentially.

The first stage is naïve reading. This part of interpretation is simply about ascertaining the key motivations, connections, and overall meaning of a text. Ricoeur describes it as "a naïve grasping of the meaning of the texts as a whole."[35] Simonÿ et al. argue that this stage in relation to empirical work is about reading and rereading transcripts and field notes. In my context, the naïve reading was developed through watching the recordings of the interviews and reading transcripts and field notes. The aim of this stage was for me to gather understandings of each of the participant's key focuses, experiences, and theologies in an open-minded, noncritical way.[36]

---

written discourse goes beyond the author differently because discourse must "speak for itself" (Ricoeur, "Metaphor and Central Problem," 45–46). However, I would argue that with the process of transcribing interviews, I as the researcher am transforming an oral discourse into a written text. I am deciding where the emphasis may lie, punctuation, paragraphs, and connections between sentences. As a result, the recording of interviews and their transcription (and the writing of field notes about the interviews) means that they cannot be understood simply as oral discourse.

34. This approach is elaborated fully in Ricoeur, *Interpretation Theory*.

35. Ricoeur, *Interpretation Theory*, 74. Cited in Simonÿ et al., "Ricoeur-Inspired Approach," 6.

36. Simonÿ et al., "Ricoeur-Inspired Approach," 5.

The second stage of the framework is structural analysis. Ricoeur argues that a text will be made up of units of significance and meaning. In many ways, these units of meaning in relation to my interviews are given by the questions asked by me, due to the semi-structured nature of the interviews. However, as Simonÿ et al. discuss, this stage is also about finding key themes, subthemes, key words, or ideas that emerge in the texts. Further, they argue that with the combination of transcripts and field notes from interviews, units of meaning can be found in relation to body language, tone of voice, emotion, etc.[37] In my approach, this process involved highlighting and color-coding interviews in relation to different themes and making notes in the margins summarizing key themes, or thoughts that arose for me during the interview. This was a necessary part of the process of analyzing the interviews to be able to compare similarities and differences between the perspectives of the various interviewees.

This leads to the third stage, the critical interpretation and discussion of the overall text. This stage of the process is where the texts are appropriated by me in such a way to move "from the individual to the universal." In other words, it is about the comparison to other interviews, field notes, and to wider theories. In the case of my work, each interview is interpreted in relation to other interviews, field notes made while observing events and activities, and wider academic discussions, such as in public theology, queer theory, etc.

I have developed a wide-ranging and varied data set, and I am therefore able to critically develop a sophisticated interpretation of Manchester Cathedral's public theology. However, it is important to reemphasize that all interpretations are open to critique, development, and being combined with other interpretations. In Ricoeur's theory no text, nor interpretation can claim to be absolute. As such, part of my critical process throughout data collection and analysis has been to work closely *with* Manchester Cathedral, to test my interpretations and help refine them. In this way, this hermeneutical process remains an intersubjective process in that the interpretations are open interpretations. The intersubjective and collaborative effort, in my view, provides credibility to my interpretations of the cathedral, even though I would not claim them to be absolute.[38] In this way, though they are not absolute, they are not arbitrary interpretations.

---

37. Simonÿ et al., "Ricoeur-Inspired Approach," 5–6.
38. Simonÿ et al., "Ricoeur-Inspired Approach," 8.

CONCLUSION: A PENTECOSTAL WALKS INTO A CATHEDRAL . . . AND BECOMES AN ANGLICAN

I began this chapter discussing my motives and experiences that led me to take on this particular piece of work. What I didn't say was that I have now been confirmed at Manchester Cathedral. The Pentecostal who walked into the cathedral has now become part of the Church of England. I finish the chapter discussing this because I think it is important to reiterate that this kind of research within public theology should operate in a two-way direction. Not only was I conducting research at Manchester Cathedral, but I was being shaped and formed in particular ways by this research. My faith journey was affected, as well as my view of ministry and what possibilities lay ahead for the church. And this is part of the gift of intersubjective methodologies in theology. The theologian opens themselves as a guest and learner even in spaces where they are playing the host. And this is one of the challenges to public theology as a field that I think is most relevant. Too much of public theology is ultimately one directional, with a theologian trying to translate an idea or concept that has been formed independently from a particular context or public. The goal of interaction in these forms of public theology is to convince others of a particular perspective.

However, part of what intersubjective ethnographic models and methods offer are a framework for learning, in the context of theological work with living communities. In this sense, to be public with theology is not just about communicating theological ideas in a way that is publicly accessible, though this is important. Rather, perhaps the task is for public theologians to foster spaces of exploration, learning, and deep listening, in ways where the theologian themselves may be transformed by the interaction. These insights will be a key theme in the following three chapters, as I explore the forms of relationships and work Manchester Cathedral has developed in relation to interfaith work, racial justice, and LGBTQIA+ inclusion.

4

INTERRELIGIOUS DIALOGUE AT MANCHESTER CATHEDRAL

ONE MONTH AFTER I had submitted my doctorate evaluating Manchester Cathedral's public theology in March 2023, the dean and chapter issued an apology. On March 29 the cathedral hosted an open iftar event. The event took place in the cathedral and included speeches from various faith and civic leaders who articulated a common concern to build community and foster friendships. However, though the iftar prayers took place in the designated place outside of consecrated space (the cathedral gardens), the *adhan* (the Muslim call to prayer) took place inside the cathedral nave. This breached the guidance given by the Church of England, which says that the *adhan* "should happen in the room allocated for prayer, rather than a consecrated space."[1]

The cathedral dean and chapter issued an apology for this. The spokesperson for the cathedral, who is not named in the *Church Times* article, stated: "In hindsight, we acknowledge the call to prayer should also have been issued outside the Cathedral and in future we will be mindful to offer our hospitality that does not interfere with the integrity of Manchester Cathedral. We apologise for this oversight. We will ensure that any call to prayer is not offered in the Cathedral at any such events in the future."[2] However, the spokesperson was quick to clarify and show that "the Dean and Chapter work hard to ensure Manchester Cathedral is a welcoming place for the entire community and for those of all faiths and none. The

1. Martin, "Apology," para. 4.
2. Martin, "Apology," para. 6.

house of God is open to all, and we offer hospitality for all communities so that we can make connections, build bridges and build friendships."[3]

I bring this story to the very start of this chapter, because it highlights key characteristics of Manchester Cathedral's public theology in relation to interreligious dialogue and engagement and raises significant questions about the nature and limits of this particular aspect of its public work. Interreligious dialogue at Manchester Cathedral is not to be understood as a separate activity among the many public activities which the cathedral is engaged in. Rather, "interreligious" is the form that much of its public activity operates within. But as the above story shows, hospitality in interreligious contexts draw out tensions and limits and raise questions of "integrity" and identity. Therefore, in this chapter, I will be examining the public theological underpinnings of these interreligious relationships and networks and interrogating and evaluating the public theology of the interreligious work at the cathedral. I will examine three aspects of the interreligious activity at the cathedral: interreligious social justice activity, interreligious worship services, and interreligious scriptural reasoning.

The approaches to publicness characterized by John Rawls, Jürgen Habermas, and Paul Ricoeur will provide frameworks for understanding the approach of the cathedral in this area. To analyze the cathedral's interreligious public theology, I will be providing descriptions and analysis of events I have attended, or watched a recording of, and interviews that I have conducted with the cathedral team who have discussed the cathedral's interreligious activity. Throughout this chapter, I will demonstrate that Manchester Cathedral's interreligious character raises questions about how the cathedral understands its own Christian identity in relation to other religions, and how it understands the identities of others as they network with them. I will show how a Ricoeurian approach to publicness in this area emphasizes the need to understand how people of different faiths are formed to see the world and ethics in various ways. This emphasis on formation in the context of religion presents a challenge to the public theology of Manchester Cathedral in this area and to public theology as a field.

THE INTERRELIGIOUS CHARACTER OF MANCHESTER CATHEDRAL'S PUBLIC THEOLOGY

Over the course of time that I conducted my research at Manchester Cathedral there had been several highly significant national and international events that had occurred to which the cathedral responded as the

---

3. Martin, "Apology," para. 7.

"spiritual hub" of the city of Manchester.[4] To name just a few of these events, the cathedral responded to the global BLM protests which began after the murder of George Floyd, the Russian invasion of Ukraine, the COP-26 conference, and the death of Queen Elizabeth II. Further, during this period the cathedral has had to navigate its ministry during a global pandemic and the subsequent cost of living crisis that are both still ongoing. In its response to these painful, troubling, and highly significant events, the cathedral has operated as a space of grief, prayer, and sometimes protest. But the cathedral operating this way is not new. For example, in 2017 after the Manchester Arena bombing, the cathedral became a national space of grief and solidarity, which was perhaps most visibly seen at the one-year anniversary service that the cathedral hosted which was broadcast internationally.

I highlight these events because despite the range of topics and issues that are engaged here the consistent characteristic in the cathedral's response to these is that the cathedral maintains an interreligious element to its responses. For example, the day after Queen Elizabeth II died, I attended the cathedral's choral evensong service, which was dedicated in honor to the queen. However, unlike other choral evensongs at the cathedral, this service included participation by representatives of other faiths. Dean Rogers Govender called representatives of different faith communities to light a candle in honor of the queen.[5] Similarly, when Russia first invaded Ukraine the cathedral quickly organized an interfaith prayer vigil, which included public prayers from different faith communities.

Demonstrated here then is that interreligious networks and activity are central to much of the important public work that Manchester Cathedral does. However, I argue that the interreligious character at Manchester Cathedral takes three distinct forms; interreligious social justice work, interreligious worship services, and interreligious scriptural reasoning events.

Manchester Cathedral's Interreligious Social Justice Activity

For Dean Rogers Govender, the interreligious work oriented towards social justice at Manchester Cathedral functions as a response to obey the "second greatest commandment" that Jesus gave to his disciples, to love their

---

4. The claim that the cathedral is the spiritual hub of the city is one made by numerous participants in my recorded interviews but is especially a claim made by the clergy.

5. There were no Jewish representatives present because the service took place during a Sabbath. However, a representative had sent a greeting showing their solidarity with those grieving at the cathedral.

neighbors as themselves (Matt 22:36–40; Luke 10:25–37). Govender said to me in one interview:

> I think our religion also teaches us to serve others to love God and to love our neighbor. . . . Jesus affirms and calls us to love and affirm and respect and include those who are not necessarily in the body of Christ, in the church. They are no less children of God than you are as a believer. . . . So my understanding is a much broader, rather than a tribal, understanding of how inclusion works. And so, you can be a person of another faith, or no faith and God still loves you. If God loves you, why shouldn't I?

When Govender was explaining to me the rationale of interreligious social justice work, he drew on the story of the good Samaritan (Luke 10:25–37) from which he argued that the duty to care for the ones who are "broken at the side of the road" transcends all potential boundaries and divisions. Just as the Samaritan saw past the ethnocentric divisions between Jews and Samaritans, so too people of faith should see past their religious divisions with others and focus on healing and helping those who are in need.

For Govender, while there are differences between faith traditions, the faith traditions are at their best when they are united in a common concern for justice and peace. Govender argues:

> To give an example, climate change. It affects all people. Not just Christians or Hindus or Muslims. It affects all of us. So, all of us have got to tackle it together because it is part of our common interest and need to preserve our environment for the good of everybody: for the common good. I think if we understand religion in a tribal insular way, then I think we have misunderstood religion and God.

For Govender, this expectation that religion should not be understood in a "tribal" or insular way applies not only to his own Christian faith but to all faiths. As he states:

> Religion is both about our personal relationship with God, but it is also about the world in which we live, it is about our relationships with others in the world, the wider world. And religion ought to be a force for good. Anything that promotes goodness and good values in society that prevents us from getting involved in crime and murder, exploitation, and violence. That's a good thing, and religion should do all it can to promote those values, for the good of all, and the good of religion itself.

One example of social justice activity at the cathedral can be seen in the work it does in Our Faith Our Planet (OFOP). OFOP is an interreligious climate change network within the wider network of the Manchester Climate Change Agency, which Govender chairs. The OFOP website formerly stated that the organization

> is an inter-faith network based in Manchester focused on climate change action through engagement and education. The group are committed to creating a green, healthy, and inclusive city that contributes to the Manchester Climate Change Strategy.[6]

On October 19, 2021, I attended the OFOP event called Make #COP26 Count, which was called in advance of the COP26 UN Climate Change Conference that took place between October 31 and November 12, 2021. The OFOP event took place in a hall at Khizra Mosque. The event started with networking and food. Dean Rogers gave the introduction to the meeting reminding the participants that we must work towards justice for all, and for our planet. He quoted Desmond Tutu as saying: "We should be concerned for those drowning, but we should also go upstream to find why people are falling in." After this introduction, the host of the meeting, Rev. Ian Rutherford from the Central Methodist Hall in Manchester, gave an overview of what COP26 is and was then followed by Caroline Lucas, the Green Party MP for Brighton, who shared her hopes for COP26.

During the event, there was a section which sought to demonstrate the joint vision of climate justice represented in the faith communities of five of the major world faiths which were: Sikhism, Islam, Judaism, Christianity, and Hinduism. Each of these representatives presented, for a minute each, a concept from their own faith tradition that they saw as connecting with the topic that motivates and inspires them to fight for climate justice.

The group was then presented with a video message from Mayor Andy Burnham, who encouraged us to give feedback to him for him to use at COP26. This was the foundation for which the next activity took place. We were split into four groups to share what we wanted to be achieved and see changed as a result of COP26. The group that I was a part of was made up of faith leaders and lay people, younger people and older people, and there were several different faiths represented.

Of interest for our discussion is the role that religion played in this interreligious network. The focus of the meeting as can be seen above was to generate thoughts about the actions those represented would want the various world leaders at COP26 to take to fight climate injustice. The most

---

6. See https://faithforourplanet.org/ for current statements.

explicitly religious section described the various motivations religious groups have for being concerned about the future of the planet. Each of the religious representatives in that section were instructed to give one minute's examination of their religious tradition's connection to the question of climate justice. The goal, it seemed to me, was to demonstrate the unity among the faiths in their motivation to fight for climate justice.[7]

Interreligious Worship at Manchester Cathedral

Manchester Cathedral's interreligious character is also expressed through its organizing and hosting of interreligious worship services. The cathedral hosts prayer services, civic services, memorial services, and celebratory services, which often include prayers, readings, and/or sermons from people of other faiths.

In an interview with Canon Marcia Wall, the canon precentor at the cathedral at the time, she described both the importance of interreligious worship in these settings and the process of writing the liturgy for such a service. She suggested that because the cathedral aims to be inclusive to people of all faiths and none, she aims to produce inclusive liturgies which include people of other faiths for special services. Acknowledging that the regular church services usually follow the Anglican authorized liturgy, Wall argued:

> Where we excel at inclusive worship is when we have special services where I have more of a free hand to prepare my own liturgy because it's not Sunday Eucharist and it's not morning or evening prayer, which are things where we must follow the Anglican authorised liturgy. We have a little bit of freedom, but we can't deviate much.

One key example she used of a special service hosted by the cathedral is the civic service which occurs after a new lord mayor is appointed. Wall said in the interview:

> That lord mayor may be a Christian, or Muslim or a Jewish person. So, I have a meeting with the new lord mayor, and we do the service together. The dean chooses the preacher, and he tries to

---

7. Much of the cathedral's interreligious social justice work often addresses concerns about racial justice. Because the cathedral's public theology of racial justice is the topic of the next chapter, I will describe events concerning racial justice there. However, for now it is worth noting that these events, such as the Challenging Hate Forum and the Thomas Clarkson Day, as just two major examples, focus on the common concerns about hate crime and racism as the uniting focus for these interreligious activities.

choose somebody of a different faith and gender to the person being appointed. Somebody who would be a good preacher. The preacher will choose the readings, but the lord mayor then chooses the hymns. The previous lord mayor to the current lord mayor is a Muslim so for his service we had a reading from the Qur'an, and he asked for one of his Muslim friends to come and read that.

Similarly, Wall described some of the choices that she made regarding the first anniversary of the Manchester Arena attack. She said:

> I prepared that service it was massive . . . so we had to be very inclusive. So, I had readings from the Qur'an, I had something from the Jewish scriptures, I involved Sikhs, Hindus, Muslims, and humanists who could take part in the service, reading their lesson or a poem or sharing a reading.[8]

I asked Wall if she found that there were ever any tensions produced in relation to maintaining the cathedral's Christian identity in this practice of including people of other religions in these services. For Wall, there are key Christian elements that always appear in the service. For example, the Lord's Prayer is always kept in, and there is usually at least one reading from the New Testament. However, she argued that while there might be tensions in maintaining their own distinctive identity, it is also important for those of other faiths to be able to remain integral to their faith too. Wall highlighted to me that a Muslim or Jewish representative will never be asked to read a prayer addressed to Jesus because they don't worship him as God in the same way Christians do. But for Wall, because the cathedral has worked with its colleagues from other faiths for a long time now, enough trust has been built up through which if there were any issues there could be open dialogue and conversation about navigating those tensions in the context of a worship service.

One example of an interreligious service at the cathedral that I attended took place on Saturday, October 2, 2021. The cathedral hosted a celebration service in honor of Mahatma Gandhi's 152nd birth anniversary, which aimed to be an "interfaith celebration of non-violence, peace, unity, compassion and hope." The event was organized by Shrimad Rajchandra

---

8. In one interview, Govender described the very deliberate choice of including Muslim representatives in all of the services that were related to the arena attack because he was aware that anger and hate could be aimed towards the Muslim community because the attacker was an Islamic extremist. For Govender, it was important to place his Muslim colleagues visibly at the front of these services, to demonstrate the solidarity and grief of the Muslim community in the city. For Govender, maintaining this kind of unity in the city was a key part of his ministry at the time of responding to this tragedy.

Mission Dharampur UK, which is a "Jain faith-based global movement that endeavors to enhance the spiritual growth of seekers and benefit society."[9]

Dean Rogers wrote a message in the order of service that every attendee received. The message summarizes the purpose of the celebration. It says:

> My prayer is that we take non-violence, peace-making and bridge-building seriously in our city region and in our country and beyond. We need to tackle knife crime, domestic abuse, and violence, and build cohesion in our diverse city. We need to champion the cause of peace in war-torn nations. As a diverse gathering here today may God bless our individual and corporate efforts to pray and work for a better, peaceful, inclusive, and just society where every person and community flourishes.[10]

The service largely consisted of various readings from different faith traditions including Hinduism, Islam, Sikhism, Christianity, and Jainism. The various readings centered upon the various tradition's teachings about peace, nonviolence, and love. The service closed with a pledge to be spoken by those in attendance.

The pledge that closed the meeting said this:

> We stand as one community, we commit ourselves to work for justice, peace, and equality by saying together:
>
> Eternal God, we believe that you have called us together to broaden our experience of you and each other.
>
> We believe that we have been called to help in healing the many wounds of society and in reconciling people to people and people to God.
>
> Help us, as individuals and as communities, to work, in love, for peace, and never to lose heart.
>
> We commit ourselves to each other with hope—in joy and sorrow.
>
> We commit ourselves to all who share our belief in equality and reconciliation—for support and solidarity.
>
> We commit ourselves to the way of justice and peace—in prayer and action. We commit ourselves to you—our guide and friend.

---

9. See Shrimad Rajchandra Mission Dharampur, "About Shrimad Rajchandraji."
10. Order of service no longer available.

After the event I wrote down the various elements of the service and wrote some initial reflections in my research journal. At one point I wrote this:

> From this service I can see how the cathedral is attempting to be a boundary destroying, bridge building space, where people from all walks of life and views can find common meaning and goals to create a more fair, just and peaceful society. If the cathedral team see a potential boundary that could cause division, it seeks to cross it. Traditional boundaries between the sacred and secular and boundaries between other religions. It has seen the old boundaries between Christians and Jews, Muslims, Hindus and Buddhists and has decided to cross them, finding more common ground between those who have been excluded through other forms of Christian relationality. Part of the cathedral's public theology is that God is found in every religion, society, tradition and individual that strives towards peace, justice and unity.

In this way, what struck me about the meeting was the way that the cathedral uses certain unifying principles, in the case of this service, peace, to identify the common ground among diverse traditions and communities. But, of course, interreligious worship practices raise questions about the cathedral's Christian identity, as part of the established church, and its desire to be available to all. This was a concern that I had raised in the first round of interviews that I did with the cathedral team about the challenge of being public and asking the question of whether Christian distinctiveness needed to be "compromised" or neutralized in any way to maintain public relevance. Or to put it another way, does the inclusive agenda of the cathedral require the marginalization or neutralization of the distinctive elements of the Christian faith? I asked this to several participants in the context of discussing interreligious work.

The cathedral administrator at the time, Stuart Shepherd, argues that because the cathedral is not trying to hide its Christian identity when it hosts interreligious events, the cathedral can resist criticisms levelled that it is compromising its Christian faith. He said:

> For example, we've had iftars in the cathedral. It's probably unheard of to invite and hold an iftar on the cathedral floor. There was no kind of shying away from the building or the presence or the kind of things around the cathedral, the icons or you know various aspects of things where you might say, "That might be a bit insensitive to leave that there." We don't do that kind of

thing. It stays as is. So, something like the iftar is held in the nave, which is the meeting space for all people. We keep the quire and the side chapels as they are, so there is no shying away from what is actually there and what we are about at the same time.

Sharples responded to the questions, saying:

> No, because I think that our number one priority is worship. Because worship is something we do every day and the worship is absolutely Christian worship, therefore that is the nonnegotiable Christian identity of the cathedral. That's its primary function. Because if you are secure in that identity and understanding and that function then I think you can afford to be generous in terms of including people of all faiths and none. It doesn't compromise our integrity in any way. And it is distinctively a Christian institution ... Because in the venue itself the people who are up front at the cathedral do so very clearly as ministers of the gospel.

Similarly, Wall responded to the question, saying:

> I think our main daily worship and Sunday worship [are] very much Christian focused because that is our job as a cathedral we have a focus on Christian faith and we have to follow the liturgy of the Anglican Church, so we use morning and evening prayer to do daily prayer, the Book of Common Prayer, and when I have prepared Sunday worship again it is based on what we have in common worship that is published by the Church of England. We are open to everyone, and we do get people from other faiths attending our Sunday service. But we do not change the Sunday services because people of other faiths are attending our worship.

There are two main responses here. The first response is to suggest that the building and aesthetic symbolism within the building provide enough Christian identity markers to also offset criticisms that the cathedral is compromising its identity. For Shepherd, the cathedral would be open to critique if it changed its aesthetic to accommodate these activities. But because the cathedral does not do this, it remains firm in its Christian identity, even while hosting, for example, a Muslim iftar. Holgate further affirmed this by pointing out that no matter what kind of interreligious engagement the dean is in, he always wears his clerical collar, which identifies him as a priest within the church.

The second type of response from Wall and Sharples suggests that the amount of Christian worship that takes place in the cathedral and is part of the cathedral's daily rhythm offsets any critiques of the cathedral compromising its identity. The worship life of the cathedral provides enough distinctiveness to justify more activities which include people of other faiths and their distinctive acts of prayer and worship.

A third type of response is given by Govender. He argues that it is the cathedral's role as part of the established church which grounds the cathedral's interreligious work. The Church of England operates as a guardian institution for all faiths in England, and, for Govender, other faith groups trust the church to represent them in the House of Lords, because the CofE is the only religious organization represented in the House of Lords.[11] In this way, Govender argued, just as the CofE has a national responsibility to people of all faiths, so its cathedrals and parishes have a responsibility to care for the freedoms, faiths, and flourishing of those in their communities who are part of different religious traditions. Thus, for Govender, it is the cathedral's Christian character, and its role as part of the established church which provides the basis of its interreligious character. Further, his own role as dean means that he is not simply the dean of Christians but is the dean of people of all faiths and none in Greater Manchester.

Scriptural Reasoning

The third and final area of interreligious engagement that I would like to explore here is the Scriptural Encounter group, where David Holgate was a keen participant as a representative of the cathedral during his time as canon theologian. The Scriptural Encounter group is a forum hosted by the Centre for Jewish studies at the University of Manchester. It is "a textual study-discussion forum to achieve mutual understanding over potentially contentious texts on particular topics." While the forum is hosted by the Centre for Jewish Studies, it is done so in "partnership with members of the Jewish, Christian and Muslim communities in Greater Manchester."[12] For

---

11. Some argue against the idea of the CofE being represented by the bishops in the House of Lords, because it can be seen to promote one particular faith community over the others in Britain. However, as John Hall, who was dean of Westminster Abbey at the time of discussing this topic, states, "It's a matter of service. The C of E exists to serve the people of the nation, and the bishops in the House of Lords are there for service" (Sherwood, "Church and State," para. 22). Further, as Martin Percy argues establishment as "being not about privilege but being a national church, rather like a spiritual NHS—providing spiritual care to all, quite independent of an individual's faith, belief or need" (para. 24).

12. See http://www.manchesterjewishstudies.org/scriptural-encounter/.

Holgate, participating in this group regularly was a key outworking of the cathedral's mission to be the cathedral for people of all faiths and none.

The Scriptural Encounter group has looked at topics, among others, of gender identity and diversity, interpretations of the binding of Isaac by Abraham, and eschatological approaches to holy places in the three faiths, to name just a few examples. Usually, the format of the forum is to take one topic over three different meetings, with each meeting being used to present texts about the topic from one of the Abrahamic faiths represented. For example, in 2021 the forum examined the topic of domestic abuse and violence within the Abrahamic religions. In the first meeting, Mahmoud Afifi presented texts from an Islamic perspective. In the following session, Dr. Rachel Starr presented the topic from the perspective of Christian texts. And in the final week for that topic, Rabbi Lee Wax presented from the perspective of Jewish texts.

The format of the meeting is usually that the presenter will speak for a set amount of time, and then participants can then enter a dialogue with the speaker and each other. Holgate sees this work as a crucial part of his own ministry because he sees the cathedral's public role as being able to comment on serious social issues of inequality. But Holgate recognizes that the cathedral itself would be limited in its perspective if it did not engage with the perspectives of those of other faiths. For Holgate, as the cathedral tries to work towards a more just and equal society, it is crucial that issues such as patriarchy, gender diversity, and inclusion are understood from diverse perspectives.

UNDERSTANDING THE PUBLIC THEOLOGICAL CHARACTER OF MANCHESTER CATHEDRAL'S INTERRELIGIOUS ACTIVITY

So far in this chapter, I have described the cathedral's three main forms that its interreligious character adopts. Each of these has had events and activities that I have described. In this section, I will evaluate this character using the approaches to publicness developed in chapters 1 and 2 and through engaging the work of theologians focusing on interreligious dialogue.

Govender claims that his approach to interreligious dialogue is intended to reclaim humanity as the first religion of the cathedral and their interreligious partners. For Govender, this emphasis on humanity as the cathedral's first religion is not despite the cathedral's Christian identity but is the natural overflow of Trinitarian theology. Govender described his understanding of the Trinity as a circle of love, in which humanity participates as it joins in loving creation because the love of the Trinity is present in every human created by the Godhead.[13]

Thus, for Govender, the theological implications of his Trinitarianism lead to an inclusive approach to Christian dialogue with other faith groups, which resists Christian superiority, because God is not seen to be an object held by the church.[14] Paul Hanson similarly argues that to foster inclusive public discourse about common concerns and public virtues acknowledges the fact that God alone reigns and that no "mortal individual or group can claim more than *partial* understandings of God's universal rule that human institutions are to mediate." Hanson further argues that because no one person or institution can claim more than partial understanding, public discourse requires multiple perspectives in order to collectively calibrate society's "moral compass."[15] For Christians to claim pure moral insight on public issues and on the decisions that society should make is to commit idolatry: the mistaking of the human for the divine.[16]

Govender and Hanson are therefore both resisting presumptions that Christians alone possess all the theological and moral insights necessary to guide society. The cathedral in this way thus resists what is often known as Christian superiority and triumphalism.[17] John Hick and feminist theologian Rosemary Radford Ruether have critiqued Christian superiority and triumphalism within the context of interreligious dialogue. Their works have been influential in discussions about Christianity and its relationships to other religions. Hick argued that all religions have the "same experiential roots in contact with the same divine reality" but because of these different experiences, they differ in the way they elaborate that divine reality.[18] For Hick, the lack of recognition of this fact has led Christians to not recognize the streams of salvation in other religions, and the Christian has been able to relate to the religious other only as one who needs to be proselytized.[19] For Hick, this attitude can be characterized as Christian superiority or triumphalism.

13. I will return to this quote in ch. 7 where I explore in more depth how the cathedral's public theology as it relates to concepts of humanness.

14. As one of the favorite Desmond Tutu quotes shared by Govender and Holgate on separate occasions to me says, "God is not a Christian."

15. Hanson, "Bible and Public Theology," 34; emphasis in original.

16. Hanson, "Bible and Public Theology," 33–34.

17. McBride, *Church for the World*, 37. McBride here defines *triumphalism* as the belief that Christians alone possess moral answers to life's questions, which can be imposed on others who do not share the same religious convictions.

18. Hick, *Philosophy of Religion*, 12.

19. Hick, *Philosophy of Religion*, 78.

Triumphalist attitudes within the Christian tradition, for Hick, led to the "practical outworking in colonialism, antisemitism, the burning of heretics and the western political and cultural superiority."[20] Hick ties the lack of publicness of older forms of Christianity to high Christological formulations which have proclaimed Christ to be more than a prophet, even though, according to Hick, the historical Jesus never made claims of divinity about himself. As a Christian pluralist, doctrines of incarnation, atonement and the trinity are alienating and can only lead to Christian superiority in Hick's perspective. Thus, he argues that this superiority demonstrates the self-evident falseness of these doctrines.[21]

Similarly, Ruether has argued that "anti-Judaism developed theologically in Christianity as the left-hand of Christology. That is to say, anti-Judaism was the negative side of the Christian claim that Jesus was the Christ."[22] She asks the question "Is it possible to say, 'Jesus is Messiah' without implicitly or explicitly saying at the same time 'and the Jews be damned'?"[23] For Ruether, the answer to this question is simply no. As a result, she calls for a revision of Christian theological teaching about Christ that refuses to claim Jesus as the Messiah, but rather claims him as a "Jew who hoped for the coming of the Kingdom of God and who died in that hope."[24] For Ruether, doing Christian theology in the shadow of the Holocaust requires a repentant theology. She argues:

> To bring this tragic history to an end will demand something like a massive repentant acceptance of responsibility by the Christian church, and a dramatic shift in the spirituality which it teaches. . . . A repentant Christianity is a Christianity which has turned from the theology of messianic triumphalism to the theology of hope.[25]

The cathedral shares the same concerns regarding historical acts of Christian persecution of those of other religions that resulted from Christian perceptions of their own superiority. However, the cathedral has never indicated that it wishes to revise the core doctrines that have historically come to be understood to make up orthodox Christian theology. They share the

---

20. Hick, *Disputed Questions in Theology*, 48.
21. Hick, *Disputed Questions in Theology*, 96.
22. Ruether, "Antisemitism and Christian Theology," 79.
23. Ruether, *Faith and Fratricide*, 246.
24. Ruether, "Christian-Jewish Dialogue," 4.
25. Ruether, "Antisemitism and Christian Theology," 92.

same concerns with Hick and Ruether but opt for a Rawlsian bracketing of potentially divisive doctrines, instead of the revision of doctrines.

By "bracketing" I mean here a kind of act of Rawlsian translation whereby certain convictions and values are not brought into focus in public settings because they are seen as hindering the shared task of fostering the common good in society. The "common good" then is assumed to be a conceptual category determined by factors outside of specifically religious convictions, though religious convictions may motivate the public theologian to articulate arguments in relation to the common good. For this reason, because a shared understanding of the common good is assumed, it is also assumed that specific religious convictions can be bracketed by individuals engaged in dialogue.

The cathedral then, through the way that the bracketing is implied in its interreligious work creates a division between the ultimate concerns of certain religions and the penultimate concerns of society. Ultimate concerns are the central beliefs that religious adherents have about God, the transcendent, etc., whereas penultimate concerns are concerned with the temporal. They are concerned with the present state of the world and problems that need to be dealt with. James K. A. Smith characterizes this distinction in the following way:

> Whether you think human beings are made in the image of God or are just sentient meat encased in skin, we can probably all agree that sewer systems are a good thing. We might not agree on the eternal destiny of the soul, or whether we have souls, but we might all be able to agree that laws requiring child car seats are a good idea. If we would only focus on the mundane, penultimate issues, we need not be bothered by the ultimate beliefs that divide us.[26]

From my reading, penultimate concerns are the primary focus of interreligious activity at Manchester Cathedral. For Govender, these penultimate concerns may be about climate change, racism, or other issues of public concern. But what matters for Govender is that the ultimate concerns of the Christian, Muslim, Jewish faith, or any faith group that wishes to engage with the cathedral, do not stop the activity which seeks to address the common concerns that pertain to many diverse people groups within the public sphere.

---

26. J. Smith, *Awaiting the King*, 20. While Smith himself does not adopt this division between ultimate and penultimate concerns, as can be seen from the tone of this passage, this paragraph nonetheless neatly characterizes the difference between the two.

John Rawls, as I showed in chapter 1, uses the language of "comprehensive doctrines" to communicate a similar meaning to the phrase "ultimate concern." He uses his theory of justice as a way of grounding the "penultimate concerns" of society, to produce an overlapping consensus which avoids a clash of comprehensive doctrines in the public sphere. The function of these words and phrases and that of "ultimate and penultimate concerns" are the same: they are a way of denoting that which may be privatized and bracketed for the sake of reaching a consensus on common issues of public concern.

In my view, Manchester Cathedral often adopts this Rawlsian approach to its interreligious social justice work and worship. Just as Rawls assumed that an overarching unifying principle such as justice could provide enough of a common ground among diverse people groups, so the cathedral presumes that categories or values, such as justice or peace, can provide the unifying ground upon which different religious groups can interact. For example, the celebration of Gandhi service discussed above was (for the most part) thoroughly Rawlsian, in that the various readings and songs were utilized to demonstrate that the different traditions are all united in their shared concern for peace.[27] Gandhi, and his commitment to nonviolence, becomes a unifying symbol, that all religious groups and nonreligious groups for that matter could also adopt in their own pursuit of peace. Similarly, in OFOP and CHF meetings, the unifying principle or factor is the common concern to find practical solutions to shared problems, namely climate change and hate crimes. In this context, religions offer support to unifying values and principles established by other, nonreligious means.

However, it is important to note that of concern for the cathedral in its interreligious character is not *only* joining with people of other faiths to find solutions to shared problems. In addition, the cathedral values developing these networks and bonds of deep trust because the cathedral team believes that the cathedral belongs to all citizens of the region of Greater Manchester. In my interviews with staff, many noted that colleagues from the Hindu, Muslim, and Jewish communities often say how welcome and at home they feel at the cathedral since Govender has been leading the cathedral to be the cathedral for people of all faiths and none. According to those I interviewed, these colleagues from other faiths comment on the contrast between how welcoming the cathedral feels under the leadership of Govender, compared

---

27. I write "for the most part" here because Govender told me that he had to have a meeting with the organizing team for this event because part of the service promoted a new book by a Jain philosopher. In Govender's terms, the service ended up becoming a promotion of Jainism, rather than a celebration of Gandhi and the call to peace.

to how it has felt in previous years. Thus, the cathedral has been successful in developing its interfaith relationships in quite a rich way.

It is important to note that in terms of trust, researchers have found a negative correlation between social trust and the importance of religion. Regarding their study Berggren and Bjørnskov write that:

> The main reason to expect a negative effect, of the kind we have identified, is that religions may cause division and rift, both in that religious people may distrust those who do not share their beliefs and who are not subject to the same enforcement mechanisms as they are, and in that non-religious people may regard with suspicion those who take religiosity seriously.[28]

As a result of both an awareness of the distrust of religious institutions in post-secular societies as described above, and the desire to continue to build relationships with a diverse network of people and groups, the cathedral resists certain practices that they perceive would lead to a loss of trust among the networks that they have developed. For example, I asked participants a question about how the cathedral navigates the tension between being inclusive in an interreligious setting, while still maintaining its distinct understanding of the Christian gospel. Canon Marcia Wall said:

> I think you can still live out the gospel without having to proselytize or try to convince people. We are careful that we are not trying to convert anybody because as soon as that is introduced, the interfaith conversation goes down the drain. And we are not actually trying to convert anyone, not in my book anyway and I don't think anybody here is. So, we are living the gospel because we are proclaiming the gospel in our worship. We are open to everybody without questions and so we show the love of God, loving our neighbor by offering hospitality to everybody not just of other faiths but in the LGBTQ+ community, or different genders and different races.

Similarly, Canon David Sharples suggested to me that an overt desire to proselytize would undo much of the ministry and aims of the cathedral. He said:

> If people came and the message was overtly evangelistic in our events and activities, the danger then is you won't get people around the table because they will say, "You're inviting us along, but actually you have another agenda, and the real agenda is to

---

28. Berggren and Bjørnskov, "Religion in Daily Life," 474.

convert people to the Christian faith." And I don't think that works. You would then cease to engage with people.

It can be seen from these quotes that the cathedral's resistance to proselytization is not simply a theological concern, but a concern about undoing the social capital, or trust, developed with other faith groups.

THE LIMITS OF A RAWLSIAN APPROACH TO INTERRELIGIOUS DIALOGUE AND ACTIVITY

A key question for my analysis and evaluation then, is whether the Rawlsian approach that the cathedral adopts presents any limits or challenges, and if so, are there other possibilities for interreligious dialogue in public? The Rawlsian approach adopted by the cathedral team depends on the assumption of there being a shared common ground among the different religious groups. However, Marianne Moyaert argues that the presumption of a common ground inhibits real dialogue rather than creating the space in which real dialogue can take place. She reasons this by saying:

> This is because real dialogue involves listening to genuinely strange ideas, whereas the assumption of common ground limits the strangeness of what can be heard. The listener who is convinced of common ground will not be able to hear the full novelty of what is said.[29]

This tendency can be seen in the example of the OFOP gathering I described. The introduction of the perspectives of different faith communities in one segment of the meeting was not with the intention of introducing the strangeness or novelty of the different religions, but to demonstrate the common ground among the religions. In many respects, this purpose would be hindered if a genuinely "strange idea" was introduced.

The limits of this approach are helpfully explored by both Habermas and Ricoeur. Habermas, like Rawls, sees one of the central problems with interreligious dialogue and relationality in the public sphere as the potential for such interactions to descend into violence, whether physical or metaphorical. For Habermas and Rawls, tolerance was established as a principle of civil society because of the wars of religion in the sixteenth and seventeenth centuries. However, as I argued in chapter 1, for Habermas, this potential for violence does not mean that religions have no ability to share their perspectives and ideas in ways that don't lead to violence. Instead,

---

29. Moyaert, *Fragile Identities*, 103.

environments should be created for religious citizens to be able to share their religious perspectives, which can provide significant moral insight that secular instrumental reason is unable to replace.

For Habermas then, while religious language and symbols must be siphoned for their relevant moral components and then translated into terms of secular reason, religion's unique perspectives must be explored to uncover moral dimensions to public issues. Without such engagement, for Habermas, the public sphere is deprived of both valuable insights and the democratic environment which treats all citizens and identities equally is diminished.[30] Hence, he is resistant to secularist theories which would seek to exclude religious perspectives from the public sphere altogether. From this perspective, Manchester Cathedral, because of its Rawlsian approach, adopts a kind of secularization approach to interreligious dialogue which limits the potential moral contributions that religious voices might be able to make.

Ricoeur's approach agrees with Habermas's critique of the Rawlsian approach but takes the argument further. Ricoeur's most extensive treatment of this topic arose in response to the Declaration of a Global Ethic in 1993, which I will describe at length. The declaration was formed by the World Parliament of Religions under the leadership of Hans Küng.[31] Küng argues that one of the main problems religious bodies and communities have to deal with is interreligious conflict and the only way to overcome religious conflict and violence is for the religions to engage in interreligious dialogue. However, Küng suggests that such interreligious dialogue should not focus on doctrines which may fuel the conflicts.[32] Instead, the religious voices should seek to find agreement on "*fundamental* issues, such as violence, global warming, and famine."[33]

While Küng acknowledges there are differences between the world religions understandings of what is good and evil, right, and wrong and what humans ought to do ethically, he thinks these differences "should not hinder us from proclaiming *those things which we already hold in common and which we jointly affirm. An ethic* already exists within the religious teachings of the world which can counter global distress."[34] Marianne Moyaert, who analyzes the debate between Ricoeur and Küng, argues that at the heart of

---

30. Ricoeur, *Time and Narrative*, 289.
31. Moyaert, *In Response to Religious Other*, 73.
32. Küng and Kuschel, *Global Ethic*, 103.
33. Moyaert, *In Response to Religious Other*, 74; emphasis added.
34. Küng and Kuschel, *Global Ethic*, 105. Cited in Moyaert, *In Response to Religious Other*, 74–75; emphasis in original.

this belief is that humans all possess inalienable rights and dignity, regardless of their differences in terms of race, class, gender, sexuality, etc.[35] As a result, the search for a global ethic is not about "one global ideology or a single unified religion beyond all existing religions, and certainly not one religion over all others." Rather the global ethic is "a fundamental consensus on binding values, irrevocable standards and personal attitudes."[36] The universal affirmation of inalienable human rights and dignity affirms that there is overlap in the religions, which should be the focus of their discussions.

Practically, the declaration affirmed that the uniting ethical factor of all the World religions is the Golden Rule: 'What you do not wish to be done to you, do not do to others.'[37] I will quote Moyaert at length where she summarizes the declarations' four minimum commitments:

> 1) "a culture of non-violence and respect for life" ("you shall not kill!"), 2) "a culture of solidarity and a just economic order" ("You shall not steal"), 3) "a culture of tolerance and a life of truthfulness" ("You shall not lie!"), and 4) "a culture of equal righthand partnership between men and women" ("You shall not commit sexual immorality"). The declaration assures the reader that the global ethic put forward cannot replace the rich ethical teachings of the Torah, the sermon of the mount or the Quran. Rather, it offers a minimum ethic that all religions can adhere to, whereas the religious traditions offer "maximum ethics."[38]

The aims and objectives of the Declaration of a Global Ethic represent a Rawlsian approach to consensus, common ground, and the separation between ultimate and penultimate concerns. The ethic assumes that every reasonable religious individual can adhere to these principles and thus find common ground with other reasonable religious individuals. Again, this approach also represents the approaches to social justice and worship in the cathedral's interreligious work.

However, Ricoeur admits that he had a "certain inner resistance to this project."[39] Ricoeur was especially resistant to Küng's suggestion that religious doctrines should be bracketed out from interreligious discussions

---

35. Moyaert, *In Response to Religious Other*, 75.

36. Küng and Kuschel, *Global Ethic*, 105.

37. Küng and Kuschel, *Global Ethic*, 106.

38. Moyaert, *In Response to Religious Other*, 75–76. See also Küng and Kuschel, *Global Ethic*, 73.

39. Küng and Ricoeur, "Religions, violence et paix," 217. Cited in Moyaert, *In Response to Religious Other*, 76.

and instead those in the discussion should focus on concrete ethical and practical matters. Ricoeur argues against this because he thinks that such a separation is both impossible and undesirable. If a Christian hears the command "Do not kill," the Christian does not hear this command separate from recognizing the image of Christ crucified, "because he is the victim *par excellence*."[40] The command not to kill, then, cannot be separated from the Christians' own stories, symbols, and doctrines. Further, he thinks that separating the commands from their religious energy, accompaniment and support will in turn produce a poor morality that relies on its own contents for sustainability rather than "a word that is entrusted to us because it comes from elsewhere."[41]

Further, he argues that if the aim of creating these minimal ethics is to end interreligious conflicts it is guaranteed to fail in its project because the formal principles cannot be accompanied by formal interpretations. So, for the formal principle "do not kill," there is the very real potential for interreligious conflict as they may each interpret the word "kill" in a variety of ways. What does one say about abortion, euthanasia, the eating of animals, or war? The formal principle has not done anything to reduce conflict.[42] Instead, Ricoeur challenges the assumption that a lack of conflict is desirable. He suggests that instead of disregarding "what separates us, the real problem is to understand what separates us."[43] As I demonstrated in chapter 1 Ricoeur does not deny the possibility of universal principles, but he does not want to adopt or emphasize these at the expense of plurality. Pluralism is one of the great universal facts for Ricoeur. His theory of the inchoate universal, or universal potential, is an attempt to strike a balance between homogenization and tribalism.[44] For Ricoeur, this can happen only within the space of encounter, where others in their difference can still gather to

---

40. Küng and Ricoeur, "Religions, violence et paix," 217. Cited in Moyaert, *In Response to Religious Other*, 77.

41. Küng and Ricoeur, "Religions, violence et paix," 218. Cited in Moyaert, *In Response to Religious Other*, 77.

42. Küng and Ricoeur, "Religions, violence et paix," 219. Cited in Moyaert, *In Response to Religious Other*, 77–78. In relation to my own interests in the topic of LGBTQ+ inclusion, which will be explored further in ch. 6, it is not clear that whether the fourth minimum commitment includes/excludes those who do not identify within the firm binary labels of "men" and "women." Does this commitment include a commitment to nonbinary, gender-fluid, and transgender people? This tension is explored further in ch. 6.

43. Küng and Ricoeur, "Religions, violence et paix," 219. Cited in Moyaert, *In Response to Religious Other*, 78.

44. Ricoeur, *Time and Narrative*, 289. Ricoeur, *Oneself as Another*, 290. See ch. 1 for my discussion of Ricoeur's theory of the inchoative universal.

discuss as humans.⁴⁵ For Ricoeur, "Universalism . . . can only be co-existive with a more or less controlled plurality."⁴⁶

Another way of putting this is in the words of Dan Stiver summarizing Ricoeur:

> To his mind, the context of our upbringing, the language that we speak, the cultural values we have interiorised, and the religion that commits us are not to be put aside as mere regrettable limitations. On the contrary, he argues that all those dimensions make it possible to live in a meaningful world, and they put us on the path to something that continually eludes the human grasp: a superabundance of meaning that can never be exhausted.⁴⁷

For Ricoeur, in contrast to Rawls and the Rawlsian approach which Küng clearly adopts, to focus only on those things which we hold in common is to mistake the way that religion is formational for the way that people understand ethics and society. The diversity of formational influences among people in the public sphere is a topic for exploration. Thus, in the context of exploring the formational aspects of the religions, the avoidance of discussing those things which separate and can potentially divide, can lead to a loss of meaning and the suppression of diverging perspectives. To draw on the theme of hermeneutics, Ricoeur argues that the way that people interpret and understand penultimate concerns is in part affected by how our ultimate concerns shape our hermeneutics.

This, furthermore, has implications for the field of public theology. Throughout this chapter, I have been evaluating Manchester Cathedral's public theology by using the three approaches of publicness that I developed in chapter 1. However, I have not engaged with public theology as a field until this point. This is mainly because public theologians have often focused on the nature of communicating with diverse publics in the context of policy making. As a result, public theologians have often emphasized concepts of "translation" to discover the most proficient ways of being convincing and persuasive in the public sphere. Therefore, the analysis of this chapter has significant implications for public theologies which seek to engage with people of other faiths in the public sphere.

As I discussed in chapter 2, the incarnational mark of public theology means that it aims towards the "welfare of the city" rather than the growth

---

45. Moyaert, *In Response to Religious Other*, 79. See Ricoeur, *Time and Narrative*, 290.

46. Changeux and Ricoeur, *What Makes Us Think*, 288.

47. Stiver, *Theology after Ricoeur*, 163. Cited in Moyaert, *In Response to Religious Other*, 33.

and benefit of the church. However, the analysis in this chapter demonstrates that "the city" is not monolithic, but made up of many different types of communities, including religious communities, which have their own unique visions and perspectives of how "the welfare of the city" should be understood. Many of these visions are formed through religious narratives and symbols. The Ricoeurian approach that I am advocating for, then, means that any kind of dialogue and translation should not come through the bracketing of these religious symbols, but through some kind of direct engagement with them. Translation in this context is not simply about finding the lowest common denominator of reason among the different religious groups, but about understanding one another's different perspectives and how these are formed. Without this kind of reflection in conversation with people of other faiths, public theology risks homogenizing both Christian perspectives and the perspectives of others, because its assumption of shared common ground could mean that a "genuinely strange idea" cannot be heard by public theologians.

However, as the staff that I interviewed demonstrated in the previous section, talking about distinctive and particular religious visions in public may sound as though the only outcome or aim is to try and convert the other. But, as is clear from my analysis of the Ricoeurian approach to publicness and interreligious dialogue, proselytization need not be the only outworking of engaging distinctive theological visions. Instead, those engaged in interreligious settings could explore in a variety of ways that religious stories, traditions and symbols influence the way that ethical life is understood by different religious individuals and communities. Such exploration need not require the domination of one religious group over others or the absorption of some identities into a larger identity. Instead, through practices of linguistic hospitality there can be an exploration of various traditions and perspectives in order for each participant to share genuinely strange ideas that may enrich the whole, or part of, the group.

Yet, it can be argued that such an approach can be adopted, only when enough trust has been developed within a diverse group over time. In a case study done on interreligious youth groups in London, Johan Liljestrand demonstrates that in one of the youth groups in particular there was an awareness that the different religious individuals represented needed to focus on their similarities for a time to develop trust to be able to then begin to discuss the differences in their perspectives. Liljestrand records one leader of a group saying:

> We haven't talked so much about differences but have focused more on similarities—we've finished with that now. We've

worked with these young people for a year or so now they are ready to take the next step and move on a bit.[48]

Nevertheless, it is not clear to me that Manchester Cathedral desires to develop its interreligious activity in such a way that the differences between the religious groups are explored. In the above example, the youth leader had the desire to develop discussion among the youth about their differences. This can be seen in his use of the phrase "move on," an indication that he perceives this development as progress in some way. The question then becomes, for the cathedral, what is the purpose of the interreligious character of the cathedral?

In her book *Fragile Religious Identities*, Marianne Moyaert argues that the purpose of interreligious activity and dialogue is to connect with the question of God. She states:

> In interreligious theology, we gropingly ask where God comes into view and do so with an open attitude of hospitality. Interreligious dialogue is a theological space only if it is related to God. Where does God reveal himself? Interreligious theology must be true theology. The quest for God is fundamental to the theological implications of interreligious dialogue.

For Moyaert, direct theological engagement is necessary for interreligious theology to truly be theology. However, from my engagement and analysis with Manchester Cathedral, they demonstrate an approach to interreligious dialogue which emphasizes similarity, shared meaning, and perspective. In this way, "the quest for God" is not central. Rather, the cathedral's approaches to both social justice-oriented interreligious work and interreligious worship can be characterized as an expression of how diverse religious traditions are united in their common concern for justice, peace, and inclusion. It is worth repeating Govender's perspective on interreligious public theology at the cathedral: "We are claiming humanity as our first religion."

However, I would argue that even in the claiming of humanity as the first religion of different faith traditions questions of God must be critically engaged. As Hick and Ruether have demonstrated, it is Christian theological interpretations and visions that have often led to some of the social ills that Manchester Cathedral seeks to challenge in public. Even if the cathedral would not go as far as revising specific doctrines such as the incarnation, or the belief in Jesus's messiahship, Ruether and Hick demonstrate the need to be challenged by and engage with these doctrines and the harmful ways

---

48. Liljestrand, "Case Study 1," 34.

these have formed communities to participate in violent practices in the church and society.[49]

Further, in the claiming of humanity as the first religion of the cathedral, there is an assumption that understandings of what it means to be human are not contested on theological or anthropological grounds. This will be especially significant in the subsequent chapters, but for now it is worth noting that the cathedral does not possess a thick theological understanding of the human. Rather, humanity functions as a category to provide overlapping consensus.

SCRIPTURAL ENCOUNTER AND SCRIPTURAL REASONING AS ONE OUTWORKING OF A RICOEURIAN APPROACH TO INTERRELIGIOUS DIALOGUE

For the most part, my evaluation has focused on two of the three aspects of the cathedral's interreligious public theology: social justice work and interreligious worship. In my perspective, both aspects of its interreligious character can be characterized as being Rawlsian in the cathedral's approach. However, the exception to this is the Scriptural Encounter and Scriptural Reasoning work that David Holgate participated in during his time at the cathedral.

In many ways, the groups follow the model of the reading of classics put forward by Tracy. By giving each perspective and religious tradition its own session to lead and explore, the groups allow for authentic articulation of the theological and ethical perspectives of that religious participant. But through the dialogue following a presentation, there is the opportunity for comparative theology and interrogation, that does not seek to harmonize the perspectives, but to understand their differences. While Holgate has been participating in these groups, he has done so as a representative of the cathedral. However, of the three areas of interreligious work at the cathedral this work is the least visible at Manchester Cathedral. The social justice

---

49. This focus on formation may be one way that public theologians can address the public of the church more effectively. Parker argues that the public of the church is the more neglected public among public theologians of the three outlined by Tracy (Parker, "Public Convergence," 448). However, public theologians could do more to engage with questions of doctrine and scriptural interpretation in light of the dialogues that they participate within in the public sphere. For example, K. Day and Kim argue that part of the dialogical nature of public theology means that there is an openness of theologians to be challenged and transformed by perspectives communicated in society ("Introduction," 15). I am arguing that this openness and transformation can take place only if the approach of public theologians is more Ricoeurian.

and public worship aspects of its interreligious engagement affect multiple departments of the cathedral. However, as Holgate himself suggested to me in an interview, it is not clear that the wider cathedral team know what happens at these Scriptural Reasoning and Scriptural Encounter groups and how these meetings could impact the practice and theology of the cathedral. There is also a question of whether any cathedral team member will continue with this type of scriptural reasoning work following the retirement of Canon Holgate.

DIVERSITY IN INTERRELIGIOUS ENGAGEMENT

Govender, and the cathedral team following his leadership, may well ask what the end result of this analysis may be. Is it the case that I am arguing that interreligious worship should not take place at the cathedral, or that it should be filled with conflicting prayers and scriptural texts and perspectives? Should the interfaith social justice events, such as OFOP, be focused on exploring the differences between faith traditions, instead of finding practical solutions to common issues? In my view, much of the cathedral's interreligious work is a viable model for Christian institutions wanting to engage in interreligious networking. The Rawlsian model it has adopted has been successful in gathering people from various traditions to not only enter the cathedral doors and feel welcome but to participate in its life in different ways. As I have argued, it is necessary to develop trust among those of other faiths to adopt Habermasian or Ricoeurian approaches to interreligious dialogue.

However, the cathedral's largely Rawlsian approach raises questions about what the purpose of its interreligious work is or could be. In my view, while the cathedral's approach to interreligious social justice work and worship successfully explores the common ground between faith traditions, its interreligious networks could be enriched through the exploration of different visions and identities even where this might produce conflict in the group. As I have argued, the aim of this is to understand our differences, and not simply bracket them.

This is not a case for an either/or approach to interreligious networking and dialogue. Instead, it is a both/and approach which can build upon the already successful and deep relationships that the cathedral has built with its neighbors of all faiths and none. Instead, the cathedral could host other activities and networks which resist the Rawlsian model's tendency towards homogenization and could draw more deeply from the perspectives of other faith traditions. Such dialogues, understood in the context of linguistic hospitality, are an opportunity for each participant to offer gifts of themselves to the wider group. By potentially bracketing distinctive identities, and focusing on more common ground, the cathedral's interreligious networks could be losing out on vital gifts from the diverse participants. As Tracy argues:

> The global culture which the present suggests, and the future demands impels everyone—every individual, every group, every culture, every religion, and theological tradition—to recognise the plurality within each self. . . . Our present situation demands that each come to the dialogue with a genuine self-respect in her or his particularity as well as a willingness to expose oneself as oneself to the other as really other. Self-exposure is merely the reverse side of the self-respect demanded by this pluralistic moment.[50]

In sum, without practices and activities through which otherness and difference of vision can be explored a public theology of interreligious relationality, both as thought and practice, is likely to be impoverished.

CONCLUSION

In this chapter I have demonstrated how and why Manchester Cathedral often adopts a Rawlsian approach to interreligious social justice work and worship. The guiding presumption is that people from different religious traditions can unite over issues of common public concern and shared values without their distinctive religious identities and understandings compromising this joint pursuit of justice and peace. However, the challenge I have tried to present to this approach as part of my critical evaluation of the public theology at play is that religion must be understood as a private entity that can be marginalized and privatized when neutrality is required.

However, such an approach does not address the ways that ethics and values are formed within the context of religion, rather than seeing them as an additional aspect of religious thought. Therefore, formation should be a primary concern of public theologies engaging with interreligious dialogues. Without this, the cathedral's public theology of interreligious dialogue could be impoverished if it does not create opportunities to hear genuinely strange ideas. Further, unless public theologians develop more Ricoeurian approaches to interreligious dialogue, the field as a whole will

---

50. Tracy, "Defending the Public Character," 352–53. Cited in Jones, "9/11 Changed Things," 209.

also suffer from this impoverishment. In the following chapter, I will explore the cathedral's public theology of racial justice and demonstrate how the concerns raised regarding formation in this chapter are also relevant regarding the topic of racism.

5

MANCHESTER CATHEDRAL'S PUBLIC THEOLOGY OF RACIAL JUSTICE

IN THIS CHAPTER, I am critically evaluating Manchester Cathedral's public theology of racial justice. I will first outline my interpretation of the state of the "racism debate" in the three publics of society (specifically the UK), church (the Church of England), and academy (the field of public theology) which demonstrate some contexts for interpreting the anti-racist theology of the cathedral. I will then analyze the racially inclusive public theology of the cathedral and describe the various aspects of its anti-racism work. Finally, after identifying the approach to publicness that the cathedral adopts in its anti-racist work, I will offer a critical evaluation of the model and explore how a different approach can build on the cathedral's already existing networks and work in this area.

RACISM AND SOCIETY, THE CHURCH, AND THE ACADEMY
British Responses to BLM 2020

In the midst of a global pandemic, the murder of George Floyd on May 25, 2020, was filmed and shared on websites and social media. Though the murder took place in the US, much of the world's population was grieved and enraged by such blatant racially-based killing by somebody meant to "protect and serve." Protests thus began in many countries around the globe. The UK Black Lives Matter protests are said to have been the "largest anti-racism rallies since the slavery era."[1] Some protesters took to pulling down British heritage monuments and statues that represent Britain's colonial past and participation in slavery. For example, demonstrators in Bristol toppled a statue of the slave trader Edward Colston.[2] The UK prime minister at the time, Boris Johnson, criticized this and other plans demonstrators had to pull down various statues and monuments of those involved in the slave trade or known to have held racist views as an attempt to "lie about our history."[3]

The protests were also the motivating factor for the Conservative Government to release a report in 2021 from the Commission on Race and Ethnic Disparities. The purpose of the report was to seek to understand the reality and existence of disparities and the causes of these across different ethnic minority groups. The report argues that much of the current public debate about racism ignores the progress we have made as a country. The introduction says, "The evidence reveals that ours is nevertheless a relatively open society. The country has come a long way in 50 years and the success of much of the ethnic minority population in education and, to a lesser extent, the economy, should be regarded as a model for other White-majority countries."[4]

With this optimistic view of the progress Britain has made, the report argues that actually, the racial group that suffers as much, if not more than ethnic minorities, is the white working class.[5] According to the report, this is because the system is not "deliberately rigged against ethnic minorities." Instead:

> The impediments and disparities do exist, they are varied, and ironically very few of them are directly to do with racism. Too

---

1. Mohdin and Campbell, "So Many People Care," para. 2.
2. Siddique and Skopeliti, "BLM Protesters Topple Statue."
3. Monbiot, "Boris Johnson," para. 1. Of course, Johnson did not reckon with the fact that by uncritically leaving the statues in place, one could also describe this as "lying about history" or "whitewashing" history.
4. The report argues that Britain's colonial history should be read with an optimistic and progressive lens. The report even, controversially, suggests that educators should adopt a new narrative for the Caribbean experience that "speaks to the slave period not only being about profit and suffering but how culturally African people transformed themselves into a re-modelled African/Britain" (Commission on Race and Ethnic Disparities, *Report*, 7). It is not too far to argue that this report does injustice to the real suffering caused by Britons during these periods, where those writing the report would rather foster a culture of blissful ignorance instead of wrestling deeply with the systemic racial injustices that have formed a large part of British history.
5. Commission on Race and Ethnic Disparities, *Report*, 7.

often "racism" is the catch-all explanation and can be simply implicitly accepted rather than explicitly examined.[6]

Predictably, the report was controversial. On April 19, the independent experts of the Special Procedures of the United Nations Human Rights Council released a statement saying that the council

> categorically rejects and condemns the analysis and findings of the recently published report by the UK's Commission on Race and Ethnic Disparities, which, among other conclusions, claim that "geography, family influence, socio-economic background, culture and religion have more significant impact on life chances than the existence of racism."[7]

Further, it states:

> The suggestion that family structure, rather than institutionalized and structural discriminatory practices are the central features of the Black experience is a tone-deaf attempt at rejecting the lived realities of people of African descent and other ethnic minorities in the UK.[8]

The protests and the report demonstrate the polarizing state of the conversation about racial justice and inclusion in highly significant arenas. This is an important context in which Manchester Cathedral performs its public theology of racial justice.

Racism and the Church of England

To begin discussing the complex state of the conversation about racial justice in the Church of England I will begin by citing Archbishop Justin Welby's admission that the Church of England is "deeply institutionally racist." Welby said this at the General Synod in 2020 in the context of a motion unanimously backed for the Church of England to "lament" and apologize for both "conscious and unconscious racism."[9]

Since then, there have been a number of moves made by the leadership of the Church of England to try and address the problem of systemic and institutional racism in the church. Part of this has been in performed visual solidarity with the Black Lives Matter protests in June 2020. For example,

---

6. Commission on Race and Ethnic Disparities, *Report*, 8.
7. Special Procedures, "UN Experts Condemn," para. 1.
8. Special Procedures, "UN Experts Condemn," para. 4.
9. Fox, "Deeply Institutionally Racist," para. 2.

the archbishop of Canterbury, Justin Welby, took the knee in Wells Cathedral with the cathedral chapter.[10]

Beyond visual solidarity with the Black Lives Matter protests, United Society Partners in the Gospel, which is an Anglican mission agency, launched a campaign called "standing in solidarity." Part of this campaign was an open letter sent to partners and churches stating:

> We acknowledge the pervasive and systemic reality of racism within ourselves, our communities, and the structures of British society. We recognise that this racism has deep historical roots, which shape our institutions, the practices of our communities and the attitudes of individuals and societies. The appalling treatment of members of the Windrush generation in recent years is just one monstrous example.[11]

However, it seems that before the protests, discussions of racial inclusion and justice were not high on the agenda in Anglican social theology. For example, in the publication *Anglican Social Theology*, edited by Malcolm Brown and released in 2014, which seeks to provide both a historical account of Anglican social theology and to pave the way for another generation of Anglican social theology, the issue of racism is not explored or addressed. Further, in his 2018 book *Reimagining Britain*, Welby claims that great changes of status have been achieved in Britain for groups that have historically been oppressed such as "women, ethnic minorities, those with disabilities, those with varieties of sexual orientation and desire."[12] Beyond this Welby does not reimagine Britain in the context of racial justice. Despite his repeated calls for economic justice in the reimagined post-Brexit Britain, racial justice seems to be "settled in his mind."[13]

I point to these texts to show that racial justice was not a priority for the Church of England before 2020 in the way that it is now. Some may argue against this claim because there have been numerous reports produced by the Committee for Minority Ethnic Anglican Concerns, and its predecessor the Committee on Black Anglican Concerns, which have been presented to synods over the last thirty-six years. Therefore, it could be argued that this demonstrates that racial justice has been on the agenda for the Church of England for at least as long as that.

However, it seems clear that the recommendations set forth in these reports have, more often than not, made little impact on the structures of

10. Lethaby, "Bishops Take the Knee."
11. Cited in France-Williams, *Ghost Ship*, 126.
12. Welby, *Reimagining Britain*, 33.
13. France-Williams, *Ghost Ship*, 126.

the Church of England. Thus, the recent anti-racism task force sought to correct this mistake by making one of the central tasks of its 2021 *From Lament to Action* report (*FLTA*):

> To review recommendations made in the previous Committee for Minority Ethnic Anglican Concerns (CMEAC) reports, noting actions taken or omitted, and to identify previous recommendations which could be implemented swiftly.[14]

One example of where recommendations have not been implemented in the past is one highlighted in the early pages of the task-forces report. In 1999 John Sentamu, an adviser on the Macpherson report, tabled "draft Agenda for Action in the Church of England, which was presented to the House of Bishops, Archbishops' Council and General Synod."[15] *FLTA* notes:

> It is telling that, more than 20 years later, the Taskforce found itself tabling a draft of its own action implementation timetable to the House of Bishops and Archbishop's council identifying strikingly similar areas to those identified by Bishop Sentamu and the Archbishops' council in 1999.[16]

Despite the reports and commissions that have taken place in the last thirty-six years, these have largely not led to changes in the Church of England's policies. For example, *FLTA* "laments" that:

> For the last decade, Sentamu alone represented that diversity. His retirement in June 2020 meant that for the first time in over a quarter of a century, there was no UKME/GMH diocesan bishop serving in the Church of England. In terms of ethnic diversity amongst diocesan bishops, when the new Bishop of Chelmsford takes up office later this year the Church of England will be back where it was 27 years ago.[17]

Further:

> At the time of writing (March 2021), the number of UKME/GMH bishops can together be counted on one hand (5 out of 111). The number of UKME/GMH Deans, archdeacons, and senior staff in the National Church Institutions only adds up to a further nine people. There are no UKME/GMH Diocesan

---

14. Archbishops' Anti-Racism Taskforce, *FLTA* 5.
15. Archbishops' Anti-Racism Taskforce, *FLTA* 11.
16. Archbishops' Anti-Racism Taskforce, *FLTA* 12.
17. Archbishops' Anti-Racism Taskforce, *FLTA* 12.

Secretaries (the most senior staff role in each diocese) or Principals of Theological Educational Institutions at all.[18]

Thus, the Church of England clearly needs to address its own institutional failings in this area. As a mother church in the Church of England, this is another significant environment that the cathedral must navigate as it seeks to be an advocate for racial justice in public.[19]

Public Theology and Race

Public theology is committed to offering theological responses to relevant social issues in a constructive manner that benefits people both inside and outside the Christian community. It would seem to be surprising then that "there are few theologians engaged with issues of race... who refer to themselves as public theologians."[20] What accounts for this lack of engagement with a topic that is deeply relevant to so much of our social experience? This question is especially pertinent in a field that is committed to engaging with topics of public relevance and including marginalized voices in the conversations. As I argued in chapter 2, Esther McIntosh's essay in the *Companion to Public Theology* is crucial for understanding this omission. Because public theology is largely focused on reaching as wide an audience as possible because it often follows a Habermasian construction of the public sphere, identity-based issues such as racism are seen as incompatible with this goal. As a result, the concerns of black and womanist theologians are rarely considered by public theologians, because these are seen as "one issue" theologies.[21] As McIntosh argues:

> It is public theology's self-definition as dialogical rather than particular that has kept issues of gender and race at the periphery of its concerns; that is, by viewing feminist theology, black theology, and queer theology as "one issue" theologies, public theology has sought to retain a broader focus on the role of theology in the public sphere.[22]

18. Archbishops' Anti-Racism Taskforce, *FLTA* 12.

19. It is important to note that both Govender and lay chapter member Dr. Addy Lazz-Onyenobi have contributed in significant ways to CMEAC and the *FLTA* report. Lazz-Onyenobi presented some of the findings of the report at the 2021 Thomas Clarkson Day described below.

20. McIntosh, "I Met God," 302.

21. McIntosh, "I Met God," 306.

22. McIntosh, "I Met God," 306–7. This type of approach could account for the denial of the existence of structural racism in society, because as soon as this concept

In this way, public theology is formally inclusive in that the dialogue is supposedly open to everybody. However, as Stephen Burns and Anita Monro argue "There are always limitations on the 'public': who may enter, speak, act, and the roles that they are allowed to play in these public spaces."[23] McIntosh further argues that "Habermas' work imagined a liberal democratic sphere in which social status could be eradicated and reasoned consensus could be reached on important matters."[24] In other words, Habermas imagined the ideal public sphere to be "color blind" in that participants are required to emphasize their common humanity and the joint task of emancipation and liberty over and above their own situations and distinctions. As a result, Habermas envisages a public sphere devoid of contestation, power or economic interests, and governed by common reason, which is neutral and as objective as can be.[25] Therefore, through the marginalization of one's own social status as a person of color in society, issues of race themselves become marginalized. It is for this reason that some black theologians are suspicious of so-called inclusive publics that they are "welcome" to enter.

For example, James Cone's classic work *Black Theology and Black Power* challenges white theology to recognize that the answer to societal racism is not integration, by which he means the inclusion of black voices into the democratic public sphere, because the requirements of such integration are such that people of color

> keep their "cool" and not get too carried away by their feelings. These men [integralists] argue that if any progress is to be made, it will be through a careful, rational approach to the subject. . . . They simply do not see that such reasoned appeals merely support the perpetuation of the ravaging of the black community.[26]

---

is introduced, the neutrality of the public sphere that liberal democratic societies pride themselves on is put into question.

23. Burns and Monro, "Which Public," 1.

24. McIntosh, "I Met God," 303.

25. Some public theologians have noted that because of the exclusionary nature of the Habermasian public sphere, this conception should be reformed. For example, Kim argues that Habermas's conception of the bourgeois public sphere was determined by stratifications of race, gender, and class. For Kim, "[Habermas's] ideas need to be revised to meet the demand of the contemporary complex situation of plural societies" (*Theology in Public Sphere*, 11). However, in this view the Habermasian approach to publicness is still assumed to be normative for public theologians. See Parker, "Public Convergence," 453.

26. Cone, *Black Theology of Liberation*, 17–18. It is worth noting here what my use of the term "Black" throughout in this book refers to. There is a wide use of the term "Black" among British and US-based theologians. Lartey, for example, uses the word in a general sense of "people of African, Caribbean, and Asian descent as well as people

In my view, public theology is often guided by the integralist presumption that rationality, reason, and scientific understanding can guide the public sphere in such a way that social and racial differences (and therefore issues of power) can be bracketed out. Consequently, there is a question then of whether public theology can be a helpful lens through which to engage with issues of racial justice for institutions such as Manchester Cathedral, or whether the field should be abandoned for a field more able to tackle these issues. Furthermore, is public theology too dependent on integralist approaches to inclusion for it to be useful for issues to do with racism? Or would a different approach to public theology yield more successful contributions in the public sphere in regard to racial justice? This will be a key question that I address in the evaluation section of this chapter. So far, I have demonstrated the complex, polarizing nature of debates about racism in British society, the Church of England, and the field of public theology. Key for my analysis will be to see how the public theology of the cathedral is practiced regarding the topic of racial justice and how such action poses challenges to society, the church, and the academy. To begin my analysis, I will explore the theology of the cathedral in regard to its focus on racial justice.

MANCHESTER CATHEDRAL'S PUBLIC THEOLOGY OF RACIAL JUSTICE

Eschatological Understanding of Racial Reconciliation

To begin this section on the anti-racist public theology of Manchester Cathedral I will start at the beginning: with my first recorded interview with Dean Rogers Govender. As I started the interview with an opening question, Govender was ready with some thoughts inspired by the sermon that he had given at the cathedral the previous Sunday, which happened to be All Saints Day in the church calendar. The question I asked was about the mission statement of the cathedral, which reads, "The Cathedral aims to build community, to make a difference in our society and the wider world through

---

who identify with 'the black experience' in terms of heritage, oppression, and domination." ("After Stephen Lawrence," 81). Jagessar and Reddie argue that "the term 'Black' does not denote one's skin pigmentation but is a political statement relating to one's sense of marginalization." Because they identify whiteness as a key aspect of racial marginalization in the West, they refer to people of color under the umbrella term "black" because they are understood to also be marginalized by oppressive, dominant white structures ("Introduction," xiii).

the good news of Jesus Christ."[27] I asked Govender, "How are the inclusive aims of the cathedral realized with the gospel of Jesus Christ when people see or hear the name Jesus Christ and often understand this as something exclusive?" Govender quickly turned and grabbed his Bible from his shelf. He asked if he could read a number of passages to me that demonstrate how he sees the gospel of Jesus Christ as inclusive. In the first round of interviews racial justice was not a key focus of my line of questioning, especially not at the very top of an interview. Yet, after just one question about inclusion and the gospel at the start of my first interview with Govender, racial justice and inclusion became front and center.

The first passage he turned to is a passage that was read at the All Saints service the day before the interview. It was from Rev 7:9–17. The key verses for our discussion are 9–10, which say:

> After this, I looked, and there before me was a great multitude that no one could count, from every nation, tribe, people, and language, standing before the throne and before the Lamb. They were wearing white robes and were holding palm branches in their hands. And they cried out in a loud voice:
> "Salvation belongs to our God, who sits on the throne, and to the Lamb."

After reading the passage Govender then interpreted the passage for me in relation to the question I had asked about the gospel. He said that in this section of Revelation:

> Jesus is sharing with John a vision of the kingdom of God and all the saints of God. He's basically saying these saints are from every nation, all tribes and peoples and languages. If anything talks about the diversity of the saints who are people who have lived on this earth as followers of Christ and citizens of heaven it is a very clear picture, a very clear vision of what it's all about. It is about a diverse church, a diverse community, and that diversity is represented through every tribe and every language and so on. So, keep in mind that Revelation is the last book in the bible so it kind of sums up and encapsulates all the teachings of Jesus, the vision of the kingdom of God which is a very diverse inclusive community.

For Govender, the kingdom of God is not the kingdom of God without full racial inclusion, equality, diversity, and representation within the community of saints. In fact, for Govender, inclusion and diversity are not

---

27. This was still visible at https://manchestercathedral.org/about-us in 2021 but was removed in 2023, subsequent to the cathedral's adoption of a vision for 2035.

simply optional extras for the Christian community in a "metropolitan" city such as Manchester, or any community for that matter. Rather they are central to what the gospel of Jesus Christ is actually about as represented by two key Trinitarian moments.

The first is the death and resurrection of Jesus. Govender pointed me to Eph 2 in which Paul is trying to address, according to Govender, a division between Gentile Jesus followers and Jewish Jesus followers. In this context Paul writes in Eph 2:11–22:

> For he himself is our peace, who has made the two groups one and has destroyed the barrier, the dividing wall of hostility, by setting aside in his flesh the law with its commands and regulations. His purpose was to create in himself one new humanity out of the two, thus making peace, and in one body to reconcile both of them to God through the cross, by which he put to death their hostility.

Govender explains:

> That very important letter of Paul is talking about Jesus bringing together Jews and Gentiles. He is abolishing the differences by saying, "You are one family in the gospel." One family in Christ that his death on the cross has brought the two of you together, creating a new humanity. In other words, one new man, one new human, one new humanity.

The second Trinitarian moment that Govender pointed to was the day of Pentecost in Acts 2. In this story, the Holy Spirit is given to the Jesus followers. The key verse from this text that Govender emphasized is verse 11, which says, "We hear them declaring the wonders of God in our own tongues."

Govender said regarding this story:

> In the New Testament with the coming of Jesus, Jesus gathers people from the four corners of the earth and pulls them into one kingdom . . . *The gospel is about bringing a very diverse humanity together in one body.*

Thus, for Govender, the gospel is not simply about individual repentance and conversion, though this can be a part of one's response to the gospel. Rather, if Christian communities are not sufficiently diverse, or at least working towards racial inclusion and diversity, the gospel is not being enacted and fulfilled. From these texts, we do not see that racial inclusion and reconciliation naturally flow from people's acceptance of Christ, but rather that racial equality and inclusion are thrust upon the newly formed Jesus followers. Indeed, issues of racially based tension make up much of the focus of New Testament ethics. In a sense, for Govender at least, an important part of what salvation is and means in the world is racial solidarity, diversity, peace, and inclusion.

Challenging Hate Forum

As Govender tells the story, he was approached several years ago by the city's chief constable who asked if the cathedral would be able to help organize activities or events to help prevent and challenge the thousands of hate crimes that take place in Greater Manchester. In response to this conversation, Govender started the Challenging Hate Forum (CHF). The CHF is a collection of individuals from a range of organizations, religious, ethnic, and cultural backgrounds who gather on a regular basis to discuss issues surrounding hate crime, hate speech, and discrimination that are relevant at the time.

Since beginning my studies in 2019 I have attended CHF's that have included members of the council presenting on British values that can unite diverse people groups, and sessions concerning racial discrimination through "Stop and Search." Shortly after the tragic events of Sarah Everard's murder in March 2021, the CHF hosted an event on laws passed to make misogyny a hate crime from the autumn of 2021. From questions about racism on social media to the challenge of human trafficking and modern slavery in Greater Manchester, the CHF commits itself to discuss both the theoretical and practical sides of challenging hate.

The events usually take place in the cathedral nave. However, during the course of the pandemic, the cathedral committed to keeping the forum running by hosting the events on Zoom.[28] The events usually take an hour and a half with the meeting starting with a greeting from Govender, and then a guest or member of the forum will give a twenty-to-thirty-minute presentation on the given topic. The remainder of the time then is for questions, debate, practical ideas, and storytelling from the participants. The purpose of this is to ensure that the topic is not simply viewed from the

---

28. In many ways the pandemic, though deeply disruptive, forced the cathedral's public theology to be starkly revealed because the cathedral was forced to prioritize certain events and activities. The fact that the CHF remained a constant part of the cathedral's life during this time demonstrates the importance of this forum in the cathedral's understanding of its public role.

perspectives of experts giving abstract information but is offered in the context of real human relationships and experiences.

Govender explained to me that the governing call of the CHF is to build peace among diverse people groups. He says:

> I'm saying as a Christian leader that we are called to live at peace. If we are to live at peace and harmony with one another in a diverse community and society then all of us need to be building peace with one another. And building peace is not a blissful experience pretending that there are no issues around us. It's about addressing those issues, trying to understand our differences, so that we can affirm and celebrate our common humanity. That's what being a peacemaker is all about; so that we can be children of God together.

At the heart of this forum is a theology of reconciliation, actualized through networking. For Govender, the cathedral's relationships and networks are one of the most significant aspects of its public ministry. The cathedral thus embodies the realities that John Atherton, a previous canon theologian at Manchester Cathedral, sought to express in his book *Public Theology in Changing Times*. He writes:

> Since the church is no longer the centre of life, particularly in Western societies, its vocation is not to respond by retreating into inward-looking, congregational-based churches, but it is about taking part with others in promoting better localities. That can be achieved by the church providing an open, "no strings attached" forum for such a coming together of different perspectives and traditions: If it has a wider role, it can only be as an inter-network, providing a forum or some common ground for other networks.[29]

Atherton relates his perspective to the work done by the Youth Justice Trust, which was set up by the Board of Social Responsibility in the Diocese of Manchester. The trust sought to address youth and crime disorder in Manchester. The trust was set up by Anglicans, but it was necessarily a collaborative project involving participation from other voluntary bodies and social service departments, the probation service, and other government departments. Atherton writes:

> Why did the church lead such a partnership? Because no one agency could now tackle such complex matters. Within such an agreed collaborative effort, the church was regarded as a body

---

29. Atherton, *Public Theology for Changing Times*, 107.

involved in various relevant aspects of the youth crime problem, from participation in deprived localities and with young people, to being an organisation with strong historic and ideological commitments to the pursuit of justice and practice of compassion.[30]

As I understand the cathedral and the ministry of CHF led by Govender, this is exactly the reputation and meaning the cathedral wants to communicate to its partners and wider society. It seeks to unite participants beyond potential barriers such as race, gender, religion, or sexuality, for the important task of creating a more just and peaceful society.

Representation: Staff and Congregation

As demonstrated above, Govender argues that diverse communities who worship together are the picture of the kingdom of God that churches should be striving for. Therefore, it is no surprise that one of the central ways that the cathedral attempts to challenge racism and foster racial inclusion is by including those from ethnic minority backgrounds into all aspects of cathedral life. For example, the congregation under the leadership of Govender has diversified in terms of ethnic minority participation in the last ten years. This is evident, in part, in the diversity of stewards and lay leaders, such as readers, intercessions, and sacristans.

Stuart Shepherd, who was the cathedral's administrator at the time, told me:

> I can say in the last five years we've made changes in the age dynamic, the age profile, the colors of people's skin that were attending . . . You might get a cathedral doing similar type of work, but my experience of cathedral congregations has generally been very middle class and very white.

He then stated that this increase in racial diversity would be one of the key markers of the cathedral's success in its ministry over the last ten years. However, from my interviews with numerous staff I have found it difficult to ascertain exactly how Manchester Cathedral has managed to do this. When I have tried to press for the cause of the cathedral's ability to attract a more diverse congregation than is typically known for cathedrals, some participants in interviews have argued that the dean being black automatically makes the cathedral look more welcoming and relevant to those from ethnic minority backgrounds who want to worship at a cathedral.

30. Atherton, *Public Theology for Changing Times*, 105.

Residentiary Canon David Sharples indicates this when he says that the "optics" of the cathedral team demonstrate the inclusivity and diversity of the cathedral. He says, "We have a dean who is from the global majority. Interestingly I am the only residentiary canon who is British. Marcia is Brazilian, and David and Rogers are South African." David Holgate says:

> But the end result is that the cathedral is led by three southern hemisphere individuals two of whom would identify as BAME and that's a hugely different environment from anywhere else in the cathedral world. In fact, there may or may not be another BAME residentiary canon in the whole of England. It's that kind of imbalance.

Further, greater diverse representation is the primary change that Govender argues the Church of England needs to make in order to begin to tackle its problem of institutional racism. In an interview, he said that "urgent and immediate action" was needed to address underrepresentation at all levels in the church and that the church needed "a massive escalation of BAME senior leaders."[31]

Thomas Clarkson Day

On October 28, 2021, under the direction of Canon David Holgate, the cathedral hosted its inaugural Thomas Clarkson Day, which is hoped to be an annual event permanently part of the cathedral's calendar. The day was a celebration of the sermon that Thomas Clarkson delivered in Manchester Cathedral on October 28, 1787. The sermon was an abolitionist sermon based around Exod 23:9, whose text was: "Thou shalt not oppress a stranger, for ye know the heart of a stranger, seeing ye were strangers in the land of Egypt" (KJV). The sermon was addressed to a famously packed cathedral, which led to massive support for the abolitionist movement in the UK. The cathedral team was surprised and dismayed that such a momentous event had never been recognized officially in the cathedral's history as an event worthy of celebration.

This event focused on issues related to modern slavery. As well as there being a number of speeches about political action being taken to both prevent and put a stop to modern slavery in Britain, there were a number of stalls representing various organizations that are involved in the struggle against modern slavery. But the event also addressed the question of the role of religious groups in tackling racism in greater Manchester, which was the

---

31. Williams, "Church Leaders Join Voices," para. 22.

basis of a presentation given by Dr. Andrew Boakye from the Department of Religions and Theology at the University of Manchester.

Boakye was asked to give an address concerning the role of faith communities in tackling racism in greater Manchester. The address began by illustrating that the early church struggled to overcome ethnic divisions, and the overcoming of these divisions was part of the church's witness to the world. Boakye then gave three areas that faith communities needed to address in order to tackle racism in their own communities and beyond. These were: (1) model honest self-critique, (2) resist the temptation to depoliticize the gospel, and (3) embrace radical love.

I had been asked to give a five-minute response to the address in relation to my own research at the cathedral. My main response to the paper attempted to make connections between racial exclusions and other exclusions often present within faith communities and society such as sexuality and gender identity. Also presenting at the event was Dr. Addy Lazz-Onyenobi, who is a BAME chapter member and also a member of General Synod and helped on the anti-racism task force of the church that produced *FLTA* and, as such, she presented some of the details of the report at the Thomas Clarkson Day.

Special Events

The CHF is the most frequent activity that has taken place at the cathedral for the last ten years that has direct engagement with issues of racial justice. In addition to the forum, the cathedral has hosted educational events in raising awareness of hate crime during Hate Crime Awareness Week. They have hosted prayer vigils under the banner of "Hope not Hate." In addition to these events around hate crime the cathedral, since 2015, hosted the launch of Black History Month for Greater Manchester until 2020.[32] The cathedral also hosted BAME church services for the diocese of Manchester in 2015 and 2016.

For the purposes of our analysis, the questions in the next section will be concerned with what is potentially missing, and what could viably be included in the cathedral's regular activities to further their passion for racial justice. It should be noted however, that Govender is much more involved with questions about racial justice within the Church of England than I can detail here. For example, I have not analyzed Govender's work during his time chairing Committee for Minority Ethnic Anglican Concerns (CMEAC) which has now been disbanded and replaced with the Anti-Racism

---

32. The cathedral was unable to host the event during the pandemic.

Task Force. Govender is also a frequent source of wisdom, advice, and solace for BAME members of the Church of England who seek his council.

While these conversations and friendships are not part of my analysis, it must be remembered as I move into some of my evaluations that much of what an institution or leader achieves in regard to racial justice cannot be quantified or articulated precisely because of the complex nature of racially based exclusions. The critiques that I have are not to suggest the cathedral is not making valuable contributions to these conversations, but rather I want to see how the cathedral can further its quest for racial justice with the various publics it engages, by potentially adopting a different approach to publicness.

EVALUATING MANCHESTER CATHEDRAL'S PUBLIC THEOLOGY OF RACIAL JUSTICE

As I have demonstrated, Manchester Cathedral has made racial justice a large part of its public message and work. However, there are several issues raised in the cathedral's approach that I will address in this section. First, I would describe the cathedral's approach to publicness in regard to racial justice as Rawlsian. This is because in the work of the CHF, for example, there are many philosophies and theologies represented, and so the conversation usually concerns very practical discussions of how to tackle hate crimes such as racism. The people who attend the CHF are seemingly all in agreement that hate crime needs to be challenged, that racism is evil, and that collectively they should be working together for peace justice and unity. Therefore, in Rawlsian fashion, participants in the CHF, including Govender, may each have their own motivations for being involved in the forum but, from my experience of the forum, these motivations are largely not presented. What is public is the articulation of a united concern for hate crime and practical ways of achieving the diminishing of hate crime in the city and beyond.

In my view, this is very similar to the Rawlsian approach to publicness. There is an assumed common ground for overlapping consensus (the desire for peace), and this provides the foundations and rules of this particular public space. All participants agree on the goal, just as in Rawls's veil of ignorance all participants are agreed that justice should be understood as fairness and that this type of justice should be established in society's institutions. As a result, religious "comprehensive doctrines" are bracketed. In some ways, the cathedral goes beyond Rawls's own approach, in that the cathedral focuses on practical manifestations of racism and injustice. One critique of Rawls's work itself is that his unwarranted political optimism also reveals the limits of his theory when one asks *how* society can move to being well-ordered from not being so. Rawls does not tell us how to proceed in transforming an "ill-ordered society" into a well-ordered society based upon the principle of justice. Rawls simply assumes that the basic tenets of his theory of justice are self-evident and that well-ordered societies will adopt them.

Charles Mills draws this critique out into the issue of racial justice. This is a topic which Rawls says very little about. Mills argues that while in theory if Rawls's principle is adopted racial justice would be automatically eliminated, there is nothing within Rawls's work to suggest a way forward in making that vision a reality in the case of racism and other such matters of present injustices.[33] In contrast, while the cathedral similarly assumes that reasonable people will already be committed to the values of peace, inclusion and justice, the cathedral recognizes that the values need to be applied to specific contexts, including the context of racial injustice. Thus, the cathedral assumes a joint common understanding of particular values and chooses to focus on the practical aspects of how these values can be applied to resist racism.

However, despite the fact the cathedral goes beyond a Rawlsian approach in this way, it adopts the Rawlsian approach in the way that it understands racial injustice. The cathedral, through focusing in on hate crime, hate speech and injustices such as modern slavery, runs the risk of framing racism in individualistic ways. As Liz Fekete argues:

> A strategy against racism that solely homes in on "hate" and "bigotry" creates a competitive environment (wherein groups vie for recognition, resources, etc.) that then militates against unity in action. And it also erases the varied ways in which Black and Brown communities, Muslims, Jews, new refugee and migrant communities, Roma, Gypsies, and travellers experience structural racism and institutional failure, not least in the policing of "hate crime." To put it simply, this new modified view oversimplifies racism.[34]

Fekete argues that the emphasis on hate crime means that analysis of the formation of structural racism is left by the wayside. In my view, this approach focuses on the effects of a racialized social vision, without addressing that vision itself. As Delgado and Stefancic argue:

---

33. Mills, "Retrieving Rawls," 11.
34. Fekete, "Reclaiming the Fight," 89.

> Formal equal opportunity—rules and laws that insist on treating blacks and whites (for example) alike—can thus remedy only the more extreme and shocking forms of injustice, the ones that do stand out. It can do little about the business-as-usual forms of racism that people of color face every day and that account for much misery, alienation, and despair.[35]

These "business-as-usual forms of racism" indicate the fact that "racism is [also] covert, incremental, and systemic . . . it is camouflaged and can be difficult to pinpoint within our education, employment, media, police, and justice systems."[36] Further, as Robin DiAngelo states, "Systems of oppression are flexible and adaptive, so we have to pay attention to their forms because the assumption is legislation eliminates inequality and oppression."[37]

Because racial systems of oppression are adaptive, flexible, and covert, "whiteness" has become a core concept in academic discussions about racism to elucidate these dynamics. Steven Garner argues that "whiteness" is a social and cultural vision "from which judgements are made about normality, abnormality, beauty and ugliness, civilisation and barbarity."[38] It is important to note that whiteness is a racial discourse and not "white people," which refers a socially constructed identity usually based on skin color.[39] As Willie James Jennings argues:

> "Whiteness" does not refer to people of European descent but to a way of being in the world and seeing the world that forms cognitive and affective structures able to seduce people into its habitation and its meaning-making.[40]

For Jennings, part of this way of being in the world is to follow the ideal of "white self-sufficient masculinity," which ultimately distorts the imaginative possibilities of life together in the context of diversity of many forms.[41] Garner further argues that whiteness depends on its own invisibility because it has the power to make itself appear "natural and unquestionable."[42] One of the ways that whiteness as invisibility develops is when "racism is taught as something which disadvantages those who are not white, but not

---

35. Delgado and Stefancic, *Critical Race Theory*, xvi.
36. Das Gupta et al., "Preface," x.
37. DiAngelo, *White Fragility*, 40.
38. Garner, *Whiteness*, 35.
39. Leonardo, *Race, Whiteness, and Education*, 169.
40. Jennings, *After Whiteness*, 13.
41. Jennings, *After Whiteness*, 13.
42. Garner, *Whiteness*, 35.

as something that structurally advantages white people over non-white people."[43]

From my engagement with the cathedral, the team would espouse an understanding of the pervasiveness of structural racism, whiteness, and white supremacy. However, the cathedral focuses on the explicit outworking of these structural dynamics, but the visions and formations of these structures of whiteness and racism are rarely, if ever, critiqued and challenged. As I will demonstrate, a public theology of racial justice must be explicitly theological, because it must address the ways that Christian theology itself has been a key formational aspect of whiteness in Britain.

Theology and the Formation of the Racial Imagination

Govender, during the BLM protests in 2020, spoke at a Manchester Diocesan meeting where he relayed a saying that is spoken in Africa about the British settlers: "When the white settlers came to Africa, they had the Bible, and we had the land. They said, 'Let us close our eyes to pray,' and we prayed. And when we opened our eyes, we had the Bible, and they had the land." This saying demonstrates that the colonizing activity of the British Empire was understood by some colonized communities to be deeply religious. The theological frameworks of colonizers provided not only legitimation for their actions, but the meaning of them.

For example, Willie James Jennings argues that theologians and intellectuals of all the colonialist nations interpreted the suffering of slaves through a Christian narrative that suggested "African captivity leads to African salvation and to black bodies that show the disciplining of faith."[44] Jennings explores different historical accounts that demonstrate the theological meanings given to colonial practices and the enslavement of African peoples. One such event that Jennings analyzes is an account given by Gomes Eanes de Azurara, Prince Henry of Portugal's chronicler, who described and interpreted the arrival of a ship containing 235 slaves taken from Africa arriving on the shores of Portugal. Azurara's account shows how the arrival and auctioning of the slaves was a ritual, a ritual deeply shaped by Christianity. For example, Prince Henry, "following his deepest Christian instincts, ordered a tithe be given to God through the church." As Jennings describes:

---

43. Garner, *Whiteness*, 37.
44. Jennings, *Christian Imagination*, 20.

> Two black boys were given, one to the principal church in Lagos and another to the Franciscan convent on Cape Saint Vincent. This act of praise and thanksgiving to God for allowing Portugal's successful entrance into maritime power also served to justify the royal rhetoric by which Prince Henry claimed his motivation was the salvation of the soul of the heathen.[45]

Jennings demonstrates here that it was a result of a particular, but dominant, theological imagination, which gave meaning and justification for practices of colonization and enslavement by empires like Britain. While (hopefully) all Christians in Britain would denounce the institution of slavery and see the theological justification of slavery as a gross distortion and mistake, in my view the church in Britain has not largely come to terms with the fact that there was an "underlying theological framework which legitimated the constructions of church ideologies which led them to supporting black chattel slavery."[46] As a result of this failure to reckon with its past, the church has also failed to interrogate how theology may be continuing to bolster whiteness as a cultural imaginative category which favors white bodies over others. As Jennings writes:

> The displacement and reconfiguration of bodies that happens . . . in slavery more broadly, becomes part and parcel to "the formation of an abiding scale of existence." Such formation is theological and relates to the formation of human identity in modernity.[47]

Emilie Townes further expounds on the dynamics of the white imagination, which she terms "the fantastic hegemonic imagination" in her book *Womanist Ethics and the Cultural Production of Evil*. The fantastic hegemonic imagination, she argues, is the way that people are formed to understand themselves, the world, and others around them. People are so formed by cultural images and narratives which bolster the status quo as "the way things really are," leading to the reproduction of evil because it cannot be recognized as such by the hegemonic imagination.[48] Theology has historically helped to construct the hegemonic imagination and the hegemonic imagination has in turn been formative for some forms of theology. Townes, for example, argues that triumphalist theologies are a result of the hegemonic imagination.[49] However, Townes also explores the ways that

---

45. Jennings, *Christian Imagination*, 16.
46. Reddie, *Black Theology, Slavery*, 1.
47. Jennings, *Christian Imagination*, 24.
48. Townes, *Womanist Ethics*, 17.
49. Townes, *Womanist Ethics*, 90–92. Townes characterizes the political theology of

this fantastic hegemonic imagination "is found deep in the cultural coding's we live with and through in U.S. society."[50]

Townes's concerns in this work, therefore, overlap with Ricoeur's in that they are both concerned with how ethical and social imaginations are formed. Townes is specifically concerned with how the fantastic hegemonic imagination is formed in societies. However, this focus on formation gives resources for addressing issues of publicness. Townes writes:

> You must take an uncompromising look at our social locations and the ways in which you are a socially constructed being. This is in response to the rampant individualism that marks contemporary U.S. life where you often hear sentences that include "I am not personally . . ." You or I may not be personally doing anything, but we are ourselves doing a great deal. None of us are in the world all by ourselves.[51]

Thus, Townes demonstrates the need to assess issues of race in relation to the way that societies and cultures are formed to think and view the world racially. One example that this can be applied to at the moment is that of racist attitudes towards immigrants and refugees in the UK, particularly as these attitudes have been exacerbated since the Brexit vote in 2016.[52] As Reddie argues, the leave campaign depended on demonstrating the potential benefits for the poor white working class in Britain if there were fewer poor ethnic minority people in Britain.[53] As a result, xenophobia and scapegoating were common in the popular zeitgeist and continue to be prevalent in discussions about migrants and refugees. As Reddie demonstrates, one reason why the poor disenfranchised white classes of the UK don't turn their critique to the discriminatory system of neoliberal economics is because whiteness "remains a sight of privilege for notions of belonging, and its concomitant subjectivity is one embedded in paradigms buttressed by superiority and entitlement."[54] In other words, it is easier to target a nefarious "other" who is seen to be a drain on public resources than to turn the

---

manifest destiny in the US as a key aspect of triumphalist theology. For example, the settlers use of the conquest narrative in the book of Joshua to justify the wars against indigenous people already in the Land demonstrates how triumphalist theology informed the domination of "the New World."

50. Townes, *Womanist Ethics*, 21. Of course, just because she is writing in the US context does not mean that the UK context does not also produce this fantastic hegemonic imagination.

51. Townes, *Womanist Ethics*, 77.

52. Reddie, *Theologising Brexit*, 5–7.

53. Reddie, *Theologising Brexit*, 102.

54. Reddie, *Theologising Brexit*, 102.

critical lens towards the systems which serve elite, "white middle-class and often public school-based privilege."[55]

However, distinctions are made in British society between migrants and refugees who are "good" and those who are "bad." As Garner argues the neoliberal agenda has meant that productivity is the key lens through which a migrant is evaluated. If the migrant can provide short-term labors, they are perceived as more desirable. Any other types of migrants are viewed suspiciously and of less value. For Garner, whiteness becomes the key framework through which these value judgments are made.[56]

Garner conducted several interviews in which white participants would discuss their views on immigration and race. One of the findings of the research, was that in the shadow of the Holocaust, racism has been developed in the way people choose to talk about culture instead of race. In this case, participants demonstrated that they had a vision of a normative ideal culture, and how well those who are coded as "other" can integrate into that culture. Thus, one participant's view of the good "integrated migrant" is partly defined as someone who actively supports local and national sporting teams. The research demonstrated that for many participants there are certain British rules that need to be abided by, even though no participant could give concrete definitions of what these rules are.[57]

This is important, because it demonstrates that there is a concept of "Britishness" that functions on an imaginative and subconscious level that provides the criteria that migrants and refugees are judged on. However, in order to address these forms of racism, there must be an exploration of how such racial visions are formed within our culture. However, I would further argue that because Britain is still perceived to be a Christian nation and has an established church, British culture, whiteness, and the Christian religion are inextricably connected in a way that one cannot be understood without the others. Because of the British church's intimate connection with empire and colonialism historically, it is crucial to interpret Christianity within Britain today by engaging these themes. Without such an approach to both Christian theology and racial justice in the public sphere, the thread of whiteness, which "is the significant thread in English Christianity,"[58] may well be left intact.

55. Reddie, *Theologising Brexit*, 103.

56. Garner, *Whiteness*, 165.

57. Garner, *Whiteness*, 166. Common among participants was the view that the adoption of British culture must be a priority for migrants, even if that means suppressing their own culture, in order for them to be considered as worthy of public resources.

58. Reddie, *Theologising Brexit*, 17.

Thus, one of the major limitations of a Rawlsian approach to racial justice, which marginalizes theology to the role of being a private motivation for a passion for racial justice, is it automatically leaves white theology bracketed, but intact. Black theologians have been arguing for decades that at the root of racism is not simply our politics, but our theologies. For example, in 1969 James Cone argued:

> The sickness of the Church in America is intimately involved with the bankruptcy of American theology. When the Church fails to live up to its appointed mission, it means that theology is partly responsible. Therefore, it is impossible to criticize the Church and its lack of relevancy without criticizing theology for its failure to perform its function.[59]

For the British church, "the theology of Empire has outlived the Empire. The Empire has gone but its theology lingers on."[60] Thus there is a need within the Christian church to wrestle with the ways theology has historically and continues to form whiteness and has been formed by whiteness. This is a need that institutions such as Manchester Cathedral are the best positioned to respond to, because of their desire for justice, inclusion and equality. Therefore, there is the question of how a public Christian institution such as Manchester Cathedral can approach racial justice in a way that critically engages whiteness and other aspects of the formation of our racial imaginations.

Towards A Ricoeurian Approach to A Public Theology of Racial Justice

As I have been arguing, theology itself is complicit in the continuing development of whiteness as a hegemonic imagination in Britain. Thus, one of the key tasks for institutions such as Manchester Cathedral is not to bracket theology in light of this, but to critically reengage, reinterpret, and rearticulate theology in the public sphere. If we take Ricoeur's understanding of the ethical life, and therefore our sociopolitical life, as primarily formed by narratives, symbols, interpretations, and metaphors, etc., then the cathedral should acknowledge that Christian symbols, doctrines, texts, and narratives cannot be neutral. Rather, they are invested with meaning by the communities that engage them. As Dan Stiver argues:

---

59. Cone, *Black Theology of Liberation*, 81.
60. Reddie, *Theologising Brexit*, 30.

> Ricoeur is critical of the idea that one can detachedly analyse scripture, tradition and their experience because they are already trained to see the world in a way of the tradition and language, they have been given that can hardly be brought to consciousness.[61]

As I have been arguing, whiteness is one such "tradition" or "language" that affects many readers, both white and people of color who have inherited a white theology. The symbols and narratives that make up the language of the church should be brought into scrutiny, in the name of discovering not only how whiteness has historically and presently affected readings of particular texts and theological understandings, but also to read these symbols in a way that is liberating and empowering for people of color.

Therefore, the kind of public theological revision necessary to resist both whiteness and decolonize God in theology cannot be performed by certain elite individuals, but rather a robust ecclesial praxis is needed in which diverse people can contribute to the task of constructing a black public theology.[62] As postcolonial theologian Emmanuel Lartey states, "Christian theology has been done predominantly utilising tools and resources developed in European countries."[63] He argues that this has led to a distortion in understanding the image of God. God is only understood in European terms because those who have been colonized were not able to contribute to the task of constructing the image of God. He, therefore, calls for the creative and radical decolonizing of God in theology, in part by including diverse, marginalized, and postcolonial voices in spaces where theology is constructed.[64]

---

61. Stiver, *Ricoeur and Theology*, 64.

62. I am following Anthony Reddie's definition of black theology here when he writes: "Black Theology can be broadly understood as the self-conscious attempt to undertake rational and disciplined conversation about God and God's relationship to Black peoples in the world, across space and time. An important dimension of Black Theology is the extent to which it attends to the lived experience of Black people within history, both in past and present epochs. This emphasis upon the lived realities of Black people is one that seeks to displace notions of theology being 'distant' and unresponsive to the needs of ordinary people in this world and is less concerned with metaphysical speculations about salvation in the next" (*Black Theology, Slavery*, 2).

63. Lartey, *Postcolonizing God*, 124.

64. Lartey, *Postcolonizing God*, 124–29. One area of theological reflection that is necessary for a public theology of racial justice is to develop black hermeneutics, such as a black revision of Christology and doctrines such as salvation and redemption. As Anthony Reddie writes about the edited volumes *A Time to Speak* and its sequel *A Time to Act* that: "What is lacking in both texts, however, is the significant development of a black hermeneutic. The writers seem to operate from the perspective that there is little that is problematic within the Christian faith. The task, therefore, for black Christians

This has implications for the field of public theology because, as I have argued, black and womanist theologies have been marginally engaged in public theology because these theologies prioritize subjectivity and distinctive identities over and above integralist approaches such as the Habermasian construction of the public sphere. The question should be raised, based on my analysis so far, that if public theology cannot engage more deeply with black and womanist theologies, then can the field truly contribute to the growing understanding of institutions like Manchester Cathedral that care deeply about racial justice? However, I want to argue that public theology could engage with these theologies and learn from them if theologians instead adopt a Ricoeurian approach to publicness.

Ricoeur's work demonstrates that these themes have always been publicly valid when publicness is not reduced to the objective and universal as in the Rawlsian and Habermasian approaches. However, I am arguing that a more Ricoeurian approach to a public theology of racial justice is possible, but it requires a turn to the subject, to understand how the subject is formed racially, and what symbols, narratives, and stories could be helpful for opening and imagining alternative worlds other than the one dominated by whiteness. However, it is worth noting that this is not a new approach, but one integral already to black theologies and womanist theologies.

Therefore, the cathedral would similarly benefit from turning more deeply to black and womanist theologies for resources in developing a public theology that includes the potential for a "radical subjectivity." Radical subjectivity places the stories and voices of those excluded on the basis of race and elevates those experiences as the primary source for discussing, debating, and revising theologies in relation to racial exclusion.[65] Of course, the cathedral is successful at gathering diverse people together in a variety of settings and also creating spaces for people to share their experiences and stories. However, as I have been arguing, these stories and experiences are often shared with the goal of finding practical solutions to racism on the ground. While this is also important, my contention is that a turn to subjectivity should also interrogate social visions and structures with the goal of understanding how these are formed within the public spheres. In my view,

---

is simply to remind white racists of their myopic perspectives in understanding the central message of Jesus Christ. This failure, for example, to highlight the need for a black British Christology or to reassess the meaning of salvation, means that these two texts, which are excellent in offering an authentic black British voice, somehow fail to demonstrate how that discourse is nothing more than a coloured façade on top of a white supremacist edifice" (*Black Theology in Transatlantic Dialogue*, 28).

65. "Radical Subjectivity" is the title of part 1 of Floyd-Thomas, *Deeper Shades of Purple*.

these activities that elevate subjectivity must make space for the possibility of the disruption of dominant theological and moral visions.

Further, the turn to subjectivity is also a way of deepening the cathedral's anthropology. As I have shown in this chapter and the previous chapter, the cathedral desires to claim common humanity as its first religion. However, the realities of whiteness present in theological and ecclesial settings, as well as in society, demonstrate that understandings of what it means to be human are affected by racial visions. Therefore, the turn to subjectivity emphasizes the individuals' own understandings of what it means for them to be human in this time and place. By doing so, they may disrupt dominant, oppressive visions of humanity that produce various exclusionary practices and theologies in public.

CONCLUSION

In this chapter, I have demonstrated that while the public work of anti-racism at Manchester Cathedral is adventurous in its partnerships with other players in the city and beyond, the Rawlsian approach it takes to this public issue could potentially limit what can be achieved in the various publics it addresses. By bracketing theological reflection in relation to racial justice, the present dynamics of whiteness within the cathedral the Church of England and wider society are left intact. I have argued in conversation with black, womanist and postcolonial theologians that such theological reconstruction can only take place within the context of diverse community-engaging discussions and practices concerning the formation of racial imaginations. These practices might include theological revision, as theology has often bolstered whiteness in Britain. I have shown how a Ricoeurian approach to racial justice would lead to integrating theological reflection, critique, and revision into the anti-racism work of the cathedral. This could produce creative forms of anti-racist work and dialogue in the cathedral and beyond. I will elaborate in subsequent chapters on how such developments could take place at Manchester Cathedral, especially to ensure that the revision of theology not only relates to racial exclusions but also serves to liberate people from multiple oppression of various intersections of identity.[66] This will be important in the next chapter as I will critically evaluate the cathedral's public theology of LGBTQ+ inclusion.

66. As Kelly Brown Douglas argues, it is not enough for a black Christ to throw off the chains of racial oppression. She argues that because of the impact of White colonial Christianity in the black church, many black communities have participated in the oppression and exclusion of women and LGBTQ+ people. As a result, the black Christ must "end the self-destructive attitudes and activities of blacks against other blacks" (*Black Christ*, 85–86).

6

MANCHESTER CATHEDRAL'S PUBLIC THEOLOGY OF LGBTQ+ INCLUSION

IN THIS CHAPTER, I will be examining Manchester Cathedral's public theology of LGBTQ+ inclusion. Manchester Cathedral is publicly and explicitly vocal and visible in its affirmation of LGBTQ+ people. This is an important topic to examine for several reasons. First, as I will discuss below, the topic of gender and sexuality questions divides often placed between the private and the public. Scholars within the field of public theology have largely not engaged with the topics of sexuality and gender diversity, because there seems to be an underlying presumption that sexual and gender ethics belong in the realm of the private.[1] However, the topic of sexuality and gender continues to have public and political relevance, not least within the Church of England.

Manchester Cathedral is one such institution which demonstrates that issues of sexuality and gender identity are important public topics. The cathedral is public in its affirmation of LGBTQ+ people, but I will be exploring how the visible and vocal affirmation in public places a level of responsibility on the cathedral to address arenas and sources of exclusion

---

1. McIntosh, "I Met God," 301–7. McIntosh argues here that it is public theology's reliance on a Habermasian conception of the public sphere that is the cause of this omission, because "Habermas' work imagined a liberal democratic sphere in which social status could be eradicated and reasoned consensus could be reached on important matters" (305). She further argues that queer theologies are perceived to be "one issue theologies" within this Habermasian form of public theology, which has led to topics relating to sexuality and gender being marginalized in the field (306). I will explore both of these points below.

both in the church and society. As we shall see, for many queer theorists and theologians a theology of inclusion can produce anaemic statements about God, church, sexual practice, and identity, without disrupting the patterns of speech and practice that make exclusions invisible or unremarkable.

To address these questions, I will first examine the cathedral's activity in this area. I will then situate the cathedral within the wider Church of England, as the cathedral has participated in work related to the *Living in Love and Faith* (*LLF*) project. I will then interrogate the cathedral's understanding of its inclusive character by engaging with two main critiques of the language of inclusiveness. I will finish by asking what a Ricoeurian approach to "queer publicness" might mean for Manchester Cathedral.

MANCHESTER CATHEDRAL'S APPROACH TO LGBTQ+ INCLUSION

In my first recorded interview with Dean Rogers Govender, Govender said to me: "Dom, one thing that you need to understand about me is that I am allergic to all kinds of discrimination." Under the leadership of Govender for more than fifteen years, Manchester Cathedral has built a name for itself as a place of welcome and inclusion. Inclusion at Manchester Cathedral is not an area of activity but a core value. As Steven Hilton,[2] who was the cathedral curate at the time, said to me in a recorded interview:

> I think inclusion, as I have come to understand it here, is simply at its best the primary lens through which we try and do everything. It isn't a discrete area of activity. We couldn't appoint a head of inclusion. We couldn't have an inclusion team, although we could of course discuss that. It is simply, under the dean's leadership, how we are all mandated to do our work. One of the lenses we do our work through, in the dean's name, is inclusion.

This inclusive character of the cathedral, which seeks to welcome people of all faiths and none, people of all nations and cultures, also underlies its desire to welcome those who identify under the LGBTQ+ umbrella and their allies. The cathedral's inclusive posture towards LGBTQ+ people is explicit and vocal. In my interpretation of the cathedral, there are three areas of LGBTQ+ engagement which are understood by the cathedral team to embody the cathedral's inclusive character in this area: the raising of the

---

2. It is worth noting that the cathedral's inclusive posture and employment policy have meant that there have been a number of key members of staff who openly identify as LGBTQ+. Steven Hilton is one such member of staff who is gay. Therefore, I engage with the interviews I conducted with Hilton frequently in this chapter.

pride flag during August's Pride Weekend, its engagement with the *LLF* project, and hosting and organizing LGBTQ+ events and activities. I will outline each of these areas of engagement here.

The Raising of the Pride Flag

Since 2015, under the leadership and direction of Dean Govender, the cathedral has hoisted the pride flag on its roof during Pride Weekend in the last week of August. The hoisting of the flag is done in a ceremony-like fashion, with representatives of the LGBTQ+ community present as well as some cathedral staff and clergy. In August 2021 the cathedral raised the progress pride flag. The progress pride flag retains the original six stripes from the common pride flag but also has a chevron along the hoist. The chevron has five stripes (black, brown, light blue, pink, and white). The colors represent marginalized people of color, trans people, those who are living with HIV/AIDs, and those whose lives have been lost to HIV/AIDS.

When the flag was first raised at Manchester Cathedral in 2015, the event was noted on their website. The website stated:

> Manchester Pride with the annual Big Weekend taking place from Friday 28th to Monday 31st of August. The theme for the Manchester Pride Parade is "devotion." Manchester Cathedral is devoted to being a welcoming, inclusive Cathedral for all who visit and to celebrating and embracing diversity in the City of Manchester.

The website went on to say that "Manchester Cathedral will show its support to Manchester's LGBT community by flying the rainbow flag from the Cathedral tower." Govender is quoted as saying:

> I am pleased to support the LGBT community on their special 25th anniversary. As a Cathedral that takes inclusivity seriously, we extend our warm good wishes to LGBT people and wish them well in the years ahead. In flying the Rainbow flag at the Cathedral, we express our solidarity and prayers. May the theme of Devotion deepen our love for God who loves all people and affirms our common humanity![3]

In my view, the raising of the flag is a performative act that produces an excess of meaning even beyond the intentions of the dean and chapter. This is partly because cathedral buildings themselves are already performing

---

3. Manchester Cathedral, "Manchester Cathedral to Fly Rainbow."

roles and producing meaning outside the control of a particular dean, chapter, or congregation. For this reason, I have connected the raising of the flag with a study that Judith Muskett conducted on the ways that metaphors shape our imaginations about cathedrals.

Three primary metaphors used for cathedrals, highlighted by Muskett, are flagship, beacon, and magnet. Each of these has been used to describe the power of the cathedral building. Muskett writes:

> Platten and Lewis . . . explain that the "flagships" image was employed to capture the ideas that Cathedrals are symbols not only of Anglicanism but also of "the loyalty of people to their city, county or region" and that they are "seen as significant by people of any Christian Church or none."[4]

In the Church Buildings Review Group in 2015, cathedrals are referred to as the "flagship" buildings of the Church of England because they "demonstrate most visibly the importance of the Church in the life of the nation."[5] Further, for Avis, the flagship role of a cathedral building is to embody an ecclesial sign to the world and provide a bridging role to the "unchurched in the community."[6]

These understandings of cathedrals as flagships are bolstered by the metaphors used to describe cathedrals as beacons. The report *Spiritual Capital* brought the beacon metaphor to prominence by reporting that two thirds (65 percent) of the respondents to the local survey agreed or strongly agreed that cathedrals are "a place of interest for tourists"; and, of those, 89 percent also agreed or strongly agreed with the proposition that "a Cathedral is a beacon of the Christian faith."[7] Half of the respondents (48 percent) to the national questionnaire agreed that cathedrals "reach out to the general public, not just to those who are part of the Church of England," with the figure rising to three quarters in the local survey.[8] Of the local sample, 88 percent agreed with the statement that "I get a sense of the sacred from the

---

4. Muskett, *Shop Window, Flagship*, 69. Citing Platten and Lewis, "Introduction," xii.

5. Church Buildings Review Group, *Report*. Quoted in Muskett, *Shop Window, Flagship*, 71.

6. Avis, *Ministry Shaped by Mission*, 112–13. Quoted in Muskett, *Shop Window, Flagship*, 68–69.

7. Theos and Grubb Institute, *Spiritual Capital*, 17. Quoted in Muskett, *Shop Window, Flagship*, 76.

8. Theos and Grubb Institute, *Spiritual Capital*, 25. Quoted in Muskett, *Shop Window, Flagship*, 76.

Cathedral building," a point echoed by those whom the team interviewed individually.⁹

The metaphor of the beacon was used by Carl Austin-Behan, who is the LGBT advisor to the mayor of Greater Manchester. Austin-Behan was present at the 2020 raising of the flag when pride events could not take place because of the COVID-19 pandemic. He said:

> Pride in 2020 may look different to years gone by but we need these celebrations more than ever. Homophobic abuse and bullying continue, even in Greater Manchester, and LGBTIQ+ communities live with direct discrimination because of sexual and/or gender identities. Manchester Cathedral, once again, *stands as a beacon of hope and of respect* and I'm proud to be raising the flag with The Dean of Manchester today.¹⁰

The beacon metaphor indicates that the cathedral building is seen as a sign of hope, of "confident open Christianity," and a signal (though a signal of *what* is open to interpretation depending on the perspective of the one viewing the signal).¹¹ Finally, the metaphor of a beacon connects with the metaphor of a cathedral being like a magnet. Cathedrals act as magnets in that they attract tourists,¹² and commercial activity, such as hosting concerts, dinners, and fairs.¹³ They also act as magnets for attracting diverse people groups, that wouldn't necessarily enter a church, because cathedrals are seen to belong to a wider public.¹⁴ As Muskett concludes in her assessment of these three metaphors:

> The group of metaphors considered in this chapter highlights the missionary potential of cathedrals as leading symbols of the Christian faith and signs of stability that shines a light in our increasingly secular world. . . . Flagship, beacon and magnet do not necessarily draw attention to activity within the cathedral walls; rather, these metaphors profess a message about the

---

9. Theos and The Grubb Institute, *Spiritual Capital*, 29. Quoted in Muskett, *Shop Window, Flagship*, 76.

10. Manchester Cathedral Website, "Manchester Cathedral Flies Rainbow"; emphasis added.

11. Muskett, *Shop Window, Flagship*, 73.

12. Platten, "Introduction," 2.

13. Jenkins, *England's Cathedrals*, xxiv–xxv. See my article "Harvey Nichols Fashion Shows" for a discussion on the commercial activity at Manchester Cathedral.

14. Poole, *Buying God*, 79.

power of the buildings themselves—to lead, to shine out and to attract.¹⁵

The team at Manchester Cathedral recognizes its potential for the building to act as a flagship, beacon, and magnet. Therefore, it is significant that it chooses annually to include the pride flag as part of the outward makeup of its message to the city. It desires to stand as a beacon of inclusion for LGBTQ+ people, a flagship of affirmation and to hopefully attract into its doors members of the community and their allies that have often felt excluded by other religious institutions.

This message of inclusion is significant within the context of how LGBTQ+ Christians feel in relation to faith communities. The 2021 safeguarding survey conducted by the Ozanne Foundation found that "only a third 'feel safe to be out' in their local churches and just one in five feel 'safe to be out to the wider Christian community.'"¹⁶ As Hilton said to me in an interview, "Like it or lump it, many people are expecting the church not to be a welcoming place to the LGBT community." Therefore, the flying of the flag operates in response to the recognition of this mistrust and aims to make a public statement, not only about the sexual politics of the cathedral but the God that is worshipped therein. In attempting to build trust with those in the city, the cathedral hopes that the hoisting of the flag on the roof may primarily proclaim the perhaps surprising message of an inclusive God, who affirms, loves, and who stands in solidarity with LGBTQ+ people of all faiths and none.

The Living in Love and Faith Process

I highlighted the raising of the pride flag first and foremost, because in my view, as an action it pronounces the cathedral as a queer spiritual space to the city of Manchester. In a sense, the raising of the flag is different to other kinds of public acts that the cathedral performs, in that its message does not require the public to enter the cathedral to hear it (or attend an online event). Rather, it is a performative, signifying act, with a surplus of meaning. The raising of the flag, therefore, is an act beyond apologetic arguments and debates about sexuality and gender identity because it is unflinching in its affirmation of LGBTQ+ people. However, recently, Manchester Cathedral has been more involved in debates about LGBTQ+ inclusion within the Church of England as it has played an important role in the *Living in Love*

---

15. Muskett, *Shop Window, Flagship*, 82.
16. Ozanne Foundation, *2021 Safeguarding LGBT+ Christians*, 5.

and Faith process (*LLF*). However, before elaborating on its role in *LLF* it is important to understand the context of how this process was first imagined and brought about.

Marriage has been solely understood as "the lifelong union between a man and a woman" for the entirety of the Church of England's history. The House of Bishops has consistently maintained that marriage, understood in this way, "remains the proper context for sexual activity."[17] According to the *LLF* book, a motion proposed by Tony Higton in 1987 is the last substantive motion on sexual behavior passed at General Synod. The motion in its amended form stated that sexual intercourse properly belonged only within a "permanent married relationship" and that fornication and adultery and "homosexual genital acts" are sins against this ideal and "are to be met by a call to repentance and the exercise of compassion."[18]

In 1991 the General Synod of the Church of England produced its own document called *Issues in Human Sexuality*, which *LLF* suggests effectively became the church's official working policy and was defended in another report made in 2003 called *Further Issues in Human Sexuality*. The 1991 report states:

> Homophile orientation and its expression in sexual activity do not constitute a parallel and alternative form of human sexuality as complete within the terms of the created order as the heterosexual. The convergence of Scripture, tradition, and reasoned reflection on experience, even including the newly sympathetic and perceptive thinking of our own day, make it impossible for the church to come with integrity to any other conclusion.[19]

The church has maintained this position throughout various legal changes in society regarding same-sex relationships. For example, the Civil Partnership Act was passed under the Labour Government in 2004, where for the first time in England same-sex couples could enter a civil partnership. The bishops issued a pastoral statement which said:

> What needs to be recognised is that the Church's teaching on sexual ethics remains unchanged. For Christians, marriage— that is the lifelong union between a man and a woman—remains the proper context for sexual activity. In its approach to civil partnerships, the Church will continue to uphold that standard, to affirm the value of committed, sexually abstinent friendships

---

17. House of Bishops, "Civil Partnerships," 1.
18. Church of England, *LLF* 141.
19. General Synod, *Issues in Human Sexuality* 5.3. The 1991 report uses the term "homophile" for "same sex," though the later report does not adopt this term.

between people of the same sex and to minister sensitively and pastorally to those Christians who conscientiously decide to order their lives differently.[20]

The bishops affirmed that clergy should "not provide services of blessing for those who register a civil partnership." Further, they explained, "Members of the clergy and candidates for ordination who decide to enter into partnerships must . . . expect to be asked for assurances that their relationship will be consistent with the teaching set out in *Issues in Human Sexuality*."[21] Further, clergy must give regular assurances to their bishop that they are celibate if they are in a civil partnership or are not married.

Similarly, when the Marriage Act of 2014 was passed making same-sex marriages legally recognized in the UK for the first time, the House of Bishops responded along the same lines as they did in the 2004 response to the civil partnership act. The bishops maintained that these marriages could not be recognized by the church and as a result clergy could not provide services where these marriages could be blessed. The bishops allowed there to be a "more informal kind of prayer" if the situation seemed appropriate to the clergy.[22]

From 2014 to 2016 a process of "shared conversations" was established, the aim of which

> was that the diversity of views within the church would be expressed honestly and heard respectfully, with the hope that, in so doing, individuals might come to discern that which is of Christ in those with whom they profoundly disagree. Neither this process of conversation nor any of those involved in facilitating it, have any authority in the decision-making of the church.[23]

The aims of the conversations were not to come to a unanimous decision that would change legislation but to help foster greater dialogue among those from different perspectives. The conversations took place in three circles: the college of bishops (Sept. 2014), regionally (Apr. 2015—Mar. 2016), and at General Synod (July 2016). There was disappointment among those in the House of Laity and the House of Clergy who were hoping that these conversations would have produced more acceptance of same-sex relationships. However, no changes were made to the church's canon law regarding

---

20. House of Bishops, "Civil Partnerships," 6.
21. House of Bishops, "Civil Partnerships," 4.
22. Church of England, "House of Bishops," paras. 20–21.
23. Church of England, "Shared Conversations Archive," s.v. "About."

same-sex marriage.²⁴ Yet, the conversations and subsequent debate in GS 2055 led to Archbishop Justin Welby calling for a "radical new Christian inclusion in the church." Welby said:

> The reality of disagreement is the challenge we face as people who belong to Christ. To deal with that disagreement, to find ways forward, we need a radical new Christian inclusion in the church, with a basis founded in scripture, tradition, reason, in theology and in good healthy flourishing relationships, in a proper 21st-century understanding of being human and of being sexual.²⁵

The result of this commitment was the development of the *LLF* project. *LLF* is a library of resources that includes a book, podcasts, video resources, and a course for groups to go through together. The project is concerned with issues of identity, sexuality, relationships, and marriage and seeks to represent and educate readers and listeners on a spectrum of perspectives and experiences. The purpose of the project is not to impose one view over another, but to help the church "live together in love and faith" in the context of a diversity of positions and identities.²⁶

The House of Bishops began formulating *LLF* in 2017. Though many from within the Church of England and beyond have been involved with the writing and producing of the book, the bishops commissioned and led the process. The five-hundred-page book is split into five parts. Part 1 is a reflection on "What Have We Received?," which examines the gifts of life, marriage, learning, and relationships. Part 2 is entitled "What's Going On?," which examines the views of sexuality and identity in science, society, and religion. Part 3 is about making connections with part 2 and "God's Story," which is understood as a singular story attested to in Scripture that makes sense of the patterns of the Christian life. Part 4 then asks how Christians receive answers about these debates. It examines various ways God speaks, such as the Bible, church, creation, and culture. Finally, the last part examines the value of learning from one another, even in disagreement. The book then finishes with an appeal and way forward for the CofE, which centers on listening to one another and striving for peace and unity even as decisions are made that some will feel resistant to. In addition to the book, there is an online library of resources such as podcasts, films, and a five-session video course.

24. Church of England, *LLF* 144. See General Synod, *Marriage and Same Sex.*
25. BBC, "Synod Debate," 00:50.
26. See introductory video by Archbishop Justin Welby at the "Living in Love and Faith" landing page: https://www.churchofengland.org/resources/living-love-and-faith.

The materials in the larger book were collectively worked on by the bishops of the CofE, who also represent a range of perspectives and views.[27] The project was released in 2020, and the cathedral has played a part in the unrolling process of the resources.[28] Each diocese was asked to appoint an advocate to promote engagement with the *LLF* materials and to give feedback on them. The advocates were advised to do this work with the help of a diverse "reference group." The Bishop of Manchester with the support of Dean Govender asked Canon David Holgate to be the *LLF* advocate for the diocese. In consultation with the bishop, Canon Holgate then convened a representative reference group to work together between April 2021 and April 2022. The purpose of the reference group was to encourage people in the diocese to study the *LLF* materials, with particular emphasis on the five-session course, which incorporates video teaching and discussion material and short story films. Notably, the bishop asked the reference group to constitute a small Christian community and to engage deeply with the course materials themselves.

Apart from discussing and publicizing the *LLF* materials, most of the members of the reference group, including the cathedral curate at the time, Steven Hilton, have also led the course, both in person and on Zoom. All participants are urged to record their feedback on their experience of working together on the *LLF* materials via the online *LLF* learning hub as a way of "listening to the whole church." The role of the advocate and the reference group concludes with a presentation to the diocesan synod structured in a way that permits synod members to experience the participatory and experiential nature of the *LLF* process. This experiential and participatory

---

27. It is difficult to say however what the balance or ratio of perspectives is; i.e., do half the bishops represent the church's historical teaching while the other half are trying to advocate for changes in the church's canon law regarding same sex marriages and civil partnerships? Or is the balance more uneven, and if so in which direction?

28. The publishing of *LLF*, both the book and other resources, was met with mixed reactions within the CofE. I will highlight a few here. The *Church Times* published an editorial on Nov. 9, 2020, entitled "*Living in Love and Faith*: It's Out, It's Long, It's Good." The piece argues that *LLF* is a solution "to the bitter, defensive, and ossified situation that the Church of England has got itself into over sexuality" (para. 3). However, the resources have come under criticism by a number of academics who argue that while there is much good within *LLF*, its treatment of the Bible is one of its major flaws. John Barton, for example, critiques *LLF* for adopting a canonical approach, which elides over contradictions on ethical issues in the Scriptures and insists reconciling the conflicting viewpoints. For Barton, the biblicist presumption that Scriptures are always above criticism, which *LLF* seems to adopt, means that discussions about sexuality in the church can go only as far as deciding what the authorial intention of a Scripture was, and then submitting to that. Thus, the *LLF* promotes open mindedness, but dodges "the really hard questions about the Bible" (Barton, "Prof John Barton," final para.).

dimension is key to the *LLF* process. As Canon Holgate told me in an interview, "The purpose is to ensure the deepest engagement possible with the materials and not simply having people read a single report and have various pressure groups respond to it."

The deadline for feedback was April 30, 2022, after which the process of discernment moved on to General Synod and the College of Bishops for the remainder of 2022. The *LLF* timetable concluded in February 2023, when General Synod considered proposals from the College of Bishops for a "clear direction of travel."[29] While David Holgate and Steven Hilton have promoted engagement with the process without advocating any particular position on the topics covered by *LLF*, they are nevertheless members of the clergy of the cathedral with its explicit position of affirmation of LGBTQ+ inclusion and the affirmation of same-sex relationships. However, they have often found it necessary within the context of this process to articulate the traditional perspective and arguments, at times when those holding the traditional view have chosen not to participate in the process.

In my view, *LLF* as an ongoing process is an attempt at a kind of publicness unlike any seen on this topic within the Church of England. The process of feedback to the bishops from the leaders of these reference groups is an attempt for the "people" to speak to the bishops about sexuality and gender identity, whereas previous formulations on this topic have been directed from the bishops to the "people." In a sense, we can see a Habermasian form in the way that *LLF* is done, in which the weak publics of the various parts of the parishes formulate views together on this topic of public concern, with the intent of presenting statements to the "strong public" of the bishops, who are a large part of the political authority of the church.

However, this form of publicness has meant that the process often takes an apologetic form, a form which some writing within the perspectives of queer theology have called into question. Significantly the book and resources engage little with queer theology itself, favoring biblical studies

---

29. Church of England, "Living in Love," s.vv. "The Roadmap: February 2023." A major result of this process was that at the 2023 synod, a vote was passed, after eight hours of debate, to endorse blessings for same-sex couples in committed relationships. However, the vote does not change the church's doctrine of marriage. As Helen King said in explaining the implications of the vote, "What has changed . . . is that we will have something that you can offer to faithful same-sex couples in our churches, which recognizes their relationship, and publicly celebrates it" (F. Martin, "Synod's Same-Sex Vote," para. 16). There have been numerous reactions to this vote. For example, the Bishop of Newcastle said that she was "pleased and relieved" that the motion had passed (para. 2). However, the Church of England Evangelical Council released a formal statement following the vote saying that its members were "deeply saddened and profoundly grieved" by the vote (para. 13).

and historical-critical methods for interpreting texts that relate to sexuality. I will elaborate more on this critique later in this chapter. Important to note now, however, is that the cathedral's participation in the *LLF* process demonstrates a different form of publicness to the one represented in the raising of the pride flag.

LGBTQ+ Affirming Activities at Manchester Cathedral

Part of the way that Manchester Cathedral expresses its affirmation and inclusive posture towards LGBTQ+ people is through various special services. On Sunday, the August 29, 2021, the cathedral led what they named a "Eucharist for Pride." I attended this event with my wife and some friends. I reflected on this event in my research journal at a later date. When I walked through the doors of Manchester Cathedral to attend this joint service that had been organized with the Open Table network, my family and friends whom I had come with were greeted with a warm smile and welcome from Canon Marcia Wall. I was immediately struck by how the space of the cathedral had been adapted. Usually, a liturgical service will take place in the nave of the cathedral, in rows of chairs all facing the quire and towering organ. However, the cathedral had been rearranged for the purposes of this service. Instead of being seated in rows facing the quire, traditionally understood to be the holiest part of the cathedral, we were to find our seats in the arrangement of chairs in the nave that were placed in a large circle. The circle was made up of three rows, and myself, my spouse, and some of our friends took our seats on one of the middle rows. I wrote in my research journal:

> There is an implicit meaning in such arrangements, that I found profound and beautiful. Instead of facing the quire and the organ, the holiest space, and profoundly large instrument, we were to face one another. We faced one another, in recognition that the gifts we were to receive from the service would not be from the "front," the place of power and holiness. But we were to receive them from one another.

The circular setup surrounded a large altar, on which the eucharistic elements were placed on top of a rainbow pride flag which covered the altar. At the center of this communal service, in which we offered one another the gifts of ourselves, and our seeing of one another, were the body and blood of Christ. As I reflected on this I wrote, "I am struck that the gifts of reconciliation and community amid difference are made possible in the Christian church, by a gift that comes from outside of us: God incarnate."

The event was also ecumenical, with many attending and participating coming from various churches and traditions. In a rare mode of worship for the cathedral a worship band from another church led some contemporary worship songs, such as Matt Redman's "10,000 Reasons," as well as a few hymns. The Bishop of Middleton, Mark Davies, preached a sermon on John 10:7–16 in which Jesus describes himself as the good shepherd. The sermon was in part a retelling of the bishop's own journey towards the affirmation of LGBTQ+ people and his belief that Jesus is the good shepherd of all people, regardless of their gender identity and sexual orientation.

The meeting produced a range of emotions for me, ranging from joy to frustration. The joy was in attending an event celebrating those often excluded by Christian communities. I have attended only a few Christian services in which LGBTQ+ affirmation was a key practice. To be in such an open and beautiful setting celebrating LGBTQ+ people also produced frustration in me that such services and attitudes are so rare. I was proud to be able to bring my friends from a conservative evangelical church to experience this service.

This blend of emotions could be felt among the congregation during the refreshment time at the end. Among my own friendship group, we reflected on how simple, yet encouraging the meeting had been. I could overhear others venting their frustrations about the state of the conversation about same-sex marriage and relationships within the Church of England. Some were discussing how great it had been to be part of such a meeting because they would never have imagined twenty or more years ago such an event taking place. Others were taking selfies with the pride flag–covered altar. All this taking place while drinking prosecco and eating crisps and biscuits.

The Eucharist for Pride service is the only "pride event" that I had personally attended at the cathedral during the data collection period, because there were fewer of these events due to the pandemic. However, before the COVID-19 pandemic the cathedral hosted several events which have sought to bless and affirm trans people. An example of this is their effort to welcome trans people attending the annual Sparkle festival in the city to the main Eucharist on the Sunday. While the service has a standard liturgy, the atmosphere of inclusion and celebration has led to it being known as the Sparkle Service.

In December 2019, the cathedral hosted a carol service that sought to raise money for a new LGBTQ+ center in Manchester run by Proud Trust. Amelia Lee, who was the former strategic director for the trust, said:

> It's open to everyone with a special welcome to lesbian, gay, bisexual, and trans people as well as our allies and our friends.
>
> People who might have not have always felt included in their religion have a chance to come here and feel welcomed and celebrated.[30]

The cathedral curate Steven Hilton is quoted in an online news article discussing this event as saying:

> We host a range of events and close to our hearts in particular are events which promote unity, inclusion and equality.
>
> We hope this can be the beginning of a great working relationship with The Proud Trust. What they do for young people is life-changing and in some circumstances lifesaving.[31]

As Hilton highlights in this quote, the unifying purpose of all of these events is to create a space in which people in the LGBTQ+ community and their allies feel welcome and included at the cathedral.

CRITICAL EVALUATION OF MANCHESTER CATHEDRAL'S PUBLIC THEOLOGY OF LGBTQ+ INCLUSION

As I have demonstrated, Manchester Cathedral understands its public engagement with LGBTQ+ people primarily through the lens of inclusion. However, in this area of public engagement, it is much more difficult to see how their approach to inclusion fits any of the three models of publicness that have been key to my analysis in this thesis. One reason for this is that each approach to publicness is all concerned with the nature of how to keep the public sphere inclusive. For example, both Rawls and Habermas aim for an overarching public sphere that is inclusive. They both desire to provide theories throughout their work that will allow diverse people groups to discover, or assume, overlapping universal values that should take priority over their differences. Such differences are then relegated to the realm of the private, meaning that they should not have an impact in the public realm and the joint pursuit of overlapping consensus and dialogue.

We have seen, however, in chapter 1, that both methods require exclusions in order, paradoxically, to be inclusive. Rawls assumes that the particulars of one's religious faith, for example, can and should be bracketed out

---

30. Northern Quota, "Carol Service," paras. 4–5.
31. Northern Quota, "Carol Service," paras. 7–8.

from the decision-making process, because the theory of justice as fairness can provide enough of a moral and political language for a diverse public to be formed. Habermas, similarly, though seeing the moral value of religions, requires social inequalities to be bracketed out, to construct a public sphere that unites various classes.[32] Ricoeur, in contrast, desires to explore the tensions of inclusion, so that neither tribalism nor homogenization develops in society. In my view, Ricoeur offers an approach to the inclusion of wild public spheres that gives space for them to be heard in their authentic dialects as they communicate their particular visions.

As I have demonstrated in chapter 1, a significant critique of Habermas's philosophy is that, though he later recognizes the existence of wild public spheres, he ultimately still wants these wild publics to be integrated into a more cohesive whole that has the power to influence the state. However, the desire for a kind of integration and common consensus in Rawls and Habermas is resisted by some queer theorists and theologians. As Lisa Isherwood and Marcella Althaus-Reid argue: "Queer theology takes its place not at the centre of the theological discourses conversing with power, but at the margins. It is a theology from the margins which wants to remain at the margins."[33] In other words, queer theory and theology are/should be formed and performed in wild public spheres and should actively resist integration/assimilation into a larger whole.

There is a significant question, therefore, about if and how Manchester Cathedral engages with a "theology from the margins that wants to remain at the margins." I would argue that this type of theological engagement is not a central way that its public theology of LGBTQ+ inclusion is performed. In my view, its engagement with LGBTQ+ people is more limited than one might expect, given its vocal and visible posture of affirmation. In one of my supervision meetings while I was writing this chapter, I retorted, "I am not sure I would have a chapter to write if the cathedral did not raise the flag on their roof." As I reflected on this statement more deeply afterwards in my research journal, I thought about how there aren't very many events that take place solely about LGBTQ+ inclusion.[34] Even in my attendance at the CHF, while there have been many forums concerning racism and a few concerning sexism, there have been none during my research period on the topic of hate crimes against LGBTQ+ people.

---

32. Fraser, "Rethinking the Public Sphere," 65.

33. Isherwood and Althaus-Reid, "Queering Theology," 3.

34. The exceptions are the annual Eucharist for Pride and the carol services conducted with other LGBTQ+ organizations and charities.

Yet, despite there being a lack of "texts" to be able to analyze in this area, the cathedral raises the pride flag on its roof, which is a highly important "quasi-text," as described above.[35] Therefore, part of how I approach the public theology of LGBTQ+ inclusion at the cathedral is to apply critical lenses to what I perceive as missing at Manchester Cathedral in this area, especially by drawing on the work of queer theorists and theologians. In particular, I will focus on the work of Marcella Althaus-Reid and Linn Marie Tonstad to explore the potential of a Ricoeurian approach to publicness that build on the cathedral's values of inclusion and desire to be a queer spiritual space.

The Anti-Social Turn in Queer Theology

While much queer theology and queer theory have centered upon a desire for same-sex couples to be able to be included in the definition of marriage and be granted equal family rights and ordination rights, this objective has been critiqued by some queer theorists. This critique is often called the "anti-social turn" or "anti-inclusion turn." Kristien Justaert summarizes this anti-inclusion turn towards the anti-social in conversation with Jack Halberstam when she writes:

> The "narrative of inclusion," indeed, is highly criticized by this new line of thought in queer theory as (in Halberstam's words) "another self-congratulatory, feel-good narrative of liberal humanism that celebrates homo-heroism and ignores the often-overlapping agendas of the state and homosexuals, or the family and homosexuals, or decency and homosexuals."[36]

For Linn Marie Tonstad, the problem with inclusion narratives is that while the category of decency is being expanded to include LGBT people in particular, the binary between decency and indecency is what needs to be deconstructed and challenged. She questions whether the aim of queer theology should be to expand the categories of decency that already exist so that they can include queer people. Or is the point "to focus our attention on the non-integrability that structures every subject and every social

---

35. Ricoeur describes quasi-texts as action, because all actions can be narrated and therefore interpreted by either the doer of the action or an observer (*From Text to Action*, xiii). See also Frey, "Preface," viii. I also discuss the narration of quasi-texts in ch. 3.

36. Justaert, "Dancing in the Dark," 230. Quoting Halberstam, "Anti-Social Turn," 143.

order—that is on the impossibility of inclusion, and the destructive effects at aiming at it?"[37]

For example, as I said earlier much of the debate around inclusion has centered upon whether same-sex relationships should be liturgically granted the status of marriage. What this approach fails to consider is whether the churches regard for the institution of marriage itself needs to be resisted and deconstructed for being the kind of institution that has favored and celebrated some bodies and forms of relationships over others, often grounded upon patriarchal assumptions and structures.[38]

Althaus-Reid's production of indecent theology is essential for understanding the possibilities of a "negative" queer theology, which does not aim for inclusion. Critiquing the notion that homosexuality should be accepted by dominant systems, she writes:

> Are we being swallowed into the old colonial mechanisms of accepting the declared "abnormal" . . . into the heterosexual normality? . . . The churches would end by openly ordaining and marrying lesbi-gays in the same way that in the sixteenth century, the Pope finally accepted that Latin Americans have souls. . . . Why does something need to be accepted? Because it belongs to the domains of the Other to the non-context which cannot be eliminated sometimes but is exploited.[39]

Commenting on this passage, Cooper argues:

> Inclusion aims to absorb the abnormal into the normal if it will agree to assimilate . . . the issue of inclusion arose around same-sex marriage, which, while enabling any two people to marry, unfortunately, left intact the model of marriage between two individuals as the basis of community.[40]

Althaus-Reid's work is important in critiquing certain forms of public theology, especially those adopting the Rawlsian and Habermasian approaches because she causes us to interrogate both how the public sphere, and that which is considered "reasonable," is formed through exclusionary processes rooted in colonialism and capitalism and how theology may be used to bolster an exclusionary public sphere. She writes, "Civil societies are spaces of hegemonic struggle amongst different interests; capitalism, racial

---

37. Tonstad, "Limits of Inclusion," 1–2.
38. Cooper, *Queer and Indecent*, 114–15.
39. Althaus-Reid, "Sexual Strategies," 47. Cited in Cooper, *Queer and Indecent*, 113.
40. Cooper, *Queer and Indecent*, 113.

and sexual injustices, fighting to determine their power."[41] As Bretherton notes further, democratic politics is ultimately about how power should be distributed to sustain a common life.[42]

As a result, following Althaus-Reid, Tonstad argues that queer theology needs to go beyond apologetics about the inclusion of LGBTQ+ people into the church or heteronormative institutions such as marriage. Rather, "queer theology is about challenging the structures of heterosexuality, which are bounded by oppressive socio-political visions and practices, used to marginalise, exclude and police the bodies of those not fitting within this socio-political vision." She argues:

> Christian theology does not need queer theory to tell it that God loves everyone, and that gay people aren't sinners. Instead, we need it for a reading strategy, a diagnostic for cultural and theological imaginative, associative relationships, hidden creations, and naturalisations and so on.[43]

The argument that I want to make is that queer theory and theology can demonstrate how Western society's sexual-ethical vision is formed. As I have argued in the previous chapters, a focus on formation is a key contribution of Ricoeurian approaches to public theology, and one that is highly relevant in this context. Thus, I am arguing with Althaus-Reid that debates around same-sex marriage and further issues of LGBTQ+ inclusion often don't interrogate how hegemonic forces of colonialism, capitalism, patriarchy, and heterosexism have shaped understandings of sex, relationality, and gender in the public spheres. Public theology then needs to explore these dynamics to serve institutions like Manchester Cathedral that seek to be inclusive towards LGBTQ+ people, because, from this perspective, the language of inclusion is not sufficient to explicate these dynamics. Therefore, I will now offer a brief exploration of how Tonstad and Althaus-Reid understand the formational powers of heterosexism within Western societies, and what implications this has for public theologies of LGBTQ+ inclusion.

Capitalism as A Social Vision in Need of Queering

Tonstad argues that capitalism needed to produce a sphere of the private that is seemingly distant from the influence of capitalist structures in our lives. Thus, the relegation of family life into the sphere of the private gave an

---

41. Althaus-Reid, *Indecent Theology*, 89.
42. Bretherton, *Christ and Common Life*, 2.
43. Tonstad, *God and Difference*, 4.

impression of a realm of freedom from social and political structures. The family then became central to the "private" life, but two things occur that benefit a capitalist system from this new division between the public and the private.[44] First, Tonstad argues, that the family needs to participate within the structures of capitalism, ideally through the purchasing of property, to protect and sustain their families. The system works for the family wealthy enough that they can produce more money through property investment. Second, parents are now producing other productive citizens who will know nothing other than capitalist structures and will thus be formed entirely by its vision of reality and values.[45]

It is within this context that the family is seen to be the bedrock and key component of a flourishing capitalist society. Yet, as Tonstad argues, all of these formative practices are happening seemingly separate from oppressive political and social structures because there is the perception of freedom and privacy. Further, the church has also historically held up the nuclear family as the foundation of flourishing societies and sanctified these "storylines" still maintaining that the pursuit of such family structures is separate from capitalist aims.[46]

A relevant and recent example is found in Justin Welby's book *Reimagining Britain*, which sets out to be a manifesto for the search for common values in post-Brexit Britain. Welby offers a chapter entitled "Family—Caring for the Core."[47] In this chapter, Welby explains, "In almost all circumstances of human life the greatest source of hope, and the main location of despair is found in the family." He writes, "We should not have illusions about families, nor should we collude in idolising them . . . yet the answer to bad families is not no families, but good families."[48] For Welby, the New Testament teachings, especially of Jesus and Paul, uphold the value of families. He writes, "Jesus upholds the value of family and the obligations of fidelity between husband and wife. In the Acts of the Apostles, households are places of worship, of conversion and of mission."[49] Because of this Welby concludes:

44. Tonstad, *Queer Theology*, 82.
45. Tonstad, *Queer Theology*, 82–84.
46. Tonstad, "Limits of Inclusion," 2.
47. Welby, *Reimagining Britain*, 63–83.
48. Welby, *Reimagining Britain*, 63.
49. Welby, *Reimagining Britain*, 64. In a footnote on this page, he also points to the household codes of Eph 5:21–33; Col 3:18–25; and 1 Pet 3:17 as examples of the New Testament teachings investment in the upholding of firm, ordered family structures. It is worth noting that he doesn't point out any of the historical abuse that has resulted from these texts that black, feminist, and womanist theologians have resisted. Instead,

> The good family is the foundational intermediate institution in society, and one to which every human being necessarily belongs in one way or another . . . it is a gift of God in any society, bearing burdens, supporting the vulnerable and stabilising both those who believe themselves to be autonomous and those who feel themselves to be failures.[50]

For Althaus-Reid and Tonstad, this type of theology of family and society is deeply connected to visions of humanity that are formed by capitalist values.[51] This is what produces the logic of exclusion of those who do not fit within the sociopolitical vision of both church and state. Tonstad and Althaus-Reid make the case, therefore, that our sexual ethics are politically formed, and yet queer theology and much of Christian advocacy do not make connections to wider political framings.[52] Thus, queer-affirming Christian institutions are often (unwittingly perhaps) making arguments for why LGBTQ+ people and their relationships can still operate successfully and healthily within the boundaries set by neoliberal capitalism, or a capitalistically influenced theology of inclusion. Instead, the oppressive

---

he sees these as positive examples of the need to conserve traditional family structures for the sake of societal flourishing.

50. Welby, *Reimagining Britain*, 65.

51. Cooper demonstrates how, for Althaus-Reid, capitalism and Christianity produce and influence one another throughout the development of capitalism. As a result, our theological concepts are often reduced to economic images, such as ontological debt and payment. To resist the capitalization of theology, we must attend to the voices of those excluded by the system, because that is where God moves and operates (*Queer and Indecent*, 63–71).

52. This is important because one argument put forward by Anglican social theologian Malcolm Brown does make connection to wider political framings, in the opposite direction. He argues that the legalization of same-sex marriage in Britain follows the trends of capitalistic consumerism. In this framing, he sees the legitimation of same-sex marriages as a move away from the selfless, non-consumeristic family values, towards consumeristic, greedy, and ultimately sinful marriages of same-sex people. Brown repeatedly refers to the advocacy of same-sex marriages as a "rejection of basic Christian conceptions" ("Anglican Social Theology Tomorrow," 183–85). However, considering the arguments made by Althaus-Reid and Tonstad, such a reading misses how heterosexual marriage, as the Christian church has come to understand and practice the institution, is also the production of consumeristic and capitalistic worldviews. The root cause of the issue then is not, as Brown would have it, the gender of the people being married, but the institution of marriage itself. It is also worth noting that the accepted definitions of marriage by the church and its emphasis on love and romance would probably have been considered heretical by theologians in the patristic era. Dale Martin recalls that Jerome and Saint Ambrose considered Jovinian a heretic because he thought that marriage was a calling equal to celibacy (*Sex and Single Savior*, 117–18). I highlight this to demonstrate that "basic Christian conceptions," concerning marriage have changed over the course of church history.

structures that form heterosexism in society need to be challenged as part of queer theology and advocacy, because these oppressive structures "separated people into the decent and indecent [and] regulates accepted orders of bodily and economic exchange." This, Tonstad argues, "is ruptured by a Christ who gave his life for all. But most particularly the despised, a Christ who died at the hands of a colonial empire."[53]

This line of argument demonstrates that "queerness" is ultimately a rupturing in dominant anthropologies that are produced within capitalist societies. As Tonstad and Althaus-Reid demonstrate, a particular vision of the human and its relationships is produced by economic frameworks. Therefore, language of "common humanity," which the cathedral often emphasizes, cannot be adopted as a guiding principle in a neutral way. Instead, as I have shown in the previous two chapters, the cathedral's own anthropology would benefit from a thicker theological understanding of the human, especially by attending to theological anthropologies of black, womanist, and queer theologians.

Ricoeurian Queer Publicness: Queer Linguistic Hospitality

Manchester Cathedral desires to be a space of welcome and inclusion for LGBTQ+ people. Considering the consistent experiences of rejection and exclusion by LGBTQ+ people in both religious and secular spaces, Manchester Cathedral offers itself as a model of affirmation, love, and hospitality towards those who do not fit within the heteronormative visions of relationality that are upheld by many Christian communities. I do not want to underemphasize the importance of the work that Manchester Cathedral has done in building trust with and proclaiming a message of love and inclusion towards LGBTQ+ people. However, I will evaluate the cathedral's public theology of LGBTQ+ inclusion in light of the critiques of inclusion developed in the previous section.

Anti-inclusion queer theorists are suspicious of inclusion at any level, whether in a religious institution, or political spaces and public spaces if the inclusion of LGBTQ+ people doesn't also consist in challenging the structures which have produced practices of exclusion in the past. From the perspectives of Althaus-Reid and those who have developed "indecent theology," any posture of inclusion which does not interrogate normative visions of the human is falling short. It is within this anti-inclusion mode of queer theology that the Ricoeurian model can prove helpful. As I described in chapter 2, Ricoeur offered his theory of linguistic hospitality as a way of

53. Tonstad, *Queer Theology*, 96–97.

framing the potential for people of different cultures to communicate and offer their unique perspectives to others.[54] For Ricoeur, each culture operates with a unique vision of the good life, formed by various symbols, stories, and experiences that drive their ethical concerns. For Ricoeur, engaging with particular cultures does not require the bracketing out of particularity, for the sake of avoiding conflict, but by discovering together where the differences of vision are occurring between different groups and why.

I would suggest that those who identify under the LGBTQ+ umbrella are embodying different cultures, as they experience and interpret the world outside of the heteronormative culture which dominates most societies. As a result, they have developed their own visions of the good, conceptions of solidarity, spaces of resistance and mutual flourishing, political navigations and unique languages that are constantly developing. While "LGBTQ+" can't be understood as a single overarching culture, the particularity of LGBTQ+ communities and individuals can be understood through the lens of "culture" (or perhaps better still, cultures), because culture, according to Ricoeur, is reflected and formed through the stories we tell one another. LGBTQ+ people tell different stories to heteronormative society, and these should be attended to.[55]

HEARING AN ALTERNATIVE QUEER WORD: A QUEER PUBLIC THEOLOGICAL TRANSFORMATION

As I have been arguing in the previous section and in the previous chapter, theology itself is not neutral and is complicit in the formation of visions of normativity that have made the exclusion of LGBTQ+ people previously intelligible. Any approach to inclusion, therefore, will also explore how theology has been complicit in the exclusion of LGBTQ+ people, and how certain constructions of God have justified and legitimated the practices of exclusion in the first place.[56] Miroslav Volf, speaking of exclusion more

---

54. Ricoeur, *On Translation*, 23–24. See ch. 2 for further discussion of linguistic hospitality.

55. However, it is important not to fall into a kind of "queer fundamentalism," which assumes that LGBTQ+ identities *should* subvert all heterosexual norms. As Lewin argues, often the preoccupation with a "queer culture" means that the actual lives of queer people are not seen or heard by theorists and theologians, and so the various intersections of culture and identity that a person may reside in are ignored. Thus, a queer social vision can become a normative social vision of the kind that Tonstad wants to resist. Thus, the potential queer *cultures* should be attended to empirically, in an intersubjective manner. See Lewin, *Filled with the Spirit*, 28.

56. It is important to note that such a strategy would generate a hermeneutic of

generally, argues that before a literal exclusion takes place, whether it be, for example, the restriction of communion on one end or genocide on the other (as the ultimate act of exclusion), what must first happen is symbolic exclusion. He writes, "Most of the exclusionary practices would either not work at all or would work much less smoothly if it were not for the fact that they are supported by exclusionary language and cognition."[57]

One site that has been noted by Marcella Althaus-Reid where this kind of symbolic exclusion has taken place is within the production of theology and the pictures of God articulated as a result. She points out that Western systematic theology has been produced through the lens of heterosexuality, as an ideology and not simply one form of sexual relationality among many. For Althaus-Reid, one theological form that heterosexual ideology takes is in the form of binary thinking and the desire for single, overriding, interpretations of Scripture.[58]

Dale Martin, a New Testament scholar, highlights how the exclusion of LGBTQ+ people has often taken place on the basis of these historical, single overriding interpretations of Scripture. For Martin, at the heart of this exclusion has been the belief that Scripture "speaks" and that Christians are to "listen" to what it has to say. Such a construction removes the reader as playing an active role in the interpretation and assumes that historical reconstruction to understand the context of Scripture, as a way of arguing for affirmation or exclusion, is a task of literary objectivity. For Martin, it is important to maintain consistently that Scripture does not "speak," and that ethical and doctrinal formulations based on Scripture are not objective. Instead, Martin argues for a form of postmodern interpretation which resists the myth of singularity or objectivity in interpretation but produces different possible readings in the context of community.

---

suspicion in regard to the *LLF* process. As Holgate has said, one of his major complaints towards the *LLF* book is that it has no engagement with queer theology proper. Instead, it offers different apologetic strategies offered by both sides, with an exploration of how culture has changed its thinking on sexuality and gender identity since the modern era. For Holgate, this lack of engagement with queer theology is one of the key failings of the resource. I would further suggest that the lack of engagement with queer theology is indicative of an understand that the Christian story described through pp. 162–260 is sexually neutral and provides the objective foundation on which sexual ethics can be built and understood. Such an approach screens out queer retellings and reformulations of that/those story/stories. Such retellings are central to the model I am proposing and therefore in tension with the apologetic emphasis of the *LLF* process. For a similar critique of *LLF*'s omission of queer theology, see Hogan, "Lesbian Living in Love," 26–27.

57. Volf, *Exclusion and Embrace*, 57.
58. Althaus-Reid and Isherwood, "Thinking Theology," 306–8.

I would argue that because Manchester Cathedral aims to be a transformative, inclusive community that seeks to transform society to be more just and inclusive, various reading strategies should be explored. While the term "reading strategies" may sound like the kind of theological work that does not make a difference on the ground, and thus irrelevant to activists such as those at Manchester Cathedral, this is not so, because as Ricoeur states:

> It must be said that we understand ourselves only by the long detour of the signs of humanity deposited in cultural works. What would we know of love and hate, of moral feelings and, in general, all of what we call the self, if these had not been brought through language and articulated by literature?[59]

It is with the hope of understanding ourselves and one another, at least in part, that we can live for one another in just institutions. However, such understanding can only take place, as Ricoeur argues, in the context of narration and articulation.[60] In my view, Manchester Cathedral is yet to explore how theology itself needs to be "queered" and reformulated in light of its commitment to inclusion. Instead, I think the current cathedral team, under the leadership of Govender, has recognized how formal Christian theology has been harmful towards LGBTQ+ people and has sought to bracket formal theology for that reason regarding this topic.[61] From my reading of the cathedral, it is only with the *LLF* process that the cathedral has actively engaged in the kinds of apologetic strategies outlined by Tonstad. Instead, the cathedral has displayed and vocalized its affirming posture unapologetically.

Even though a particular theology of a spacious and inclusive God is very much at the heart of this action and activity, and there is an excess of theological meaning in its actions and activities in this regard, in my view a more imaginative and consistent engagement with "queering" formal theology with LGBTQ+ people can be a transformative act of justice. Such activities would liberate the text from hegemonic singularity and objectivity, which can lead to the transformation of vision within the community. Not only does it liberate the text from hegemonic singularity but allows for the exploration of God outside the text and in the realm of human experience

---

59. Ricoeur, *Hermeneutics and Human Sciences*, 143.

60. Ricoeur, *Hermeneutics and Human Sciences*, 60. See also Stiver, *Ricoeur and Theology*, 113.

61. This argument is very similar to the argument I made in ch. 5 regarding the cathedral's Rawlsian approach to racial inclusion. However, I will explore the overlaps and connections between the two chapters in the following chapters.

and relationality. The purpose of this approach to theology is not simply to produce a single overarching queer theology. Rather, queer theology and practice as I have understood them produce a plethora of visions, readings, and understandings which in turn produce different imaginings and hopes for the way that bodies can live, move, and love together in the world. Without such a transformation of theological images and categories, it is not clear that heterosexism can be overcome in the church. As Mary Hunt states:

> The love of a merciful, tender, maternal God/ess pales by comparison in a culture in which power is prized. The image of a macho God-Father, with his amazing Son and their sidekick Holy Spirit, has so dominated the Christian consciousness since the Middle Ages that we have had few other images. Without a change in the concept of God, I am convinced that there is little hope for overcoming heterosexism/homophobia.[62]

IS A QUEER MOTHER CHURCH POSSIBLE IN THE CHURCH OF ENGLAND?

Throughout this chapter, it is apparent that the Ricoeurian model of public theology of inclusion of LGBTQ+ people that I am advocating for stands in tension with the wider approach of the CofE in regard to this topic. I have argued that LGBTQ+ inclusion requires going beyond apologetics and to queer theology and doctrines themselves, rather than simply making already existing spaces more welcoming without significant transformations taking place as a result.

This poses the question of whether it is possible for the cathedral as the mother church of the diocese to make this queer turn to its inclusive approach. Even as the cathedral operates in its approach to inclusion now there are tensions between the cathedral and the diocese. Holgate highlighted to me in one recorded interview that certain members of the diocese complain that the cathedral's vocal and visible approach excludes them because their view is not being represented by the mother church. Therefore, I asked Govender how he navigated the tension between being the dean of the cathedral which is unapologetically affirming and being part of a diocese that is divided on this topic. Govender responded by saying that the cathedral is completely in step with the national church. He reminded me first that the

---

62. Hunt, "Overcoming Fear of Love," 159. Cited in Graham, *Transforming Practice*, 179.

cathedral, because of its place within the Church of England, was unable to be "liturgically inclusive" to people in same-sex relationships. The dean can say prayers with a same-sex couple who have already been married by the state, outside of the church. So, within the laws and liturgical restrictions of the Church of England, the cathedral remains "in sync" with the church, while striving to be inclusive of same-sex relationships.

Govender said, however, that even though the cathedral is so visible and vocal in its affirmation of LGBTQ+ people it is not out of sync with the vision and direction of the national church. Govender referenced Justin Welby's speech at the 2017 General Synod, as he announced the development of the *LLF* document and process. As I wrote earlier in this chapter, Welby called for a "radical new Christian inclusion," which does not exclude anybody amid disagreement. For Govender, this places the cathedral well within the national church's vision for the future of the Church of England, because the cathedral sees itself as being committed to this kind of radical inclusion in relation to the LGBTQ+ community. I asked Govender if he felt that he and Welby agreed about what it meant for the church to adopt this "radical new Christian inclusion." From my interpretation, it seems that Welby's vision of radical inclusion is about holding the diverse CofE together in the midst of competing viewpoints on sexuality and gender. However, for Govender inclusion is the unapologetic affirmation of LGBTQ+ people and their relationships. But Govender was emphatic in his view that he as the dean does not hold a view of radical inclusion that is out of sync with the national church in this way, saying:

> No, I am not. I would be speaking about radical inclusion at both levels. One at making space for LGBTQ+ people, but also making room for difference within the body of Christ. Because one of our ministries as Christians is the ministry of reconciliation and that is learning to live together despite a difference. And the whole teaching of "strive to preserve the unity of the spirit," I think is a very important one because the fact you have that teaching in the New Testament and we know from Corinthians and Acts and so on, and so the apostles had to fight to keep the church together. And they did make compromises, e.g., the council in Jerusalem in Acts 15. So, when I say radical inclusion, it is at both levels.

For Govender, the cathedral excludes nobody, including those Christians who would disagree with their affirmation of LGBTQ+ people. Instead, he argues that others exclude themselves from joining in with the life, worship, and work of the cathedral because of its posture towards LGBTQ+ people. For Govender, the space is open and welcome to all people, including those who disagree with the cathedral's posture and stance.

For Hilton and Holgate, this is a very real challenge that presents issues with the language of inclusion at the cathedral. Hilton said:

> One of the major difficulties, when you are here, is that people hear "Manchester Cathedral is about inclusion," and I wonder how inclusive the space feels when you speak to Diocesan Evangelical Fellowship, for example, when they see the pride flag going up. I wonder how inclusive their cathedral feels to them. So, the big challenge to us who are open hearted and on the right side of the angels from my point of view, and something I have learnt from Canon David as part of *LLF*, is I am not an inclusivist unless I am welcoming those people who disagree with me vehemently. Inclusion has to mean everyone. But if we are serious about the gospel and serious about what inclusion means, at a very big macro picture level, if they are not here then we are incomplete.

Holgate added to this by saying that the Pastoral Principles Course produced by the Church of England alongside *LLF*

> invites people to deal with ignorance, power, fear, prejudice, silence and hypocrisy. And what we are finding is when we try to get into the more substantive matters of sexuality, gender, orientation, view of marriage and so on, the problems that crop up are problems caused by those elements.[63]

Holgate suggested that to be inclusive of the wider church, the cathedral would have to engage with these topics, with those it disagrees with, in order to be radically inclusive. However, he pointed out there would be limits to what this could entail. He suggested, for example, the cathedral would not allow an event or external booking to take place which might not be inclusive towards people within the LGBTQ+ community. To some, this may be seen as going against the value of inclusion that the cathedral desires to uphold. However, I do not think this is the case. As Judith Butler argues in the context of discovering who "the people" are who should be listened to by the state:

> Even when we say "everyone" in an effort to posit an all-inclusive group, we are still making implicit assumptions about who is included, and so we hardly overcome . . . "the constitutive

---

63. For more information, see Church of England, "Pastoral Principles Course."

exclusion" by which any particular notion of inclusion is established.[64]

Butler's argument here concerns the issue of whether white supremacist and anti-refugee public demonstrations and discourse should be treated with respect and seriousness by a state oriented towards justice. Her point here is that inclusion as a value constitutes an exclusion of those whose posture is one of exclusion. For the cathedral this means that its commitment to inclusion as a value does not necessitate it elevating certain viewpoints to equal validity.[65] Instead, its inclusive approach can be understood to be a certain kind of liberation theology. Just as liberation theologies operate with a preferential option for the poor, so too can the cathedral operate with a preferential option for those who have been the historical victims of colonialist, exclusionary theology, such as the LGBTQ+ community. Part of the outworking of this "preferential option" is to elevate the voices and experiences of LGBTQ+ people and enable them to formulate, shape, and challenge dominant theological concepts such as sin, redemption, atonement, glory, healing, and others.

Such a public theology of inclusion may take a long period to establish. As Govender said to me in my final interview with him, "The trick is not to do too many radical things at once, so you don't cause ten ruptures in ten weeks." However, he suggested alongside this that the genius of English cathedrals is that they can be spiritual laboratories, in which priests, theologians, and activists can experiment together and take risks to push boundaries and get people thinking. The approach to a public theology of LGBTQ+ inclusion that I am proposing is radical, risky, and experimental. However, it is one that Manchester Cathedral, in my view, can adopt in the long run, to do justice to the flag it raises on its roof every Pride Month.

In this framework then, the value of inclusion is a good starting point at Manchester Cathedral. It indicates that the space is open to people whom religious institutions have often excluded. However, it isn't a sufficient value. Inclusion cannot be an end in and of itself. As Tonstad has argued, queer theology has often taken the form of apologetics, debating whether or not

---

64. Butler, *Performative Theory of Assembly*, 4.

65. For example, as Martin argues regarding reading strategies with a fundamentalist proof-texting style, "we must simply stop giving that kind of argument any credibility" (D. Martin, *Sex and Single Savior*, 49). See also C. Smith, who demonstrates that evangelical appeals to the "plain sense" of Scripture fail to come to terms with the plurality of interpretations of various topics and verses by other Evangelicals who approach Scripture in the same way. Smith argues that this pervasiveness of the plurality of interpretations among Evangelicals should automatically demonstrate the falsity of appealing to the plain sense of Scripture (*Bible Made Impossible*, 3–26).

same-sex relationships could or should be granted the status of marriage or whether those in same-sex relationships or who are trans, could or should be ordained. However, she further argues:

> Both sides in Christian debates over sexuality often take similarly bankrupt forms. Opponents of the full participation of queer persons commonly resort to proof-texting—tearing texts out of place, space, context, and history to deploy them as weapons, shutting down debate. Proponents of the full participation of queer persons tend to respond by an anaemic assertion of historical difference between sexuality now and then, followed by self-congratulatory statements about God's love for everyone. These debates produce exhaustion and boredom and have done little to advance thinking about sexuality or to deepen theological reflection.[66]

In a sense, while Tonstad's assessment of the state of the debates may be harsh, though in my experience accurate, the Ricoeurian model that I am proposing for the cathedral to adopt is a way of avoiding an anaemic inclusion. A more theologically and politically enriching and transformative inclusion will provide space to explore questions of how visions of human sexuality is constructed politically and will elevate the voices of sexual and gendered minorities to call into question standard practices and discourses, both in the church and in society, that produce normative visions of the human. In this model, the cathedral would be resisting the theology of a welcoming God who operates within the cathedral, calling LGBTQ+ people in, but would instead uphold the notion of a God who is already present in the margins with the LGBTQ+ people, who longs to enter the cathedral, with an alternative, queer word.

CONCLUSION

In this chapter I have sought to analyze and evaluate the public theology of LGBTQ+ inclusion at Manchester Cathedral. I began by highlighting the cathedral's approach and activities that relate to LGBTQ+ inclusion. I then highlighted how queer theology and theory present challenges to the ways

66. Tonstad, *God and Difference*, 4. In Lewin's study, one of her participants in an interview who was a congregant of a Pentecostal affirming church in the US stated, "I don't want to come to church to hear over and over that it's okay to be gay. I know that. I come to worship God. I want to talk about God." She argues based on this that what is transformative for LGBTQ+ people are not simply the repeated message that queer people are included and loved, but rather to participate in the joint discovery of God through spiritual practice and theological reflection (*Filled with the Spirit*, 27).

inclusion is often understood and performed by different institutions. I attempted to make connections between queer theology, public theology, and the cathedral's activity as I demonstrated the need for a Ricoeurian public approach to LGBTQ+ inclusion. Such an approach goes beyond simply creating a welcoming environment for marginalized people, though that is important for Manchester Cathedral. Instead, the Ricoeurian model I put forward opens the cathedral's theology and practice to a place of vulnerability so that it can be shaped and challenged by the visions and understandings of queer people. The purpose of this is to challenge the formative elements that produce heterosexism in the church and society and to be formed by alternative visions and symbols that are liberating for LGBTQ+ people.

This challenges public theologies of LGBTQ+ inclusion to recognize that formative symbols and practice should be interrogated by theologians in relationship with various public spheres. This chapter has not sought to provide answers to the questions raised, but it has been an attempt to indicate the types of questions that need to be engaged and the direction their public theology should take if the cathedral truly desires to be inclusive of LGBTQ+ people and stand in solidarity with them. In the following chapter, I will explore the connections between the previous chapters analyzing these areas of public engagement at the cathedral and demonstrate how a Ricoeurian approach to public theology can address the challenges raised by my analysis.

7

CRITICALLY EVALUATING MANCHESTER CATHEDRAL'S PUBLIC THEOLOGY

INCLUSION, IDENTITY, AND LINGUISTIC HOSPITALITY

HAVING ANALYZED AND EVALUATED the cathedral's public theology in relation to interreligious dialogue, racial justice, and LGBTQ+ inclusion, I will in this chapter explore two categories that I think are common and foundational to the cathedral's public theology in these areas. These are the categories of common humanity and human flourishing. I explore how the cathedral thinks theologically about these categories, and how the three case studies demonstrate that these categories can't be understood to be neutral, objective, or universal because each is open to particular interpretations arising from different perspectives. As I will show, there are tensions between inclusive approaches to publicness and approaches to theology that emphasize distinctiveness. Therefore, after exploring these tensions I will demonstrate how a Ricoeurian approach to publicness can help the cathedral in its aims of contributing to the flourishing of humanity.

THE RAWLSIAN CHARACTER OF MANCHESTER CATHEDRAL'S APPROACH TO PUBLICNESS

In the previous three chapters, I have demonstrated that much of the cathedral's approach, though there are exceptions, can be characterized as adopting a Rawlsian model of publicness. As I have argued, the Rawlsian approach to public theology is characterized by emphasizing common values in order to provide the ground for overlapping consensus. For the Rawlsian approach to public theology, the particular aspects of a religion should be bracketed and considered a part of private belief if these are considered to distract from the overlapping common ground. The main principle that Rawls himself considered to be truly public is the principle of justice as fairness. For Rawls, this principle has the capacity of appealing to all reasonable people within a democratic society. For Rawls, religious discourse can potentially enter the public sphere if it serves to bolster this uniting principle.

Different concepts and values can serve the same function as Rawls's "justice as fairness." I argued, for example, in chapter 5, that the cathedral can emphasize particular issues of common concern, such as hate crime, to provide sufficient ground for overlapping consensus. By emphasizing hate crime as a key uniting issue, the cathedral is theologically motivated to engage others in this topic, but explicit theology is not required to guide or contribute to these discussions.

Similarly, in chapter 4, I demonstrated that regarding interreligious dialogue and partnership the value of peace and inclusion play a dominant role in providing the overlapping consensus for the cathedral's engagement with different religious groups. This is in part because Dean Rogers Govender assumes that true religion, of any tradition, should aim towards peace. It is this common ground of peace which provides the overlapping consensus, despite different beliefs about God. As Govender said in the first recorded interview that I conducted with him:

> Religion is both about our personal relationship with God, but it is also about the world in which we live, it is about our relationships with others in the world, the wider world. And religion ought to be a force for good. Anything that promotes goodness and good values in society that prevents us from getting involved in crime and murder, exploitation, and violence is a good thing. And religion should do all it can to promote those values, for the good of all, and the good of religion itself. And dare I say, in order for my faith to thrive and flourish, all of us need to flourish.

In this quote, we see that the primary public function of religion ought to be, from Govender's perspective, to promote good values in a way which leads people to want to embody those values in their lives.[1]

1. Holgate's work in Scriptural Reasoning and Scriptural Encounter reading groups

Finally, in chapter 6, I demonstrated that the cathedral's discourse and practice in regard to LGBTQ+ people are characterized by the value of inclusion. I would argue this approach to this topic could be understood to be Rawlsian in some ways because while inclusion is a theologically motivated category at the cathedral, the cathedral assumes that the contents of what the value of inclusion means is shared both within the church and in wider society and thus provides the grounds of an overlapping consensus. For example, Anthony O'Connor argued that though some members of the diocese complain to the dean when the cathedral hoists the pride flag during Pride Month, the city affirms and celebrates the act because the cathedral is aligning with the city's values of inclusion and diversity.

However, there is a public theology of humanity that is at the heart of all the cathedral's activities, even beyond the three areas that I have elaborated on here, that unite all of the cathedral's core public values. I will explore the cathedral's public theology of humanity, particularly the cathedral's core concepts of common humanity and human flourishing.

"WE WANT TO CLAIM OUR HUMANITY AS OUR FIRST RELIGION": HUMAN FLOURISHING AND COMMON HUMANITY AS PUBLIC THEOLOGICAL CATEGORIES AT MANCHESTER CATHEDRAL

In the recorded interview I conducted with both Hilton and Holgate, Holgate argued that the inclusion of LGBTQ+ people into the church causes the whole church to flourish, not just the person being included. Hilton responded:

> One of the things that David has said is "flourishing." For me, that's my bar. We make it so complicated in the Church. Where

---

represents a different approach, more Ricoeurian in form, in that those groups seek to understand the different approaches to penultimate issues, including how beliefs about the ultimate affect the way one interprets the penultimate. This demonstrates that the cathedral's approach cannot be characterized as Rawlsian absolutely. Further, Holgate has a keen interest in biblical and missional hermeneutics. In his 2006 book, the SCM Studyguide called *Biblical Hermeneutics*, co-authored with Rachel Starr, it is argued that "the ultimate purpose of biblical interpretation is not understanding, but healing, transformation, and liberation. It is to enable people to live and flourish.... The Bible is about human encounters with God. When we interpret the Bible, we participate in the ongoing exploration of the many ways in which God's liberating and transforming love is revealed to humanity" (190–91). Thus, I would argue that Holgate's hermeneutical approach can often be characterized as Ricoeurian. Nonetheless, the Rawlsian approach characterizes much of the cathedral's interreligious networking.

> I see people flourishing, I know I can see it, I can smell it, see it, taste it. I know what flourishing looks like and I know what non-flourishing looks like . . . It has to be about human flourishing because that seems to be at the absolute heart of creation.

For both Holgate and Hilton, flourishing is universal in the sense that flourishing takes place both within and outside the church and may be a result of having faith in Christ, but they also recognize that nobody *needs* the gospel or faith in Christ in order to flourish. Hilton stated:

> No one needs the gospel to flourish. Nobody needs the church to flourish. People are flourishing without the things that I hold dear. Its tough love to say that, but that would seem to be the evidence . . . I happen to believe that life walking with Jesus Christ is life-giving and transformative for my life, but I have to recognize in the lives of nonbelievers, their lives do not seem to be impoverished because they have a different take. Human flourishing is above what I see and understand.

This concept of human flourishing is at the heart of the public theology of Manchester Cathedral.[2] The primary understanding of God consistently publicly articulated at Manchester Cathedral is a God who desires, above all else, humanity to flourish in their relationships, in their cities, and in their cultures. As a result, the concept of the human becomes the overarching category that makes all other possible distinctives secondary.

Therefore, the cathedral is passionate about social justice in the public sphere. Justice, at Manchester Cathedral, is understood to be the work necessary to ensure the potential for the flourishing of all people equally. Each area of public engagement that I have examined, and those that I haven't, seems to converge on this theme.[3] The cathedral is passionate about racial

---

2. Holgate showed in the interview that the theological concept of human flourishing is derived from feminist theologies. See Jantzen, "Flourishing"; Santos, "That All May Enjoy."

3. There are numerous public issues that the cathedral engages and public activities that it hosts that I have not been able to give space to in this thesis. Some examples include engagement with issues surrounding homelessness and migration, long-term unemployment, and faith and well-being. One significant charity that was launched by Manchester Cathedral is Volition. Volition is chaired by Govender and directed by Anthony O'Connor. The charity identifies volunteer roles for unemployed people, in partnership with Jobcentre Plus to give people experience, training, and skill building, and support to help them find employment. At Manchester Cathedral, volunteers take part in beekeeping of the bees on the cathedral roof and stone masonry, among other things. The charity is increasingly successful, and the team desire to establish this model across the UK. Hilton said to me in one interview that Volition is the "unsung hero of the cathedral." In addition, in 1995 a charity called the Booth Centre was established. The

justice in public because racism leads to human non-flourishing. It is a dehumanizing act that creates a false picture of reality in which some humans are worth less than others. LGBTQ+ exclusion is similarly an act that suggests people's sexuality and/or gender identity can result in their worth and place within society and other networks of relationality being called into question. For Manchester Cathedral, practices of LGBTQ+ exclusions are unacceptable for the church, because it assumes that some people are more worthy of flourishing in their chosen relationships and/or identities than others.

This also relates to the interreligious activity of the cathedral. The cathedral is able to invite colleagues from other religions, into the space and to use the space, because as the cathedral sees it, while there may be disagreements about God and doctrinal issues, all the religions (should) aim towards the same end: the flourishing of humanity. If this theme is kept at the center of its networking activity, as we have seen, the possibility of working together across diversity is possible. As Dean Rogers said to me in our final recorded interview:

> It means we care for one another equally, respect one another equally, and try to include one another where possible, recognizing our doctrinal and religious differences, and our different convictions about God, notwithstanding all of that. We want to claim our humanity as our first religion. Our common humanity.

Following Ronald Preston, John Atherton argues that questions about human flourishing are central to the beliefs of the Christian faith. He writes:

> For at the heart of Christian belief are questions of what it now means to be human, of what is our understanding of social flourishing, of what is the right and wrong way of promoting human living in and through its environments. The commitment to human flourishing in all its fullness is both a human and divine imperative inspired and informed by the Christ-like God who "came that they may have life and have it more abundantly."

---

charity helps support homeless people in Manchester. Originally, the center operated from Manchester Cathedral. However, in 2014, the center moved from the cathedral to different premises in the city. Govender, however, is an ex officio trustee whom Holgate represented on the board. Thus, the cathedral has maintained keen involvement with the center despite its moving to other premises. See https://www.boothcentre.org.uk/. Though I have not explored these areas of the cathedral's work in depth, the theology of human flourishing is central to the cathedral's understanding of how Volition connects with its wider ministry and public witness. See https://volitioncommunity.org/about-us/.

(John 10:10) It is the acknowledgement that "Christians have every reason to suppose God wishes human life to flourish and has put us in this world in the first place not as Christians but as human beings.[4]

The dean of the cathedral follows this line of theological thought, and thus leads the cathedral with a view of the universal scope and impact of God's trinitarian rule, which participates within the life of each and every human. Govender's favorite theological image is Rublev's Trinity icon, which for him highlights the universal scope of the Trinity's love in each human life. For Govender, this universal dimension of the work of God, which is the result of pure grace, is the basis for the cathedral's engagement with the wider world. For Govender, because God's love is universal, unconditional, and indiscriminate, the cathedral's public engagement must similarly be expansive and inclusive.

This kind of universalism is captured by Kathryn Tanner in a similar way, as she argues that the Trinitarian shape of life, understood through the lens of an incarnational Christology, demonstrates that God's gifts towards us are not a result of our work towards him, but are the result of pure grace. As a result, she argues:

> The community of concern to human beings as the ministers of divine benefit should therefore be as wide as God's gift-giving purview. In this universal community, humans should try to distribute the gifts of God as God does without concern for whether they are especially deserved by their recipients. Without bothering themselves, for example, with distinctions between the deserving or undeserving poor, they should give their full attention, instead, to the various needs of members of this worldwide community. They must offer special protections, moreover, as these become necessary, to those most likely to be left out of the community of concern at any point in time the outcast and strangers in their midst.[5]

Manchester Cathedral embodies this universal concern, seeking to include all within its walls and work with diverse networks for the causes of social justice that it is passionate about. The cathedral also offers special recognition and action towards those who are "the most likely to be left out of

---

4. Atherton, *Marginalization*, 3–4. Atherton quotes Preston, *Confusions*, 148. It is important to note that Preston and Atherton were both canon theologians at Manchester Cathedral and thus predecessors of Canon Holgate. In many ways, Holgate's theology is in continuity with the AST tradition that Preston and Atherton represent.

5. Tanner, *Jesus, Humanity, and Trinity*, 90.

the community of concern." However, as I have argued in the previous three chapters, the cathedral's thin theological anthropology means that it doesn't demonstrate an awareness of how various visions of humanity compete in the public sphere. Therefore, I will demonstrate some challenges posed to approaches to human flourishing that take place outside of a theological, and specifically a Christological interpretation, of flourishing.

HUMAN FLOURISHING AND EPISTEMOLOGICAL CHALLENGES

As I argued in chapter 2, post-liberal theologians have critiqued public theology for being accommodationist in their approach to theology, seeking to be influential in society, resulting in the bypassing of the church as a significant public space and not maintaining a faithful witness to the particularities of the Christian tradition. As Dan Bell, a critic of public theology, argues:

> Although their [public theologians] political views range widely from progressive to conservative, these theologians share a commitment to resisting the sectarian impulses in Christianity that would acquiesce in the disintegration of the moral consensus that has underwritten Western liberal policies for generations. These theologians derive from Christianity a "public philosophy" or "public theology" capable of underwriting the moral consensus necessary to sustain the health and vitality of Western liberal society.[6]

For post-liberal theologians, Christ is the ultimate vision of human flourishing that the church should bear witness to, even if this is not acceptable or relevant to wider society. Wider categories of flourishing or humanness are not required, or even legitimate for the church, because Christology and biblical narrative reveal all that is needed to understand what it means to flourish. While Manchester Cathedral recognizes that the presence of God in relation to all humanity is the source of flourishing, post-liberals argue that flourishing can only occur when this relation is actualized through worship practices, such as participation in the liturgy, in the context of the Christian community.

One key example relevant to my work is found in an article by James K. A. Smith, where Smith argues that the belief that marriage should be between one man and one woman alone is a matter of faith, revealed in Christ.

---

6. Bell, "State and Civil Society," 432.

For Smith, the case of same-sex marriage is useful in demonstrating how society cannot see how same-sex marriage is naturally disordered. He argues that maintaining the traditional view of marriage must be proclaimed in the public sphere and argued for as a matter of faith because those outside the church cannot recognize how their relationships may be disordered. This is because he thinks that nature, order, and disorder are known only in Christ and through the resurrection. For Smith, Christians approach the public sphere with the revelation of Christ and the revelation of what it means to be human, which does not require the church to be influenced by society.[7] Thus, the church, in a sense, stands above the world, even as it interacts with it, because the church alone, as the body of Christ, possesses the truth about human flourishing.[8]

I return once again to the debate between public and post-liberal theologians because this is a particularly important debate within the context of Anglican social theology (AST). As I argued in chapter 2, much of Anglican social theology has followed the so-called Temple tradition and adopts a middle-axiom approach to engaging with public issues. However, Hughes argues that there has been a renewal of AST, sparked by the global economic crash in 2008–9. This recession led to questioning from multiple spheres and disciplines about the political and economic systems that the Western world is built upon.[9] According to Hughes, the Occupy movements in particular led to Anglicans returning to their own traditions and resources to address social and economic questions.[10] As a result, there has been a turn to post-liberal theologies and philosophies in AST.

In his essay, Hughes highlights Alasdair MacIntyre and Stanley Hauerwas as key figures whom Anglicans have drawn on for their social theology in recent years. This turn towards the post-liberal critique of liberalism in turn towards a renewed interest in the church itself embodying an alternative social vision. MacIntyre's work in *Three Rival Versions of Moral Enquiry*

---

7. J. Smith, "Beyond Creation and Natural Law."

8. Similarly, though not himself identified with either public or post-liberal theologians, Miroslav Volf argues that Christians should not, and cannot, hide from the belief that true human flourishing comes when humans center their lives on the true, the good, and the beautiful. But for Volf, this means that Christians believe that God, who is the source of all truth, goodness, and beauty, is the secret to the flourishing of our lives, cultures, and cities. As a result, for Volf, Christians must place God at the center of a vision of human flourishing, because if not, other, more harmful visions of flourishing will dominate (*Public Faith*, 57–65).

9. Hughes, "After Temple," 74.

10. Hughes, "After Temple," 75. For example, Cloke et al. argue that Occupy exposed and protested the inequalities that are embedded within the structures of liberal capitalism across the world ("Postsecularity," 497).

and *After Virtue* critiques modernity's presumption that enlightened reason can provide neutral, universal moral truths that all can adhere to once arbitrary commitments (usually religious) have been bracketed out from their fundamental frameworks of moral and social inquiry.[11] For MacIntyre, the future of ethics would be "sustained through a new dark ages by small communities with disciplines and virtues such as St Benedictus religious houses."[12] For MacIntyre, this is not, however, withdrawal into irrationalism. Instead, institutions and individuals should engage with one another through "tradition-based reasoning" where truth is not perceived from "nowhere." Instead, the tradition-based reasoning should be open to dialogue, but truly tradition-based dialogue, rather than presuming dialogue must take place under the rubric of a neutral, universally accessible rhetoric.[13]

Hauerwas further developed MacIntyre's work in relation to the church's ecclesial ethics, in which he has emphasized that ethics is not the study of universal moral principles, "but embedded ways of life and material practices, or traditions."[14] This approach leads Hauerwas to emphasize the distinctiveness of the church as an alternative social body or public, that narrates the world in light of the Christian narrative, leading to his conclusion that "the first task of the church is not to make the world more just, but to make the world the world."[15] In other words, Hauerwas's theology emphasizes the community of the church, and the narrative it is formed by, as the source and mediator of true justice and flourishing. Hauerwas writes further:

> To be Christian is surely to fulfil the most profound human desires, but we do not know what such fulfilment means on the basis of those desires themselves.... While the way of life taught by Christ is meant to be an ethic for all people, it does not follow that we can know what such an ethic involves "objectively" by looking at the human.[16]

Importantly, the philosophy of MacIntyre and the theology of Hauerwas both resist key aspects of the Temple tradition, which has been dominant for serval decades in AST.[17] Yet, it is these very tensions with the

11. Hughes, "After Temple," 80.
12. MacIntyre, *After Virtue*, 58.
13. Hughes, "After Temple," 80–81.
14. Hughes, "After Temple," 81.
15. Hauerwas, *Peaceable Kingdom*, 99.
16. Hauerwas, *Peaceable Kingdom*, 58.
17. The main tension being that natural law is not a category that post-liberals adopt, unless "nature" is being interpreted christologically. According to Hughes,

Temple tradition that are proving to be fruitful for the future of AST. John Hughes states:

> Between them, MacIntyre and Hauerwas have changed the landscape of British Christian ethics and given birth to a post-liberal generation much more sceptical about the capacities of "neutral secular reasons" or of achieving a universal consensus. This new generation of theologians has learned to be particularly sceptical towards the principal ideology of Western consumer capitalism, namely the belief in freedom as abstract choice without any orientation to shared goods or ends.[18]

If Hughes is correct in his analysis of the renewal of AST, then I conclude that the cathedral stands in contrast to this development. From my interpretation, Manchester Cathedral, by and large, sees the Christian tradition as the motivating factor in the pursuit of this common vision of human flourishing. Because of the belief of the universality of God's love, presence, and work in the world, the cathedral assumes that the Christian tradition is not the sole arbiter of what it means to be human and to flourish. As a result, as I have demonstrated in this thesis, the cathedral has developed key networks with people of different faiths, and those with no faiths. It has partnered with institutions in task of addressing common concerns in the city of Manchester, such as the city council, Greater Manchester Police, and numerous charities. It emphasizes shared values and the reality of the God-given common humanity as the ground on which all people can be united.

In this way, the cathedral resists the kind of "ecclesiocentrism" of post-liberal thought. However, I would argue that the main contribution of post-liberal theologians is their demonstration that ethics is not abstract, universal, or "natural" and doesn't "come from nowhere" as MacIntyre has argued. Instead, the post-liberal school of thought emphasizes the importance of formation of ethical visions and communities, rather than the search for universal principles or values. As Hauerwas states: "All reading is embedded in a politics."[19] As I have tried to argue throughout my chapters analyzing the areas of public engagement, a Ricoeurian approach to

---

Hauerwas further argues, that to adopt any kind of natural theology is to split morality, ethics, politics, and theology into dimensions of publicness and privateness. In this case, there are on the one hand a universal set of principles available to all people, and on the other hand particular principles available to the Christian based on revelation. This is known as two-tier ethics, which characterizes middle-axiom approaches. Hauerwas deems this a theological failure, because all theology should be understood as public. Hughes, "After Temple," 94.

18. Hughes, "After Temple," 82–83.
19. Hauerwas, *Unleashing the Scriptures*, 15.

publicness affirms the exploration of the formative visions and narratives which shape the ethical life. Thus, a Ricoeurian approach will also affirm that ethics are not done in a vacuum, but develop within particular contexts, which are made up of distinctive symbols, narratives, and practices.

However, the major weakness of much post-liberal thought is that the theologians often adopt an "ecclesiocentrism," in which the post-liberal exclusivists imagine the Christian tradition ought to be the only source of formation for Christians. Post-liberal theologians are not under the impression that a perfect church exists, yet they argue that the church can only look like Christ in the world if it is formed by the resources, traditions, and theologies of the church. As a result, all hermeneutics, whether that be of Scripture, ethical actions, politics, etc., are to submit to the authority and teaching of the church.[20]

Thus, the post-liberal position recognizes the reality of reading texts, and quasi-texts, as a phenomenon that produces multiple readings and interpretations. However, their solution is an ecclesial governance of interpretation.[21] There are several reasons why this approach is inadequate. First, there is the question of which church tradition interpretation must submit to. In the writings of post-liberals "the church" is often described in broad generic terms, but what is often missing is an analysis of particular church traditions and their divergent interpretations. Smith, for example, points to the ecumenical creeds as being the governing foundations of interpretation but does not seek to explicate how there are multiple traditions and denominations that all affirm the creeds, and yet have significantly different interpretations of various texts and doctrines. Thus, if "the church" becomes the criterion of interpretation, interpretation is already present in a Christian's formed understanding of what the symbol "the church" signifies.

Second, the ecclesial approach to interpretation and ethics requires the absorption of individual Christians into a larger whole or "body," in such a way that their perspectives and interpretations are required to "submit"

---

20. For example, Stanley Hauerwas challenges the assumption that lay Christians have a spiritual obligation or even right to interpret Scripture and suggests instead, "The 'right' reading of scripture depends on having spiritual masters who can help the whole church stand under the authority of God's Word" (*Unleashing the Scriptures*, 15). Similarly, James K. A. Smith argues, in light of the fact that no interpretation can be neutral or objective: "The communal determination of contexts and horizons of expectation lead the ecclesial community to approach it as *canon*—and hence *one* book in some sense—and to receive it as a book in and through which the Triune God uniquely speaks... in other words, our hermeneutics of scripture will require, first and foremost, an ecclesiology" (*Fall of Interpretation*, 219–20; emphasis in original).

21. Hauerwas, *Unleashing the Scriptures*, 25. See also J. Smith, *Fall of Interpretation*, 217–20.

to the perspectives and interpretations of the church as a whole.²² This is starkly seen in Hauerwas and Samuel Well's opening chapter of *The Blackwell Companion to Christian Ethics*, where they argue that Christians are not entitled to bodily integrity or privacy. Rather Christians are reminded that in baptism they are "called to give up any sense that they 'own' their bodies. . . . The Body of Christ . . . sees itself as being genuinely a body, rather than a mass of discrete individuals."²³

Junker-Kenny argues in relation to this ecclesiological position that there is no acknowledgment that the institutional church, which is ultimately how they define the body of Christ, could actually fail. Thus, the post-liberal position places the church in a totalitarian and hence authoritarian role in relation to individual members but has no criteria by which to evaluate its practices.²⁴ In my view, this is a dangerous approach to theological ethics, especially in light of the three case studies in this thesis. Given the church's history of anti-Semitism, colonialism, supporting of slavery and other forms of racial exclusion, and violent ideologies that have harmed women and LGBTQ+ people, it seems to me that the church, or any institution, cannot sustain itself morally on its own criteria. Rather, what is required is an openness to correction from those within and outside of the church. This is where alternative visions of flourishing can challenge dominant visions of human flourishing within the church when those visions produce harm instead of good.

Thus, the potential positive contributions of post-liberal theology for public theology are overridden by the totalitarian tendencies which assume that maintaining distinctiveness and boundaries are the key tasks of the church. As Moyaert argues in relation to the post-liberal rejection of the possibility of translation:

> Theologically, the most important question is: When is the loss the greatest—when the Christian tradition is translated and brought into the public sphere or when its particularity is

---

22. There is a present irony in my use of the word absorption here because this is a metaphor adopted by post-liberals. However, they tend to use this in the sense of the church being absorbed by the world if it does not maintain its own distinctiveness. Therefore, it seems to me that post-liberals resist this kind of absorption, through another kind of absorption, not recognizing the dangerous consequences of the latter. As D'Costa argues: "Worryingly [this metaphor] suggests a rather unilateral process whereby the world has nothing to offer to the church and does not in any way disrupt and challenge the narrative traditions of the Church, its reading and practice of scripture" (*Theology in Public Square*, 142). Cited in Moyaert, *Fragile Identities*, 174.

23. Hauerwas and Wells, "Christian Ethics," 6. Cited in Junker-Kenny, *Approaches to Theological Ethics*, 121.

24. Junker-Kenny, *Approaches to Theological Ethics*, 121.

protected from the danger of loss of meaning by abandoning the public aspect of theology? . . . The cultural-linguistic model (postliberal) loses sight of an essential dimension of Christian faith precisely in its urge to protect it, i.e. the ad extra calling of the church that consists in, among other things, explaining the Christian faith to "outsiders."[25]

The question becomes then, are the only two options for an institution such as Manchester Cathedral that desires to be public in its theology to either assume that Christianity is ultimately a motivational energy in public engagement or to maintain boundaries in the name of protecting its Christian identity? Of course, Manchester Cathedral would, rightly in my view, opt for the former of these options. Yet, these are not the only two options available, despite the debate between post-liberals and public theologians. In the next sections, I will explore an alternative to both of these approaches that I envisage as being constructive for Manchester Cathedral's public theological approach.

BETWEEN EXCLUSIVISTS AND INCLUSIVISTS

Jennifer McBride explores the tension between inclusive theologies, such as the kind of theology at Manchester Cathedral, and exclusive theologies, such as post-liberal theologies. She describes this tension in terms of the "inclusive" Christians' tension and compromise and "exclusive" Christians' tension and triumphalism. She argues that inclusive Christian communities tend to offer a general sense of acceptance and love from God, but don't emphasize the particular ways that God is known through the person and work of Christ. In this approach, she argues, Jesus is a prime example of how to love God. The exclusive Christian approach on the other hand understands the church's task to be primarily about conversion because it believes that only Christians contain the necessary knowledge for eternal salvation.[26]

For McBride, the latter compromises faith in Christ, because exclusivists do not trust in the expansive lordship of Christ. In regard to the former, she argues they compromise faith in Christ because the Christian witness loses its potential to be disruptive of our visions and to challenge believers in the way they must be transformed by the word of God. Instead, Christianity simply becomes one path or expression of the same truths and values

---

25. Moyaert, *Fragile Identities*, 225.
26. McBride, *Church for the World*, 33.

that other people groups hold dear, even while inclusive Christians hold that Jesus is the supreme example of these truths and values.[27]

I argue with McBride that another approach can be adopted in which high Christology (or in her terms, exclusive Christology) can become the very means and foundation of a non-triumphal, hospitable public theology. She argues:

> Instead of a *religious* exclusivity that inadvertently makes an idol of its own beliefs, a nontriumphal proclamation of the lordship of Christ arises from *christological* exclusivity.... Public witness based on a "non-religious" exclusivist Christology is *inclusive* as it appeals to the expansive accomplishment of Christ, who ... has reconciled "all things" to God. It is *without compromise* because it maintains that the ultimate significance of Christ is a nonnegotiable foundation for Christian faith, discipleship, and witness.[28]

Following Dietrich Bonhoeffer, she argues that because of the expansive lordship of the crucified Christ, the word of God could be spoken through the secular to the church, the latter of which should always adopt the posture of repentance.[29] The church, in this posture of repentance, according to McBride, ought to practice this through confession publicly. She argues that such confession and repentance is not simply about offering statements from religious leaders apologizing but transforming structures that those in the institution now deem to be sinful. This can be understood as a public theology of repentance.[30]

My argument, following McBride and in contrast to post-liberal theologians, is that theology itself can be part of those structures if it is not continually transformed, revised, and creatively produced in conversation with those affected by the sinful structures that the church is repenting of. In this way, the Christian tradition should not be understood as self-correcting, but itself continually needs repentance.[31]

---

27. McBride, *Church for the World*, 31. This kind of approach is reflected at Manchester Cathedral and can be seen clearly in articulations of the cathedral wanting to adopt humanity as its first religion.

28. McBride, *Church for the World*, 26; emphasis in original.

29. McBride, *Church for the World*, 29.

30. McBride, *Church for the World*, 17.

31. Leonardo Boff captures this sentiment in some ways when he writes. "Jesus Christ had been made a prisoner of the church, of its ecclesiastical interpretations and its dogmatic casuistry. The mystery and fascination of Jesus had been lost. He had been locked within the frame of reference of an ecclesial structure. We must liberate Jesus from the church so that he can speak once again and create community, community that can justifiably be called the church of Christ" (*Jesus Christ Liberator*, 30).

Of course, there is the question of whether traditions and doctrines should be abandoned or revised when they produce suffering. This is the question raised by John Hick and Rosemary Radford Ruether, which I explored in chapter 4. They called for a decentering of Christ altogether, to the point of revising Christology in such a way that the proclamation of his divinity be regarded as something to be resisted. For Ruether in particular, emphasis on Christ's divinity is foundational to Christian anti-Semitism, which has been characteristic of a long and dark portion of the Christian church's history.

In contrast to Hick and Ruether, while I think that a non-triumphalist theology is vital for churches and Christian institutions to adopt, I do not necessarily think that this entails the complete bracketing or abandonment of the particulars of the Christian faith, because of the historical abuses these have generated. Part of this is because it is in the distinctive elements of the Christian faith that marginalized people groups, such as people of color, women, and LGBTQ+ people have found the resources for liberation and flourishing.[32] Instead, part of a public theology of repentance and Christological exclusivism would include the examination and hearing of traditions of Christianity formed within excluded and marginalized communities, which can challenge dominant traditions within the church.

Theology in this way remains central to the task of justice because theology is a vision-forming activity and process which can change the way people interact and act within the world. However, the traditions of the church can be challenged by other traditions and experiences. Part of the task, therefore, is to recognize that public theologies should not be formed outside of conversation and interaction with the bodies of the excluded, whom the cathedral try to include. Otherwise, inclusion simply becomes the expansion of what is already theologically assumed, and the exclusionary structures and powers are not challenged or transformed.[33] In my view, Ricoeur's approach to linguistic hospitality is helpful for navigating these tensions between being inclusive while also maintaining the importance of distinct identities and perspectives within the public sphere.

---

32. For a detailed discussion of how marginalized communities have turned to Christian symbols and biblical narratives for resources of liberation, see Bohache, *Christology from the Margins*. See also, Althaus-Reid, *Queer God*; Douglas, *Black Christ*; Cone, *Black Theology of Liberation*.

33. Tonstad, *God and Difference*, 256.

LINGUISTIC HOSPITALITY: BETWEEN EXCLUSIVISM AND INCLUSIVISM

As I have argued, McBride's Christological exclusivism provides a corrective to both inclusive and exclusive theologies. However, there must be a further development of what such an approach may mean both in theory and practice. Thus, I am arguing for a Ricoeurian form of linguistic hospitality, that affirms both the ability for diverse peoples to communicate with one another, and yet also maintains a level of distanciation between different people groups. In this section I will elaborate on this approach more explicitly in terms of Ricoeur's theory of linguistic hospitality.

As I demonstrated in chapters 1 and 2, Ricoeur, similarly to many public theologians, envisages the notion of translation as a key metaphor for the interaction of diverse people groups. Ricoeur argues for "linguistic hospitality," which rests on the presumption that the task of translation is never completed, because there is no single language that can communicate every perspective of every culture. As Ricoeur argues that this "translation ethic" is to generate space "where the pleasure of dwelling in the other's language is balanced by the pleasure of receiving the foreign word at home, in one's welcoming home."[34]

Luke Bretherton expands on his own theological account of political hospitality as he demonstrates the necessities of both toleration and hospitality in the public sphere. He argues that toleration is a necessary part of justice, for democratic societies to flourish, but hospitality is required to go beyond this to fulfil the theological demands of neighborly love.[35] Bretherton argues that to build a common life, toleration is not enough. Toleration is the means of negotiating between that which we find objectionable and intolerable, but it doesn't give us resources for building other virtues into our political frameworks, and communities. He thus presents hospitality as a political necessity in order to foster community between people who may consider one another friends, or strangers.[36] For Bretherton, hospitality is a non-state-centric form of relation. He writes, "It involves offering gifts from

---

34. Ricoeur, *On Translation*, 10.

35. Bretherton argues that toleration involves the willingness to accept differences (whether religious, moral, or cultural) that one might, as an individual our community, find objectionable or that conflict with one's own beliefs and practices. However, rather than a refusal to judge, toleration entails a suspension of judgment about one thing—prosecution of the truth as one sees it here and now—in favor of a judgment for maintaining an ongoing relationship. Toleration thereby hangs precariously between power, morality, community, and truth (*Christ and Common Life*, 271).

36. Bretherton, *Christ and Common Life*, 272.

one's customs and traditions as a way of calling forth reciprocal recognition from others."[37]

Drawing on Kant, MacIntyre, and Derrida, Bretherton argues that hospitality requires both hosts and guests. But in order to avoid the potential exclusionary and patronising practices that hospitality has been critiqued for in the past, hospitality should decenter the host, and make possible the transformation of the host as the host makes room for encounters with others.[38] However, this act of openness does not require the denial of the self. This is precisely what Derrida's reading of hospitality as a paradox highlights. To be hospitable, there must be a circle or group in which the guest already does not belong, yet such a circle must exist by necessity through exclusionary means. The challenge becomes how to open the circle. For Bretherton, this opening requires not only the opening of space for people to enter but the willingness of the host tradition to have their conceptions of God and right practice challenged by the stranger.

Post-liberal theologians, who follow the cultural-linguistic model proposed by Lindbeck, resist models of ecclesiology that create space for the stranger and outsider to challenge the Christian church because there is a present risk that the church will lose its distinctiveness. In the cultural-linguistic model, the protection and preservation of the church's distinctive speech and practice is of paramount importance. However, the problem with this approach is that it imagines language as static and fixed, and produces a picture of religions as monolithic "blocks characterised by coherence and continuity."[39] As a result, Moyaert follows Ricoeur's theory of linguistic hospitality and translation, arguing:

> Translation acknowledges the diversity on the one hand but denies, on the other hand, that this diversity divides the different communities from one another. Translation is a matter of moving between the strange and the familiar, between the particular and the universal, between diversity and unity. From a theological perspective, translation is the preeminent recognition of the fact that the particularity of the Christian identity

---

37. Bretherton, *Christ and Common Life*, 273.

38. For example, Bretherton highlights that in the context of interreligious hospitality Rabbi Jonathan Sacks argues that many Christian institutions adopt a "country-house" model, which demands assimilation. In this approach, the Christian church is always the host, and never the guest. The approach I am advocating for aims to decenter the cathedral as host. See Bretherton, *Christ and Common Life*, 279. See also Sacks, *Home We Build Together*, 15–18.

39. Wijsen, "New Wine," 43. Cited in Moyaert, *Fragile Identities*, 198.

can never be safeguarded by establishing and promoting closed symbolic communities.[40]

This approach to theology and Christian identity can be understood biblically, by paying attention to times when strangers and outsiders influence and change the perspectives of the people of God. Bretherton, for example, points to Rahab, Tamar, and Ruth, who despite being outside of the tribe of Israel influence it for the good in various ways. He writes:

> The heretic Samaritan and the pagan Syrophonecian woman, no less than the faithful Jewish man, can teach us something about God, how to live well, and that God can be present in "their" form of life, despite it being very different from "ours." . . . Enemies and those we find scandalous can know better who God is and teach those self-identified as the people of God what it means to be faithful, loving and just.[41]

Thus, a linguistic hospitable approach to public theology requires an openness to the other, in a way that does not absorb otherness, and yet maintains that there can be genuine interaction, critique and mutual building up in the midst of that diversity. However, this approach resists a tendency within the cathedral's current public theological approach, which tends to minimize the importance of maintaining otherness in its interactions.

THE "OTHER" AS GUEST AND HOST

The elevation of the concept of common humanity and human flourishing leads Govender to challenge the language of "otherness." During the final interview with Govender, we had been talking about the connections between the cathedral's relationships with LGBTQIA+ people and people of different faiths. Govender pointed out to me that I should notice that throughout the interview he had been deliberately avoiding the language of "others." For Govender, the language of otherness is problematic because it assumes an essential difference between groups of people, which then shapes people's actions towards those they perceive to be other. Govender told me in this interview that it is important to affirm and uphold that "there are no others," there is only one common humanity. The inclusive ministry of the cathedral, therefore, is to model that reality to the diverse visitors and participants that enter its doors. However, the philosophy of Paul Ricoeur, and the subsequent Ricoeurian approach to public theology, which I have

---

40. Moyaert, *Fragile Identities*, 225–26.
41. Bretherton, *Christ and Common Life*, 40.

been advocating for throughout this thesis, pose significant challenges to this perspective.

Junker-Kenny quotes an important passage in this regard from Ricoeur's essay "Universal Civilization and National Cultures." He states:

> The strange thing, in fact, is that there are many cultures and not a single humanity. The mere fact that there are different languages is already very disturbing and seems to indicate that as far back as history allows us to go, one finds historical shapes which are coherent and closed, constituted cultural wholes. Right from the start, so it seems, man is different from man; the shattered condition of languages is the most obvious sign of this primitive incohesion. This is the astonishing thing: humanity is not established in a single cultural style but has "congealed" in coherent, closed historical shapes: *the* cultures. The human condition is such that different contexts of civilization are possible.[42]

For Ricoeur, the fact of different languages is the first indication that otherness cannot be eliminated by appeals to "a single humanity." Each culture and its language produce vision and symbols through which distinctive convictions about human relationality, flourishing, time, and space are generated.[43] As a result, the dialogical task cannot reduce these convictions to cultural "conventions." Ricoeur writes:

> If subjects called to argumentation must lay aside everything that our moralists hold for simple conventions, then what remains of the singularity and otherness of the partners in the discussion? If their convictions are only conventions, then what distinguishes the partners from the other, apart from their interests? Only a vivid sense of the *otherness* of persons can safeguard the dialogical dimension against any reduction to a monologue conducted by an undifferentiated subject.[44]

This perspective challenges the Rawlsian model that the cathedral often adopts for its public activity. For the purpose of modeling inclusion and the oneness of humanity, the cathedral, unintentionally perhaps, practices these convictions in such a way that the distinctive convictions of different people groups are sometimes treated as conventions. By resisting the language of otherness, Govender is attempting to maintain the possibility of mutual dialogue, work, and unity across various potential divides, which

---

42. Ricoeur, "Universal Civilization and National Cultures," 280; emphasis in original. Cited in Junker-Kenny, *Religion and Public Reason*, 199.

43. Junker-Kenny, *Religion and Public Reason*, 192.

44. Ricoeur, "Theonomy," 296; emphasis added.

I have tried to argue is a deeply important and significant work. However, from a Ricoeurian perspective, this may often depend on a kind of homogenization, which presumes that no matter how different people may be, we are all *essentially* the same.

But the Ricoeurian perspective, while emphasizing plurality, diversity, and otherness, shouldn't be mistaken as an anti-public model, which would presume all cultures and religions are incommensurable with one another. While Ricoeur does not think that the task of various individuals and cultures within a democratic society is to find the singular moral foundation on which society should be built, he thinks it is adequate to admit to a plurality of foundations. This admittance of multiple foundations allows religious traditions to be co-foundational in the public sphere, offering their sources and interpretations as having potential moral energy that others can draw from for their imagination and motivation. No prior decisions can be made about what these types of engagement might produce (as in Rawls and Habermas), but this should not deter individuals and groups from exploring these moral sources. As Junker-Kenny summarizes:

> Ricoeur's discussion of the origins of authority, of different theories of democracy, of political governance and of civic action from different co-foundational traditions has spelt out a basic anthropology in which religions appear alongside other historical sources for self-understandings. It has also given a role to them on the enunciation level of the public sphere where they can offer a perspective that is relevant not only to their own communities, but for the future of the democratic project since it concerns basic questions of selves and their capability to act.[45]

When the particulars of culture, religion, or other identity categories are taken purely as potentially divisive, Manchester Cathedral could be limiting the way these distinctive perspectives, traditions, and sources can produce new imaginings of human relationality. Without a commitment to otherness in this way the cathedral runs the risk of operating with a hermeneutical closedness and being unable to be linguistically hospitable. In part, my three case study chapters demonstrate in different ways the importance of navigating inclusion through the tensions of particularity and otherness, in order that inclusion does not become the absorption of the other, producing an implicitly exclusionary publicness.

---

45. Junker-Kenny, *Religion and Public Reason*, 249.

OTHERNESS AND FORMATION: CHALLENGES FROM THE THREE AREAS OF PUBLIC ACTIVITY

The approach to publicness that I am advocating for aims to explore the complex and multifaceted ways that the kinds of exclusionary practices that Manchester Cathedral seeks to resist are first formed within the imagination of citizens. One of the implications of this approach is that public theology cannot simply be understood as an attempt to translate from religion to society, as the various sources of imaginative influence are dynamically present in both as to make a strong divide between these two categories firmly intelligible. Much of public theology assumes that the Christian tradition possesses the moral resources to create a just and peaceful society and that the main task is to make these resources intelligible to a wider audience than the Christian church. However, I have been trying to demonstrate that this is too simplistic an understanding of the relationship between the Christian tradition (or better yet, traditions), ethics, and society.

As Ricoeur argues, the religious map is an

> intersection of influences radiating out from the centres, the sources that are defined by their creativity and by their capacity to influence and to generate sources of response within others. It is thus through this phenomenon of an intersection of effects of illumination forming dense networks that the notion of the inter-religious would be defined, in opposition to the notion of a boundary.[46]

While this passage is first related to interreligious dialogue, it can also be applied to the relationship between religion and society. Rather than understanding these as fixed categories with clearly defined boundaries with their own languages, as in the post-liberal school of thought, they are often united by other influences. Thus, to try and bracket certain aspects of a tradition, in the Ricoeurian framework, is to fail to understand how certain doctrines, narratives, and perspectives are forming the interpretations of certain public issues.

This is significant in relation to the interreligious character of the cathedral. I have already highlighted the concerns of Ricoeur concerning Hans Küng's view that in order for faith communities to interact, they must bracket their divisive doctrines. But it is worth repeating at this point that Küng's concerns are similar to Govender's, in that he is attempting to eliminate the potentially divisive doctrines, in order to emphasize the commonalities between them and their common humanity. The "otherness" of

---

46. Ricoeur, "Cultures." Cited in Moyaert, *In Response to Religious Other*, 137.

one's religion is considered commonly as a potential source of violence and division.

However, two important consequences of this approach to the otherness of one's religion and the religion of another are important to highlight. The first is that religious doctrines and distinctiveness are reduced to their potential for violence. The use of public reason in this view is often to tame the otherwise inevitably violent tendencies of the religion. It is, therefore, implied that religions are inherently triumphalist in nature, seeking to dominate the public sphere with their own reason and doctrine at the expense of all others. Public reason, understood as finding the things different religious groups have in common, and bracketing those distinctives, plays the role of mediator between fundamentally violent groups. This is to ironically adopt the presumptions of a secularist ideology, which seeks to remove religion from the public sphere altogether as religions are interpreted as violent and incommensurable with modern reason.[47] The result is that even in inclusive interreligious settings suspicion is the primary way that those from different traditions relate to one another.

The second weakness of this approach is that it misses the potentially productive elements of one's own and another's faith in fostering common moral energy in democratic societies. If, for example, I interpret the distinctive elements of another religion such as Islam only as a potential source of disagreement and violence, the result is an implicit enforcement of a bracketing principle. To do this is to operate with the assumption that the public realm already operates with an adequate moral framework to achieve justice in society and that religions can simply offer tacit support to that language and framework. Habermas himself is critical of this kind of approach because he argues religious traditions perform the function of

> articulating an awareness of what is lacking or absent. They keep alive a sensitivity to failure and suffering. They reduce from oblivion the dimensions of our social and personal relations in which advances in cultural and social rationalisation have caused utter devastation. Who is to say that they do not contain encoded semantic potentialities that could provide inspiration

---

47. I am using here Luke Bretherton's distinction between secularity and secularism. *Secularity*, he understands, is the democratic form that pluralism in society takes, which can foster dialogues between both religious and nonreligious groups. *Secularism*, on the other hand, is a problematic singular phenomenon. Secularism "becomes the basis of a post-Christendom liberal regime of governance often imposed beyond the West through colonial means" (*Christ and Common Life*, 251).

if only their message were translated into rational discourse and their profane truth contents were set free?[48]

While I would resist characterizing religious traditions as simply having "encoded semantic potentialities" in need of being freed by secular reason, I would join with Habermas in affirming that the unique perspectives and insights from the diverse traditions can be an invaluable resource in the context of the exploration of public morality and meaning. However, this potentiality is reduced when the diverse traditions are reduced to their commonalities.[49]

Another area that I tried to demonstrate the importance of maintaining otherness and distinctive perspectives is in the area of racism and racial justice at Manchester Cathedral. I attempted to demonstrate, using the womanist theory of Emilie Townes, that the hegemonic imagination which contributes to the cultural production of evil is one that is formed both within the church and in UK society. Such imagination is produced through a range of media, political discourses and theologies. I argued with Townes and Jennings that whiteness is both a social vision and discourse through which particular diverse bodies are evaluated in terms of their ability to conform to a particular racialized norm, by the dominant, white group. As I identified, whiteness operates both in church and society, both in political and social discourse, and theologies. Thus, any approach to racial justice must interrogate the notions of whiteness present within institutions, discourses, and legislation.

As a result, attention to otherness and particularity must be maintained to resist assimilating diverse bodies into a "white" framework of legitimation. By assuming a posture of inclusion that doesn't interrogate whiteness and racially based standards of legitimation there is the potential for inclusion to become a form of absorption of the racial other. It is because of this that Townes argues, "Inclusion does not guarantee justice."[50] One way of examining this could be through the analysis of black and womanist theologies and how they critique and resist white theologies. Further, analysis and networks with black churches that emphasize liberation and resist white hegemonic theology would also be desirable, in order to interrogate

---

48. Habermas, *Divided West*, 6.

49. It is important to note that the Scriptural Reasoning and Scriptural Encounter groups both seek to discover the potentially productive elements of the different faith traditions. However, as I argued in ch. 4, the place of these groups within the wider life of the cathedral, especially since the retirement of Canon David Holgate, is yet to be seen.

50. Townes, *Womanist Ethics*, 58.

how these churches distinguish themselves from wider white theological frameworks, ecclesiologies, and practices.

Further, in relation to LGBTQIA+ inclusion, it may seem counterintuitive to emphasize the distinctive identities of LGBTQIA+ people while desiring to be inclusive. However, there are significant limits to inclusion that seeks to eliminate the otherness of LGBTQIA+ people. For example, as Rachael Huegerich argues, to be transgender goes beyond our "contextually articulated, but firmly grasped, conceptualisations of the universe."[51] I would argue this is true for all those identifying under the LGBTQIA+ umbrella. As a result, queer people are often marginalized and excluded in both religious communities and secular institutions within society. However, it should not be imagined that in order to include queer people in a religious institution like the cathedral that the strategy should be to demonstrate how queer people fit within dominant, status-quo conceptualizations of the universe. The danger with adopting a strategy that emphasizes similarity at the cost of otherness is that the gendered conceptualizations that made such exclusions intelligible are left intact.

As I demonstrated in chapter 6, heterosexuality and patriarchy are dominant hierarchical visions which have and continue to shape both society and the church. Heterosexuality as an ideology is a particular vision of the way humans ought to relate and reproduce that is enforced implicitly or explicitly in various contexts. The problem is that heterosexuality, which is at the heart of LGBTQIA+ exclusion which the cathedral seeks to resist, is part of a social imaginary which needs to be deconstructed on multiple levels, because it is formed both by our economic organization as a society (neoliberal capitalism) and our ecclesial and theological organizations. As I have argued, "inclusion" may be a good starting point for this work, but in itself is not sufficient if inclusion does not lead to the transformation of the visions of those who are doing the including and the structures that upheld exclusive practices.

Thus, while the concept of common humanity is an important first principle, it is not sufficient for understanding how different visions of humanity are formed and articulated within theology, politics, economy, and other areas which involve the production of knowledge and power. Instead, to remain with the example of trans people, while recognizing the trans person as a fellow human being who must be treated with respect, dignity, and love, it should not be assumed that this entails perceiving trans people as immediately intelligible. To be hospitable towards a trans person is to engage in a "genuine embrace" which "entails the ability-not-to-understand

---

51. Huegerich, "Sacred Self-Expression," 183.

but to accept the other as a question." Huegerich argues, "They are a question because the aim of flexible gender systems is not to make one understandable or intelligible, but [to maintain] that the gender systems are always open to new possibilities."[52]

Therefore, my analysis of the public theology of Manchester Cathedral demonstrates that any inclusive public approach to people of all faiths and none, to people of diverse racial and cultural backgrounds, and to those within the LGBTQ+ community requires an approach that seeks to engage their unique perspectives and maintain their otherness, while seeking to develop loving trust with these communities.

CONCLUSION

My analysis has demonstrated the importance of linguistic hospitable approaches to publicness, which also emphasize the exploration of how ethical and social imaginations are formed in particular contexts. Such an approach requires deep relationships with others in order to explore and challenge exclusionary symbols and narratives. This shows that part of the public theological task, therefore, is to create space where theology and traditions themselves can be challenged and reformed by those people and groups often marginalized and excluded from dominant public spheres and the church. I have demonstrated how an emphasis on common humanity, and other unifying principles, can be implicitly exclusionary when diverse social visions are bracketed. My argument in this chapter has been to demonstrate the necessity of engaging these unique visions rather than bypassing these unique perspectives in the search for "common ground." Indeed, it could be that an emphasis on common values, common humanity, or even human flourishing can be a way to absorb unique hermeneutics, and thus identity, into a larger, abstract whole.

In contrast, I have argued that a more Ricoeurian linguistically hospitable approach to publicness is maintained through practices in which the cathedral is not only the host of diverse people but their guests. To be a guest is to enter into a relationship of risk in which there can be significant transformations that take place through hearing "a foreign word at home." Such risk entails the possibility of repentance, theological revision, and the development of new practices. As I have shown in this book, this is a necessary aspect of any truly inclusive public theology.

52. Huegerich, "Sacred Self-Expression," 184.

CONCLUSION

LESSONS LEARNED

At the east end of the south quire aisle at Manchester Cathedral is a stained glass window called "The Healing Window." This was installed in 2004 to commemorate the restoration of the cathedral after the IRA bombing in 1996.[1] Five words are etched into the stone at the bottom of the window: diversity, healing, glory, wholeness, and inclusion. Whenever I go to the cathedral, I always walk up to this window and have a moment to reflect on it. If I ever bring friends or family to the cathedral, I make sure at some point I bring them over to this window. I think what draws me to this window is that it sums up and reflects Manchester Cathedral's public theology as I have come to understand it. The cathedral prides itself on being a place of welcome and inclusion, for people of all faiths and none; for people from all cultures and nations; and for people of all gender and sexual identities. It is a place primarily of prayer and worship and as such offers itself as a space for healing and glory for individuals and communities as they interact with the Living God who welcomes all into the kingdom.

In this book, I have sought to understand how Manchester Cathedral practices this public theology in a variety of contexts. In doing so, I have presented Manchester Cathedral as a model of religious public engagement that others can learn from, while also exploring how the cathedral's practice and discourse could develop through engaging different approaches to publicness and theology. The arguments that I have made throughout this thesis seek to elucidate the fact that engaging with humans within any sphere for the causes of justice and inclusion is never straightforward and requires a variety of practices and deep reflection. Here I would like to offer some of

---

1. For more information on the stained glass windows at Manchester Cathedral, see Morris, "Cathedral, 1983 to Present," 295–301.

the lessons I have learned in my time at Manchester Cathedral and in writing this book.

THERE ARE MULTIPLE APPROACHES TO PUBLIC THEOLOGY

Public theologians aim to contribute to issues of common concern in the public sphere in order to promote "the welfare of the city" (Jer 29:7). As such, public theology often adopts a discourse-based approach, seeing the primary context that it operates in as arenas of moral debate and policy-making. One of the key tensions that public theologians navigate is how to make their perspectives and contributions intelligible and convincing to those outside of their religious communities. However, in chapters 1 and 2 I argued that there are diverse understandings of the nature of the public sphere, and thus the nature of publicness, that impact the way public theologians may understand their roles and methods in the public sphere. Each of these approaches assumes different views on the role of religion within society and religion's potential publicness, though these assumptions are not always explicated and analyzed.

Chapter 1 demonstrated that these approaches to publicness largely differ in their understanding of what grounds religious arguments and contributions can be made in public. For John Rawls, a theory of justice and a commitment to political liberalism provide the unifying ground for consensus in the public realm, which religions can offer tacit support to, so long as they translate their concepts into these unifying terms. Jürgen Habermas suggests that religions can contribute moral energy to the public sphere that secular reason has not been able to replace. However, he suggests that the religious doctrines, symbols, and narratives should be demythologized in order for the religious contribution to be translated in a way that can be convincing to a secular public.

In contrast to Rawls and Habermas, Paul Ricoeur's philosophy does not reduce the public sphere to spaces of policy making. Rather, publicness is related to spaces of formation because each culture, tradition, and language contains its own systems of meaning and ethical legitimation which shapes the way the good and the right are understood. For Ricoeur, part of the public religious task is to explore these differences in order to discover common grounds and understanding, rather than presuming them. Ricoeur, then, sees the most valuable contributions of religion in the public sphere as resulting from unique religious perspectives.

The Ricoeurian Approach to Public Theology: We Are Hermeneutical All the Way Down

The Ricoeurian approach that I have held up as the most constructive approach to publicness throughout this thesis demonstrates that exploration of social issues in the public sphere requires multiple forms of engagement. This is because our social visions and hermeneutical interpretations of social issues are formed by multiple sources. Because these social visions are present in both church and society, any activity or practice that seeks to engage these imaginative forms should be considered public. Thus, the Ricoeurian approach to public theology challenges public theologians to not only contribute to public debates but to explore how the imagination of citizens is formed in public. As a result, a focus on practices as well as discourse is a crucial aspect of the Ricoeurian approach.

In this way, the Ricoeurian approach has been helpful in developing and shaping my own methodological approach to public theology. I have offered a unique approach to public theology which I have called a "publicness-ethnographic approach." This approach has resisted primary definitions of public theology which emphasize discourse and debate as the overall scope of public theology. Such definitions of public theology have meant that ethnographic studies of religious communities that aim for publicness have not been largely conducted within the field. However, this study of Manchester Cathedral demonstrates that much of this institution's, and other religious institutions, important public theological work is practice as well as discourse.

The Ricoeurian approach that I have adopted also challenges public theology to explore the exclusionary nature of the Habermasian public sphere that many public theologians adopt when producing their work. I argue this because public theology has largely not engaged with the topics of racial justice and LGBTQ+ inclusion. One of the reasons for this is that each of these topics requires engagement with particular social issues which affect particular social groups more than others. Because public theology often adopts a Habermasian approach to publicness, it attempts to relate wild or weak public spheres into an overarching strong public sphere.

However, as I have shown in this book such approaches to an "inclusive" public sphere are actually exclusive. These public spheres depend on approaches to public reason that stronger groups have predetermined. As a result, the dynamics present within the political spheres that lead to the production of wild public spheres and their separation from the dominant groups are not explored. Instead, I have demonstrated how a Ricoeurian approach to wild publics enables these groups to communicate with other publics, including strong publics, without the demand that they be translated into the terms of reason set by the strong public. Instead, the margins can "remain at the margins," to use Lisa Isherwood and Marcella Althaus-Reid's phraseology.[2] Thus the Ricoeurian approach seeks to understand how to engage the diversity of publics in an inclusive manner which simultaneously resists homogenization. This is significant for Manchester Cathedral because of its emphasis on inclusion as a primary lens through which the team understand cathedral activities. The consistent challenge throughout this thesis has been to promote inclusion without that inclusion becoming homogenizing.

WE MUST FOCUS NOT ONLY ON WHAT TO SAY, BUT HOW WE ARE FORMED

The Ricoeurian approach to public theology, which focuses on the formation of the subject in the context of their culture gives resources to Manchester Cathedral to further explore how diverse publics should be engaged. Each of the evaluations of key areas of engagement demonstrated the importance of attending to the particularity of an individual or public because each of the topics addressed is rooted in competing social and ethical visions. These visions can only be accessed by a deep engagement with members of various worldviews and cultures, attempting to elevate their subjective experiences and interpretations of particular social issues.

For example, I demonstrated that the cathedral often adopts a Rawlsian approach to its interreligious character. This is because it tends to ground its interreligious engagements on areas of common ground and unifying principles such as justice or peace. As a result, penultimate concerns are kept as the primary concern of interreligious engagements, and ultimate concerns are largely kept out of discussions. I argued that part of the reason the cathedral opts for this approach is to avoid any practices and discourses of triumphalism which could lead to other religious groups feeling excluded. However, I also demonstrated that a religious individual's interpretation of a penultimate concern and the good cannot be divorced from their understanding of ultimate concerns. In other words, their religious formation affects the way that ethical social issues are interpreted and understood. Thus, a public theological task is to understand these visions.

Further, in my analysis of the cathedral's public theology of racial justice I demonstrated that the cathedral often approaches racism in terms of individualistic acts rather than treating racism as systemic. For example,

2. Isherwood and Althaus-Reid, "Queering Theology," 3.

the cathedral often focuses on racially based hate crimes and modern slavery. However, I demonstrated that racism is formed in the imagination of citizens through a variety of sources, and whiteness is an interpretive lens formed within British culture. I also argued that whiteness is intertwined with theology, particularly the theology of the CofE, given its history of racism. As a result, I argued that a focus on the formation of racial structures would also include an exploration of the role that theology has played in that formation, and thus potentially lead to alternative theologies formed in dialogue with those often excluded because of racial discrimination.

Likewise, in chapter 6, I demonstrated that the cathedral's approach to LGBTQ+ inclusion assumes that the language of inclusion provides a shared moral ground between the cathedral and wider society. Thus, one of the primary understandings of God at the cathedral is that God is inclusive. Thus, the language of inclusion is the primary lens that the cathedral uses to understand its work in regard to this topic, and thus its primary discourse in public. However, I showed that while inclusion is a helpful value and a good starting point, it is not a sufficient value because it does not necessarily interrogate how patriarchy and heterosexism function structurally in church and society. As a result, the theological and social symbols which justified exclusion are not necessarily dismantled. I thus argued that the public theological task of affirming communities in this area must also include the interrogation and revision of theology because theology is understood to be a formative practice.

THEOLOGY DOESN'T JUST NEED TO BE TRANSLATED, IT NEEDS TO BE DECOLONIZED

Therefore, my analysis has demonstrated that theology itself is part of the social vision of Christians and that theology itself must be interrogated in public. Rather than seeing theology and faith simply as motivators for public engagement, this study shows that theological reflection and revision, when connected to practices of justice, are required to resist harmful imaginative forms both within the church and outside of it. Thus, direct engagement with theological themes, texts, and symbols shouldn't be seen as a matter of private faith and devotion. Rather, it should be seen as a necessary aspect of religious public activism because public activism is formed by visions of what it means to be human and what a just society looks like. Theology shapes and informs these visions for Christians, just as theology is shaped and informed by these visions. In other words, there is a dynamic connection between theology and practice in public that should not be undermined.

For this reason, I have demonstrated that part of the need for a Ricoeurian approach to public theology so that the legacies of harmful theologies can be confronted and interrogated. I demonstrated, for example, that anti-Semitism, racism, and homophobia in the church have been historically (and presently) theologically motivated and legitimated. As a result, harmful theologies can't simply be bracketed in a Rawlsian fashion because they are recognized to be harmful. Rather, I have offered an alternative framework which engages voices often excluded (e.g. black, womanist, and queer theologies) to explore to understand what work public theologians need to do to form and articulate theologies that are healing, rather than harmful.[3]

Thus, black, womanist, and queer theologians emphasize the need for communities to wrestle with the ways we have talked about God, sin, salvation, decency, and ethics have all contributed to great evils in the church and beyond. And it must be noted that theological wrestling, revision, and decolonization is nothing less than the pursuit of the living God who is present to those most harmed by the churches' toxic colonial theologies. In this way, public theological reflection should be conducted with direct input and critique from those who have experienced various forms of exclusion and harm.

Importantly, as I argued most strongly in chapter 7, these practices of inclusion should resist forms of homogenization which assume a common ground, or sameness, which eliminates otherness. While the cathedral is right to emphasize the value of common humanity as a way of affirming equality in the public sphere, it should not assume that the categories of common humanity and human flourishing affirm an essential sameness between all humans. Thus, common humanity should be affirmed, while also maintaining a sense of otherness, in order to truly hear a strange word from the "other."

---

3. One area in which this framework can be applied in the context of future study is to explore how the liturgical practices of a cathedral or church, understood as formational practices, can be evaluated and revised within the context of forming a more just and inclusive ethical vision. In this way, future study could combine liturgical studies, public theology, and the theologies of marginalized communities by applying a Ricoeurian framework to theology and formation.

A FINAL WORD

The complexity of Manchester Cathedral itself is only exceeded by the complexities that shape the public realm, social discourse, and the public imagination. And this book has focused exclusively on just one institution. Therefore, time and effort must be taken to discover how exclusions and prejudices are formed socially and theologically in multiple arenas, denominations and religious groups, in order to resist those discourses and theologies which continue to cause human and nonhuman harms. Yet only a hospitable approach to the other has the potential to contribute constructively within these complex dynamics. I have shown in this thesis that theologies and philosophies that engage with questions about justice, inclusion, and the role of religion in post-secular, pluralist societies give Christian institutions like Manchester Cathedral resources to draw on as they engage multifaceted and diverse publics with various needs and desires. Therefore, it is my hope that this book can inspire and challenge those who have read, to be a guest as well as a host, to listen as well as speak, to revise their theology, and not just translate it. I also hope that many will be inspired by the public work of Manchester Cathedral, to engage with a variety of issues of common concern in society, while upholding the values of diversity, healing, glory, wholeness, and inclusion.

BIBLIOGRAPHY

Althaus-Reid, Marcella. *Indecent Theology: Theological Perversions in Sex, Gender and Politics.* London: Routledge, 2000.
———. *The Queer God.* London: Routledge, 2003.
———. "Sexual Strategies in Practical Theology: Indecent Theology and the Plotting of Desire with Some Degree of Success." *Theology & Sexuality* 7 (1997) 45–52.
Althaus-Reid, Marcella, and Lisa Isherwood. "Thinking Theology and Queer Theory." *Feminist Theology* 15 (2007) 302–14.
Archbishops' Anti-Racism Taskforce. *From Lament to Action: The Report of the Archbishops' Anti-Racism Taskforce.* Church of England, Apr. 22, 2021. https://www.churchofengland.org/sites/default/files/2021-04/FromLamentToAction-report.pdf.
Arel, Stephanie N., and Shelly Rambo. *Post-Traumatic Public Theology.* Cham, Switzerland: Springer, 2016.
Atherton, John. *Marginalization.* London: SCM, 2003.
———. *Public Theology for Changing Times.* London: SPCK, 2000.
Augustine. *City of God.* Translated by Henry Bettenson. Penguin Classics. London: Penguin, 2003.
Avis, Paul. *A Ministry Shaped by Mission.* London: T&T Clark, 2005.
Barton, John. "Prof John Barton: The Bible in *Living in Love and Faith*." Modern Church, Nov. 25, 2020. https://modernchurch.org.uk/prof-john-barton-the-bible-in-living-in-love-and-faith.
BBC. "Synod Debate: Justin Welby Calls for 'Radical New Inclusion.'" BBC, Feb. 15, 2017. https://www.bbc.com/news/av/uk-38987882.
Bell, Daniel M., Jr. "State and Civil Society." In *The Blackwell Companion to Political Theology*, edited by Peter Scott and William T. Cavanaugh, 423–38. Blackwell Companions to Religion. Hoboken, NJ: Wiley, 2019.
Benne, Robert. *The Paradoxical Vision: A Public Theology for the Twenty-First Century.* Minneapolis: Fortress, 1995.
Berger, Peter L. "The Desecularization of the World: A Global Overview." In *The Desecularization of the World: Resurgent Religion and World Politics*, edited by Peter Berger, 1–18. Grand Rapids: Eerdmans, 1999.
———. *The Sacred Canopy: Elements of a Sociological Theory of Religion.* Garden City, NJ: Doubleday, 1969.

Berggren, Niclas, and Christian Bjørnskov. "Is the Importance of Religion in Daily Life Related to Social Trust? Cross-Country and Cross-State Comparisons." *Journal of Economic Behavior & Organization* 80 (2011) 459–80.

Bevans, Stephen B. *Models of Contextual Theology*. Faith and Culture. Maryknoll, NY: Orbis, 2002.

Blundell, Boyd. *Paul Ricoeur Between Theology and Philosophy: Detour and Return*. Bloomington: Indiana University Press, 2010.

Boer, Theo., et al. "Legal Euthanasia in Pastoral Practice: Experiences of Pastors in the Protestant Church in the Netherlands." *IJPT* 14 (2020) 41–67.

Boff, Leonardo. *Jesus Christ Liberator: A Critical Christology for our Time*. London: SPCK, 1978.

Bohache, Thomas. *Christology from the Margins*. London: SCM, 2008.

Breitenberg, Harold E. "To Tell the Truth: Will the Real Public Theology Please Stand Up?" *Journal of the Society of Christian Ethics* 23 (2003) 55–96.

Bretherton, Luke. *Christ and the Common Life: Political Theology and the Case for Democracy*. Grand Rapids: Eerdmans, 2019.

———. *Christianity and Contemporary Politics: The Conditions and Possibilities of Faithful Witness*. Chichester: Wiley-Blackwell, 2010.

———. "A Postsecular Politics? Inter-Faith Relations as a Civic Practice." *JAAR* 79 (2011) 346–77.

———. "State, Democracy & Community Organising." In *A Companion to Public Theology*, edited by Sebastian Kim and Katie Day, 93–118. Companions to Modern Theology 1. Leiden: Brill, 2017.

Brown, Malcolm. "Anglican Social Theology Tomorrow." In *Anglican Social Theology: Renewing the Vision Today*, edited by Malcolm Brown et al., 175–89. London: Church House, 2014.

———. "The Case for Anglican Social Theology Today." In *Anglican Social Theology: Renewing the Vision Today*, edited by Malcolm Brown et al., 1–27. London: Church House, 2014.

———. "Establishment: Some Theological Considerations." *Ecclesiastical Law Journal* 21 (2019) 329–41.

———. "Politics as the Church's Business: William Temple's Christianity and Social Order Revisited." *Journal of Anglican Studies* 5 (2007) 163–85.

Budhi-Thornton, Dominic. "Harvey Nichols Fashion Shows, Vintage Fairs, and the Holy Eucharist: Manchester Cathedral as Post-Secular Place." *Networking Knowledge* 16 (2023) 63–75.

Burns, Stephen, and Anita Monro. "Which Public? Inspecting the House of Public Theology?" In *Public Theology and the Challenge of Feminism*, edited by Anita Monro and Stephen Burns, 1–14. Gender, Theology and Spirituality. London Routledge, 2015.

Butler, Judith. *Notes Toward a Performative Theory of Assembly*. Cambridge, MA: Harvard University Press, 2015.

Cady, Linell. "Public Theology and the Postsecular Turn." *IJPT* (2014) 292–312.

Calvert, Arran J. "Durham Cathedral Can Be Whatever You Want It to Be: Examining the Negotiation of Space and Time." *Ethnography* 20 (2019) 523–40.

Cameron, Helen, et al. *Talking About God in Practice: Theological Action Research and Practical Theology*. London: SCM, 2010.

Carter, Craig A. "The Legacy of an Inadequate Christology: Yoder's Critique of Niebuhr's Christ and Culture." *Mennonite Quarterly Review* 77 (2003) 387–401.
Cartledge, Mark. "Public Theology and Empirical Research: Developing an Agenda." *IJPT* (2016) 145–66.
Cavanaugh, William T. "Ecclesial Ethics and the Gospel Sine Glossa: Sacramental Politics and the Love of the World." *Modern Theology* 36 (2020) 501–23.
———. "Is Public Theology Really Public? Some Problems with Civil Society." *Annual of the Society of Christian Ethics* 21 (2001) 105–23.
———. *Theopolitical Imagination: Discovering the Liturgy as a Political Act in an Age of Global Consumerism*. London: T&T Clark, 2002.
Changeux, Jean-Pierre, and Paul Ricoeur. *What Makes Us Think? A Neuroscientist and Philosopher Argue About Ethics, Human Nature, and the Brain*. Princeton, NJ: Princeton University Press, 2000.
Church Buildings Review Group. *Report of the Church Buildings Review Group*. Church of England, Sept. 2015. https://www.churchofengland.org/sites/default/files/2017-12/church_buildings_review_2015.pdf.
Church of England, The. "House of Bishops Pastoral Guidance on Same Sex Marriage." Church of England, Feb. 15, 2014. https://www.churchofengland.org/media/press-releases/house-bishops-pastoral-guidance-same-sex-marriage.
———. *Living in Love and Faith: Christian Teaching and Learning About Identity, Sexuality, Relationships and Marriage*. London: Church House, 2020.
———. "The Living in Love and Faith Journey." Church of England, n.d. https://www.churchofengland.org/resources/living-love-and-faith/living-love-and-faith-journey.
———. "Pastoral Principles Course." Church of England, Apr. 30, 2021. https://www.churchofengland.org/media-and-news/press-releases/pastoral-principles-course.
———. "Shared Conversations Archive." Church of England, n.d. https://www.churchofengland.org/about/general-synod/structure/house-bishops/shared-conversations-archive.
Church Times. "*Living in Love and Faith*: It's Out, It's Long, It's Good." *Church Times*, Nov. 9, 2020. https://www.churchtimes.co.uk/articles/2020/13-november/comment/leader-comment/llf-it-s-out-it-s-long-it-s-good.
Clifford, James, and George E. Marcus, eds. *Writing Culture: The Poetics and Politics of Ethnography*. Berkeley: University of California Press, 1986.
Cloke, Paul, et al. "Postsecularity, Political Resistance, and Protest in the Occupy Movement." *Antipode* 48 (2016) 497–523.
Commission on Race and Ethnic Disparities. *The Report of the Commission on Race and Ethnic Disparities*. Gov.UK, Mar. 31, 2021; last updated Apr. 28, 2021. https://www.gov.uk/government/publications/the-report-of-the-commission-on-race-and-ethnic-disparities.
Comstock, Gary. "Two Types of Narrative Theology." *JAAR* (1987) 687–717.
Cone, James H. *Black Theology and Black Power*. New York: Orbis, 1989.
———. *A Black Theology of Liberation*. Philadelphia: Lippincott, 1969.
Cooper, Thia. *Queer and Indecent: An Introduction to the Theology of Marcella Althaus Reid*. London: SCM, 2021.
Cornwall, Susannah. "'State of Mind' Versus 'Concrete Set of Facts': The Contrasting of Transgender and Intersex in Church Documents on Sexuality." *Theology & Sexuality* 15 (2009) 7–28.

———. "Stranger in Our Midst: The Becoming of the Queer God in the Theology of Marcella Althaus-Reid." In *Dancing Theology in Fetish Boots: Essays in Honour of Marcella Althaus Reid*, edited by Lisa Isherwood and Mark D. Jordan, 95–112. London: SCM, 2010.

Cronshaw, Darren. "Exploring Local Church Praxis of Public Theology." *IJPT* 14 (2020) 68–96.

———. "Resisting the Empire in Young Adult Fiction: Lessons from Hunger Games." *IJPT* 13 (2019) 119–39.

Das Gupta, Tania, et al. "Preface." In *Race and Racialization: Essential Readings*, edited by Tania Das Gupta et al., ix–xiii. Toronto: Canadian Scholars, 2018.

Davison, Andrew, ed. *Imaginative Apologetics: Theology, Philosophy and the Catholic Tradition*. London: SCM, 2011.

Dawkins, Richard. *The God Delusion*. London: Bantam, 2006.

Day, Katie. "The Construction of Public Theology: An Ethnographic Study of the Relationship Between the Theological Academy and Local Clergy in South Africa." *IJPT* 2 (2008) 354–78.

Day, Katie, and Sebastian Kim. "Introduction." In *A Companion to Public Theology*, edited by Sebastian Kim and Katie Day, i–xx. Companions to Modern Theology 1. Leiden: Brill, 2017.

Day, Benjamin S., et al. "Scholarly Circles: A Practice for Thinking Christianly in the University." *IJPT* 14 (2020) 389–97.

D'Costa, Gavin. *Theology in the Public Square: Church, Academy and Nation*. Challenges in Contemporary Theology. Oxford: Blackwell, 2005.

Delgado, Richard, and Jean Stefancic. *Critical Race Theory: The Cutting Edge*. 2nd ed. Philadelphia: Temple University Press, 2000.

DiAngelo, Robin. *White Fragility: Why It's So Hard for White People to Talk About Racism*. Boston: Beacon, 2018.

Doak, Mary. *Reclaiming Narrative for Public Theology*. New York: State University of New York Press, 2004.

Douglas, Kelly Brown. *The Black Christ*. 25th anniv. ed. New York: Orbis, 2019.

———. *Sexuality and the Black Church: A Womanist Perspective*. Maryknoll, NY: Orbis, 1999.

Elan, Priya. "Pride Rainbow Merchandise Is Everywhere, but Who Gets the Pot of Gold?" *Guardian*, June 13, 2021. https://www.theguardian.com/world/2021/jun/13/pride-rainbow-merchandise-is-everywhere-but-who-gets-the-pot-of-gold.

Emerson, Robert, et al. "Participant Observation and Fieldnotes." In *Handbook of Ethnography*, edited by Paul Atkinson et al., 352–68. London: SAGE, 2001.

Fackre, Gabriel. "Max Stackhouse: A Collegial Appreciation." In *Public Theology for a Global Society: Essays in Honor of Max L. Stackhouse*, edited by Deirdre King Hainsworth and Scott R. Paeth, 238–51. Grand Rapids, Eerdmans, 2010.

Fekete, Liz. "Reclaiming the Fight Against Racism in the UK." *Race & Class* 61 (2020) 87–95.

Floyd-Thomas, Stacey M., ed. *Deeper Shades of Purple: Womanism in Religion and Society*. Religion, Race, and Ethnicity. New York: New York University Press, 2006.

Fox, Aine. "Church of England 'Deeply Institutionally Racist,' Admits Archbishop of Canterbury." *Independent*, Feb. 11, 2020. https://www.independent.co.uk/

news/uk/home-news/justin-welby-church-england-windrush-racism-christianity-a9330606.html.

Forrester, Duncan B. *Christian Justice and Public Theology*. Cambridge Studies in Ideology and Religion. Cambridge: Cambridge University Press, 1997.

———. "The Scope of Public Theology." *Studies in Christian Ethics* 17 (2004) 5–19.

France-Williams, A. D. A. *Ghost Ship: Institutional Racism and the Church of England*. London: SCM, 2020.

Fraser, Nancy. "Rethinking the Public Sphere." *Social Text* 8 (1990) 56–80.

Fretheim, Kjetil. *Interruption and Imagination: Public Theology in Changing Times*. Eugene, OR: Pickwick, 2016.

Frey, Daniel. "Preface." In *Hermeneutics*, by Paul Ricoeur, edited by Daniel Frey and Nicola Strickler, vii–xii. Vol. 2 of *Writings and Lectures*. Cambridge: Polity, 2013.

Fulkerson, Mary. "Ethnography in Theology: A Work in Process." In *Lived Theology: New Perspectives on Method, Style, and Pedagogy*, edited by Charles Marsh et al., 115–33. Oxford: Oxford University Press, 2016.

Fulton, Brad, and Richard L. Wood. "Interfaith Community Organizing: Emerging Theological and Organizational Challenges." *IJPT* 6 (2012) 398–420.

Garcia, Leovino. "On Paul Ricoeur and the Translation—Interpretation of Cultures." *Thesis Eleven* 94 (2008) 72–87.

Garner, Steve. *Whiteness: An Introduction*. London: Routledge, 2007.

Geanellos, Rene. "Exploring Ricoeur's Hermeneutic Theory of Interpretation as a Method of Analysing Research Texts." *Nursing Inquiry* 7 (2000) 112–19.

General Synod. *Marriage and Same Sex Relationships After the Shared Conversations: A Report from the House of Bishops*. Equal, Jan. 2017. GS 2055. https://cofe-equal-marriage.org.uk/wp-content/uploads/2022/12/marriage-and-same-sex-relationships-after-the-shared-conversations.pdf.

General Synod of the Church of England. *Issues in Human Sexuality: A Statement by the House of Bishops*. London: Church House, 1991.

Giordano, Chiara. "'Boris Johnson Says Attacking Statues Is 'Lying About Our History' and Protests Have Been 'Hijacked by Extremists.'" *Independent*, June 12, 2020. https://www.independent.co.uk/news/uk/politics/boris-johnson-statues-churchill-mandela-colston-protests-black-lives-matter-a9562626.html.

Goode, Lee. *Jürgen Habermas: Democracy and the Public Sphere*. Modern European Thinkers. London: Pluto, 2005.

Goto, Courtney T. *Taking on Practical Theology: The Idolization of Context and the Hope of Community*. Theology in Practice 6. Leiden: Brill, 2018.

Graham, Elaine. *Apologetics Without Apology: Speaking of God in a World Troubled by Religion*. Didsbury Lectures. Eugene, OR: Cascade, 2017.

Graham, Elaine, and Anna Rowlands, eds. *Pathways to the Public Square: Practical Theology in an Age of Pluralism; International Academy of Practical Theology, Manchester 2003*. International Practical Theology. Münster: LIT, 2003.

Graham, Elaine L. *Between a Rock and a Hard Place: Public Theology and the Post-Secular Turn*. London: SCM, 2013.

———. *Transforming Practice: Pastoral Theology in an Age of Uncertainty*. Eugene, OR: Wipf and Stock, 1996.

Green, Chris. *Toward a Pentecostal Theology of the Lord's Supper*. Cleveland: Center of Pentecostal Theology, 2012.

Gregory, Jeremy, ed. *Manchester Cathedral: A History of the Collegiate Church and Cathedral, 1421 to the Present*. Manchester: Manchester University Press, 2021.

Grey, Jacqui. "'Princess Theology' and the Promotion of Women Within Pentecostalism." In *Public Theology and the Challenge of Feminism*, edited by Anita Monro and Stephen Burns, 75–85. Gender, Theology and Spirituality. London Routledge, 2015.

Guinness, Os. "A Biblical Basis for Apologetics." Be Thinking, 2010. Part 2 of "The Essence of Apologetics." https://www.bethinking.org/apologetics/the-essence-of-apologetics/2-biblical-basis.

Habermas, Jürgen. *Between Facts and Norms: Contributions to a Discourse Theory of Law and Democracy*. Translated by William Rehg. Studies in Contemporary German Social Thought. Cambridge, MA: MIT Press, 1992.

———. *Between Naturalism and Religion: Philosophical Essays*. Translated by Ciarin Cronin. Cambridge: Polity, 2008.

———. *The Divided West*. Edited and translated by Ciarin Cronin. Cambridge: Polity, 2006.

———. *The Future of Human Nature*. Translated by William Rehg et al. Cambridge: Polity, 2003.

———. "Notes on Post-Secular Society." *New Perspectives Quarterly* 25 (2008) 17–29.

———. *The Structural Transformation of the Public Sphere: An Inquiry into a Category of Bourgeois Society*. Translated by Thomas Burger with Frederick Lawrence. Studies in Contemporary German Social Thought. Cambridge: Polity, 1962.

Habermas, Jürgen, et al. *An Awareness of What Is Missing: Faith and Reason in a Post-Secular Age*. Translated by Ciarin Cronin. Cambridge: Polity, 2010.

Halberstam, Judith. "The Anti-Social Turn in Queer Studies." *Graduate Journal of Social Science* 5 (2008) 140–56.

Hanson, Paul. "The Bible and Public Theology." In *A Companion to Public Theology*, edited by Sebastian Kim and Katie Day, 23–39. Companions to Modern Theology 1. Leiden: Brill, 2017.

Hart, David Bentley. "Quentin Tarantino's Cosmic Justice." *New York Times*, Aug. 6, 2019. https://www.nytimes.com/2019/08/06/opinion/quentin-tarantino.html.

Hauerwas, Stanley. *After Christendom?* Nashville: Abingdon, 1991.

———. "The Church's One Foundation Is Christ Her Lord; or, In a World Without Foundations All We Have Is the Church." In *Theology Without Foundations: Religious Practice and the Future of Theological Truth*, edited by Stanley Hauerwas et al., 143–62. Nashville: Abingdon, 1994.

———. *A Community of Character: Toward a Constructive Christian Social Ethic*. Notre Dame, IN: University of Notre Dame Press, 1981.

———. *The Peaceable Kingdom: A Primer in Christian Ethics*. London: SCM, 1984.

———. *Unleashing the Scriptures: Freeing the Bible from American Captivity*. Nashville: Abingdon, 1993.

———. *Vision and Virtue*. Indiana: University of Notre Dame Press, 1974.

———. "Will the Real Sectarian Stand Up?" *Theology Today* 44 (1987) 87–94.

Hauerwas, Stanley, and Samuel Wells. "Christian Ethics as Informed Prayer." In *The Blackwell Companion to Christian Ethics*, edited by Stanley Hauerwas and Samuel Wells, 3–12. Companions to Religion. Oxford: Blackwell, 2004.

Hauerwas, Stanley, et al., eds. *The Wisdom of the Cross: Essays in Honor of John Howard Yoder*. Grand Rapids: Eerdmans, 1999.

Heyer, Kristin. "How Does Theology Go Public? Rethinking the Debate Between David Tracy and George Lindbeck." *Political Theology* 5 (2004) 307–27.
Hick, John. *Disputed Questions in Theology and the Philosophy of Religion*. London: Macmillan, 1993.
———. *Philosophy of Religion*. London: Prentice-Hall International, 1973.
Hogan, Jennie. "A Lesbian Living in Love and Faith." *Crucible* (July 2021) 20–29.
Holgate, David, and Rachel Starr. *Biblical Hermeneutics*. SCM Studyguide. London: SCM, 2006.
House of Bishops, The. "Civil Partnerships—a Pastoral Statement from the House of Bishops of the Church of England." Church of England, July 25, 2005. https://www.churchofengland.org/sites/default/files/2017-11/house-of-bishops-statement-on-civil-partnerships-2005.pdf.
Huegerich, Rachael. "Sacred Self-Expression: Love and Trans Authenticity." *Feminist Theology* 29 (2021) 170–86.
Hughes, John. "After Temple? The Recent Renewal of Anglican Social Thought." In *Anglican Social Theology: Renewing the Vision Today*, edited by Malcolm Brown et al., 74–101. London: Church House, 2014.
Hunt, Mary E. "Overcoming the Fear of Love." In *Sermons Seldom Heard: Women Proclaim Their Lives*, edited by Annie Lally Milhaven, 157–67. New York: Crossroad, 1991.
Ipgrave, Julia. "Interreligious Engagement in Urban Spaces: An Introduction." In *Interreligious Engagement in Urban Spaces: Social, Material and Ideological Dimensions*, edited by Julia Ipgrave, 1–15. Cham, Switz.: Springer, 2019.
Isherwood, Lisa, and Marcella Althaus-Reid. "Introduction: Queering Theology." In *The Sexual Theologian: Essays on Sex, God, and Politics*, edited by Marcella Althaus-Reid and Lisa Isherwood, 1–15. Queering Theology. New York: T&T Clark, 2004.
Jagessar, Michael N., and Anthony G. Reddie. "Introduction." In *Postcolonial Black British Theology: New Textures and Themes*, edited by Michael N. Jagessar and Anthony G. Reddie, xii–xvii. Peterborough, UK: Epworth, 2007.
Jantzen, Grace. "Flourishing." In *An A to Z of Feminist Theology*, edited by Lisa Isherwood and Dorothea McEwan, 92–93. Sheffield: Sheffield Academic, 1996.
Jenkins, Simon. *England's Cathedrals*. London: Little, Brown, 2016.
Jennings, Willie James. *After Whiteness: An Education in Belonging*. Theological Education Between the Times. Grand Rapids: Eerdmans, 2020.
———. *The Christian Imagination: Theology and the Origins of Race*. New Haven, CT: Yale University Press, 2010.
Johnson, Keith L. *The Essential Karl Barth: A Reader and Commentary*. Grand Rapids: Baker Academic, 2019.
Jones, Katherine Janiec. "9/11 Changed Things: The (Post-Traumatic) Religious Studies Classroom." In *Post-Traumatic Public Theology*, edited by Stephanie N. Arel and Shelly Rambo, 193–216. New York: Palgrave Macmillan, 2016.
Junker-Kenny, Maureen. *Approaches to Theological Ethics: Sources, Traditions, Visions*. London: T&T Clark, 2019.
———. *Habermas and Theology*. Philosophy and Theology. London: T&T Clark, 2011.
———. *Religion and Public Reason: A Comparison of the Positions of John Rawls, Jürgen Habermas, and Paul Ricoeur*. Praktische Theologie im Wissenschaftsdiskurs 16. Berlin: De Gruyter, 2014.

Justaert, Kristien. "Dancing in the Dark: Marcella Althaus-Reid and Negative Queer Theory." *Feminist Theology* 26 (2018) 229–40.
Kant, Immanuel. *The Conflict of the Faculties*. Translated by Mary Gregor. New York: Abaris, 1979.
———. *"Religion Within the Boundaries of Mere Reason": And Other Writings*. Translated by Allen Wood and George di Giovanni. Cambridge Texts in the History of Philosophy. Cambridge: Cambridge University Press, 2018.
Kim, Sebastian. "Editorial." *IJPT* 1 (2007) 1–4.
———. "Public Theology in the History of Christianity." In *A Companion to Public Theology*, edited by Sebastian Kim and Katie Day, 40–66. Companions to Modern Theology 1. Leiden: Brill, 2017.
———. *Theology in the Public Sphere: Public Theology as a Catalyst for Open Debate*. London: SCM, 2011.
Koopman, Nico. "Public Theology in the Context of Nationalist Ideologies: A South African Example." In *A Companion to Public Theology*, edited by Sebastian Kim and Katie Day, 150–63. Companions to Modern Theology 1. Leiden: Brill, 2017.
———. "Public Theology in (South) Africa: A Trinitarian Approach." *IJPT* 1 (2007) 188–209. https://doi.org/10.1163/156973207X207335.
Küng, Hans. *Global Responsibility: In Search of a New World Ethic*. Translated by John Bowden. London: SCM, 1991.
Küng, Hans, and Karl-Josef Kuschel, eds. *A Global Ethic: The Declaration of the Parliament of World's Religions*. London: SCM, 1993.
Küng, Hans, and Paul Ricoeur. "Les religions, la violence et la paix: Pour une éthique planétaire." *Sens* 5 (1998) 211–30.
Kurien, Christopher. "Globalization: An Economists' Perspective." In *Public Theology for the 21st Century: Essays in Honour of Duncan B. Forrester*, edited by William Storrar et al., 195–212. London: T&T Clark, 2003.
Landman, Christina. "A Public Theology for Intimate Spaces." *IJPT* 5 (2011) 63–77.
Lartey, Emmanuel Y. "After Stephen Lawrence: Characteristics and Agenda for Black Theology in Britain." *Black Theology in Britain: A Journal of Contemporary Praxis* 3 (1990) 80–91.
———. *Postcolonizing God: New Perspectives on Pastoral and Practical Theological Theology*. London: SCM, 2013.
Lee, Hak Joon. "Public Theology." In *Cambridge Companion to Christian Political Theology*, edited by Craig Hovey and Elizabeth Phillips, 44–65. Cambridge Companions to Religion. Cambridge: Cambridge University Press, 2015.
Lee, Samuel. "Living Out Being a Public Church in Selma, Alabama." *IJPT* 13 (2019) 360–73.
Legge, Marilyn J. "'In the Company of God and One Another': Feminist Theo-Ethics, Heterogeneous Politics and Intercultural Churches." In *Public Theology and the Challenge of Feminism*, edited by Anita Monro and Stephen Burns, 46–62. Gender, Theology and Spirituality. London Routledge, 2015.
Leonardo, Zeus. *Race, Whiteness, and Education*. Critical Social Thought. London: Routledge, 2009.
Lethaby, Tim. "Bishops Take the Knee in Wells Cathedral in Solidarity with Black Lives Matter Campaign." *Wells Nub News*, July 16, 2021. https://wells.nub.news/n/bishops-take-the-knee-in-wells-cathedral-in-solidarity-with-black-lives-matter-campaign.

Lewin, Ellen. *Filled with the Spirit: Sexuality, Gender, and Radical Inclusivity in a Black Pentecostal Church Coalition*. Chicago: University of Chicago Press, 2018.

Liljestrand, Johan. "Case Study 1: Maintaining and Transforming Bridging Capital in a Swedish Interreligious Youth Project." In *Interreligious Engagement in Urban Spaces: Social, Material and Ideological Dimensions*, edited by Julia Ipgrave, 29–38. Cham, Switz.: Springer, 2019.

Lindbeck, George A. *The Nature of Doctrine: Religion and Theology in a Postliberal Age*. Philadelphia: Westminster, 1984.

MacIntyre, Alasdair. *After Virtue: A Study in Moral Theory*. Notre Dame, IN: University of Notre Dame Press, 2007.

———. *Three Rival Versions of Moral Enquiry: Encyclopaedia, Genealogy, and Tradition*. Notre Dame, IN: University of Notre Dame Press, 1990.

Manchester Cathedral. "The Bishop, Dean and Canons of Manchester Take the Knee." YouTube, June 20, 2020. https://youtube.com/watch?v=LiD4ylIBAuw&feature=s hares.

———. "Manchester Cathedral Flies the Rainbow Pride Flag." Manchester Cathedral, 2020. https://www.manchestercathedral.org/news-events/news/manchester-cathedral-flies-rainbow-prideflag. Link discontinued.

———. "Manchester Cathedral Strengthens Ties with Portugal." Manchester Cathedral, 2022. https://www.manchestercathedral.org/news-events/news/manchester-cathedral-strengthens-ties-with-portugal/. Link discontinued.

———. "Manchester Cathedral to Fly the Rainbow Flag for Manchester Pride." Manchester Cathedral, 2015. https://www.manchestercathedral.org/news-events/news/manchester-cathedral-to-fly-the-rainbow-flag-for-manchester-pride/. Link discontinued.

Mansbridge, Jane. "The Long Life of Nancy Fraser's 'Rethinking the Public Sphere.'" In *Feminism, Capitalism, and Critique: Essays in Honor of Nancy Fraser*, edited by Banu Bargu and Chiara Bottici, 101–18. Cham, Switz.: Springer, 2017.

Marshall, Aarian. "Churches Unusual: Worship and Broad-Based Organizing in Two Brooklyn Congregations." *IJPT* 6 (2012) 435–66.

Martin, Dale B. *Sex and the Single Savior: Gender and Sexuality in Biblical Interpretation*. Louisville: Westminster John Knox, 2006.

Martin, Francis. "Apology Follows Iftar at Manchester Cathedral." *Church Times*, Apr. 6, 2023. https://www.churchtimes.co.uk/articles/2023/6-april/news/uk/apology-follows-iftar-at-manchester-cathedral.

———. "Synod's Same-Sex Vote: First Reactions." *Church Times*, Feb. 10, 2023. https://www.churchtimes.co.uk/articles/2023/17-february/news/uk/synod-s-same-sex-vote-first-reactions.

Martinez, Gaspar. *Confronting the Mystery of God: Political, Liberation, and Public Theologies*. New York: Continuum, 2001.

Marty, Martin E. *Religion and Republic: The American Circumstance*. Boston: Beacon, 1989.

———. "Two Kinds of Civil Religion." In *American Civil Religion*, edited by Russell Richey and Donald Jones, 139–60. New York: Harper and Row, 1974.

McBride, Jennifer M. *The Church for the World: A Theology of Public Witness*. New York: Oxford University Press, 2012.

———. "Public Discipleship, Constructive Theology, and Grassroots Activism." In *Lived Theology: New Perspectives on Method, Style, and Pedagogy*, edited by Charles Marsh, et al., 208–16. Oxford: Oxford University Press, 2016.

McCann, Dennis P. "A Second Look at Middle Axioms." *Annual of the Society of Christian Ethics* 1 (1981) 73–96.

McElroy, Robert W. *The Search for an American Public Theology: The Contribution of John Courtney Murray*. Mahwah, NJ: Paulist, 1989.

McIntosh, Esther. "'I Met God and She's Black': Racial, Gender and Sexual Equalities in Public Theology." In *A Companion to Public Theology*, edited by Sebastian Kim and Katie Day, 298–324. Companions to Modern Theology 1. Leiden: Brill, 2017.

———. "Issues in Feminist Public Theology." In *Public Theology and the Challenge of Feminism*, edited by Anita Monro and Stephen Burns, 63–74. Gender, Theology and Spirituality. London Routledge, 2015.

Metz, Johannes. *Theology of the World*. London: Burns & Oates, 1969.

Milbank, John. *Theology and Social Theory: Beyond Secular Reason*. Oxford: Blackwell, 1990.

Miller, David. "The Faith Friendly Company: An Idea Whose Time Has Come?" In *Public Theology for a Global Society: Essays in Honor of Max L. Stackhouse*, edited by Deirdre King Hainsworth and Scott R. Paeth, 74–86. Grand Rapids, Eerdmans, 2010.

Mills, C. Wright. "Retrieving Rawls for Racial Justice? A Critique of Tommie Shelby." *Critical Philosophy of Race* 1 (2013) 1–27.

———. *The Sociological Imagination*. New York: Oxford University Press, 1959.

Mohdin, Aamna, and Lucy Campbell. "'So Many People Care!' The Young Britons Whose Lives Were Changed by Black Lives Matter." *Guardian*, Nov. 13, 2020. https://www.theguardian.com/world/2020/nov/13/how-black-lives-matter-has-inspired-a-generation-of-new-uk-activists.

Moltmann, Jürgen. *God for a Secular Society: The Public Relevance of Theology*. London: SCM, 1997.

Monbiot, George. "Boris Johnson Says We Shouldn't Edit Our Past. But Britain Has Been Lying About It for Decades." *Guardian*, June 16, 2020. https://www.theguardian.com/commentisfree/2020/jun/16/boris-johnson-lying-history-britain-empire.

Morris, Jeremy. "The Cathedral, 1983 to the Present." In *Manchester Cathedral: A History of the Collegiate Church and Cathedral, 1421 to the Present*, edited by Jeremy Gregory, 272–309. Manchester: Manchester University Press, 2021.

Moschella, Mary Clark. "Ethnography." In *The Wiley-Blackwell Companion to Practical Theology*, edited by Bonnie J. Miller-McLemore, 224–33. Wiley Blackwell Companions to Religion. Chichester: Wiley-Blackwell, 2012.

Mouffe, Chantal. "The Limits of John Rawls' Pluralism." *Theoria* 56 (2009) 1–14.

Moyaert, Marianne. *Fragile Identities: Towards a Theology of Interreligious Hospitality*. Currents of Encounter 39. Amsterdam: Rodopi, 2011.

———. *In Response to the Religious Other: Ricoeur and the Fragility of Interreligious Encounters*. Studies in the Thought of Paul Ricoeur. Lanham, MD: Lexington, 2014.

———. "Ricoeur and the Wager of Interreligious Ritual Participation." *International Journal of Philosophy and Theology* (2017) 173–99.

Muskett, Judith A. *Shop Window, Flagship, Common Ground: Metaphor in Cathedral and Congregation Studies*. SCM Research. La Vergne, UK: Hymns Ancient & Modern, 2019.
National Initiative for Reconciliation. "The Kairos Document: A Challenge to Action (1985)." NG Kerk in SA: Argief, 1985. https://kerkargief.co.za/doks/bely/GD_Kairos.pdf.
Newitt, Mark. "New Directions in Hospital Chaplaincy: Chaplains—the Church's Embedded Apologists?" *Theology* 117 (2014) 417–25.
Niebuhr, H. Richard. *Christ and Culture*. 50th anniv. ed. San Francisco: Harper One, 2001.
Northern Quota, The. "Carol Service at Manchester Cathedral Raises Money for New LGBT Centre." Northern Quota, Dec. 17, 2019. https://thenorthernquota.org/news/carol-service-manchester-cathedral-raises-money-new-lgbt-centre.
O'Donovan, Oliver. *Resurrection and Moral Order: An Outline for Evangelical Ethics*. 2nd ed. Grand Rapids: Eerdmans, 1994.
Oldham, John. "The Function of the Church in Society." In *The Church and Its Function in Society*, edited by Visser't Hooft and John Oldham, 191–216. Chicago: Clark and Company, 1937.
Ozanne Foundation. *2021 Safeguarding LGBT+ Christians Survey*. Ozanne Foundation, 2021. https://drive.google.com/file/d/14shCbJWoCa_gEyTZWookh-o8_rpfZ4Tl/view.
Paeth, Scott R. *Exodus Church and Civil Society: Public Theology and Social Theory in the Work of Jürgen Moltmann*. Ashgate New Critical Thinking in Religion, Theology and Biblical Studies. Aldershot, UK: Ashgate, 2008.
———. "Public Theology in the Context of Globalization." In *A Companion to Public Theology*, edited by Sebastian Kim and Katie Day, 185–210. Companions to Modern Theology 1. Leiden: Brill, 2017.
Parker, Dylan. "A Public Convergence: Embracing the Congregation as a Place of Difference." *IJPT* 16 (2022) 447–65.
Parliament of the World's Religions. "Declaration of a Global Ethic." *Studies for International Dialogue* 2 (1993) 101–13.
Patta, Raj Bharat. *Subaltern Public Theology: Dalits and the Indian Public Sphere*. Cham, Switz.: Palgrave Macmillan, 2023.
Penney, James. *After Queer Theory: The Limits of Sexual Politics*. London: Pluto, 2014.
Percy, Martyn. "Anglican Cathedrals in a Secular Society: David Martin and the Sociology of English Religion." *Society* 57 (2020) 140–46.
Platten, Stephen. "Introduction—Dreaming Spires?" In *Dreaming Spires? Cathedrals in a New Age*, edited by Stephen Platten and Christopher Lewis, 1–11. London: SPCK, 2006.
Platten, Stephen, and Christopher Lewis. "Introduction." In *Flagships of the Spirit: Cathedrals in Society*, edited by Stephen Platten and Christopher Lewis, xi–xvi. London: Longman and Todd, 1998.
Poole, Eve. *Buying God: Church, Consumerism and Theology*. London: SCM, 2018.
Preston, Ronald H. *Confusions in Christian Social Ethics: Problems for Geneva and Rome*. London: SCM, 1994.
Rahner, Karl. *Foundations of Christian Faith: An Introduction to the Idea of Christianity*. Translated by William V. Dych. Milestones in Catholic Theology. London: Longman and Todd, 1978.

Rauschenbusch, Walter. *A Theology for the Social Gospel*, New York: Macmillan, 1918.
Rawls, John. *Political Liberalism*. Columbia Classics in Philosophy. New York: Columbia University Press, 1996.
———. *A Theory of Justice*. Oxford: Oxford University Press, 1999.
Reddie, Anthony G. *Black Theology in Transatlantic Dialogue*. Black Religion/Womanist Thought/Social Justice. Basingstoke: Palgrave Macmillan, 2006.
———, ed. *Black Theology, Slavery and Contemporary Christianity: 200 Years and No Apology*. London: Routledge, 2010.
———. *Theologising Brexit: A Liberationist and Postcolonial Critique*. Routledge New Critical Thinking in Religion, Theology and Biblical Studies. London: Routledge, 2019.
Reynolds, Terrence. "A Closed Marketplace: Religious Claims in the Public Square." *IJPT* (2014) 201–22.
Ricoeur, Paul. "Cultures: Du deuil à la traduction." *Monde*, May 24, 2004.
———. *Freedom and Nature: The Voluntary and the Involuntary*. Translated by Erazim V. Kohak. Studies in Phenomenology and Existential Philosophy. Evanston, IL: Northwestern University Press, 1996.
———. *From Text to Action: Essays in Hermeneutics, II*. Translated by Kathleen Blamey and John B. Thompson. Studies in Phenomenology and Existential Philosophy. Evanston, IL: Northwestern University Press, 1991.
———. *Hermeneutics and the Human Sciences: Essays on Language, Action, and Interpretation*. Edited and translated by John B. Thompson. Cambridge: Cambridge University Press, 1981.
———. *Interpretation Theory: Discourse and the Surplus of Meaning*. Fort Worth: Texas Christian University Press, 1976.
———. "Metaphor and the Central Problem of Hermeneutics." In *Hermeneutics*, edited by Daniel Frey and Nicola Strickler, 45–64. Vol. 2 of *Writings and Lectures*. Cambridge: Polity, 2013.
———. *Oneself as Another*. Translated by Kathleen Blamey. Chicago: University of Chicago Press, 1992.
———. *On Translation*. Translated by Eileen Brennan. Thinking in Action. London: Routledge, 2006.
———. *Political and Social Essays*. Edited by David Stewart and Joseph Bien. Athens: Ohio University Press, 1974.
———. "The Problem of Double Meaning." In *The Conflict of Interpretations: Essays in Hermeneutics*, edited by Don Ihde, 62–78. Studies in Phenomenology and Existential Philosophy. Evanston, IL: Northwestern University Press, 1974.
———. *Reflections on the Just*. Translated by David Pellauer. Chicago: University of Chicago Press, 2007.
———. "Theonomy." In *The Future of Theology: Essays in Honour of Jürgen Moltmann*, edited by Miroslav Volf et al., 284–97. Grand Rapids: Eerdmans, 1996.
———. *Time and Narrative*. Translated by Kathleen McLaughlin and David Pellauer. 3 vols. Chicago: University of Chicago Press, 1990.
———. "Universal Civilization and National Cultures." In *History and Truth*, 271–84. Studies in Phenomenology and Existential Philosophy. Evanston, IL: Northwestern University Press, 1965.
Roberts, Stephen. "Beyond the Classic: Lady Gaga and Theology in the Wild Public Sphere." *IJPT* 11 (2017) 163–87.

Rowland, Christopher, ed. *The Cambridge Companion to Liberation Theology*. Cambridge Companions to Religion. Cambridge: Cambridge University Press, 2007.

Ruether, Rosemary Radford. "Antisemitism and Christian Theology." In *Auschwitz: Beginning of a New Era? Reflections on the Holocaust*, edited by Eva Fleischner, 79–92. New York: Ktav, 1974.

———. "Christian-Jewish Dialogue: New Interpretations." *ADL Bulletin* 30 (1973) 1–10.

———. *Faith and Fratricide: The Theological Roots of Anti-Semitism*. Eugene, OR: Wipf & Stock, 1996.

Sacks, Jonathan. *The Home We Build Together: Recreating Society*. London: Continuum, 2007.

Santos, Patricia H. "That All May Enjoy Abundant Life: A Theological Vision of Flourishing from the Margins." *Feminist Theology* 25 (2017) 228–39.

Scharen, Christian, and Anna Marie Vigen. "The Ethnographic Turn in Theology and Ethics?" In *Ethnography as Christian Theology and Ethics*, edited by Christian Scharen and Anna Marie Vigen, 28–46. T&T Clark Studies in Social Ethics, Ethnography and Theologies. London: Bloomsbury, 2011.

———. "What Is Ethnography?" In *Ethnography as Christian Theology and Ethics*, edited by Christian Scharen and Anna Marie Vigen, 3–27. T&T Clark Studies in Social Ethics, Ethnography and Theologies. London: Bloomsbury, 2011.

Sherwood, Harriet. "Church and State—an Unhappy Union?" *Guardian*, Oct. 7, 2018. https://www.theguardian.com/global/2018/oct/07/church-and-state-an-unhappy-union.

Shrimad Rajchandraji Mission Dharampur. "About Shrimad Rajchandraji." SRMD, n.d. https://www.srmd.org/en-US/shrimad-rajchandraji/.

Siddique, Haroon, and Clea Skopeliti. "BLM Protesters Topple Statue of Bristol Slave Trader Edward Colston." *Guardian*, June 7, 2020. https://www.theguardian.com/uk-news/2020/jun/07/blm-protesters-topple-statue-of-bristol-slave-trader-edward-colston.

Sikka, Sonia. "On Translating Religious Reasons: Rawls, Habermas, and the Quest for a Neutral Public Sphere." *Review of Politics* 78 (2016) 91–116.

Simms, Karl. *Paul Ricoeur*. Edited by Robert Eaglestone. Routledge Critical Thinkers. London: Routledge, 2003.

Simonÿ, Charlotte, et al. "A Ricoeur-Inspired Approach to Interpret Participant Observations and Interviews." *Global Qualitative Nursing Research* 5 (2018) 1–10.

Skeie, Geir. "Introduction: Interreligious Dialogue and Social Capital." In *Interreligious Engagement in Urban Spaces: Social, Material and Ideological Dimensions*, edited by Julia Ipgrave, 19–28. Cham, Switz.: Springer, 2019.

Slee, Nichola. "Speaking with the Dialects, Inflections and Rhythms of Our Own Unmistakable Voices: Feminist Theology as Public Theology." In *Public Theology and the Challenge of Feminism*, edited by Anita Monro and Stephen Burns, 15–24. Gender, Theology and Spirituality. London Routledge, 2015.

Smit, Dirk J. "Does it Matter? On Whether There Is Method in the Madness." In *A Companion to Public Theology*, edited by Sebastian Kim and Katie Day, 67–92. Companions to Modern Theology 1. Leiden: Brill, 2017.

Smith, Christian. *The Bible Made Impossible: Why Biblicism Is Not a Truly Evangelical Reading of Scripture*. Grand Rapids: Brazos, 2012.

Smith, James K. A. *Awaiting the King: Reforming Public Theology*. Cultural Liturgies 3. Grand Rapids: Baker Academic, 2017.

———. "Beyond Creation and Natural Law: An Evangelical Public Theology." Comment, Mar. 26, 2015. https://comment.org/beyond-creation-and-natural-law-an-evangelical-public-theology/.

———. *Desiring the Kingdom: Worship, Worldview and Cultural Formation*. Cultural Liturgies 1. Grand Rapids: Baker Academic, 2009.

———. *The Fall of Interpretation: Philosophical Foundations for a Creational Hermeneutic*. 2nd ed. Grand Rapids: Baker Academic, 2012.

Smith, Maddy. "Manchester Cathedral Location Shoot Event." Born, n.d. https://born.uk.com/manchester-cathedral-shoot/.

Special Procedures of the United Nations Human Rights Council. "UN Experts Condemn UK Commission on Race and Ethnic Disparities Report." OHCR, Apr. 19, 2021. https://www.ohchr.org/en/press-releases/2021/04/un-experts-condemn-uk-commission-race-and-ethnic-disparities-report.

Stackhouse, Max L. *Globalization and Grace*. Vol. 4 of *God and Globalization*. Theology for the 21st Century. New York: Continuum, 2007.

———. "Public Theology and Ethical Judgment." *Theology Today* 54 (1997) 165–79.

———. "Reflections on 'Universal Absolutes.'" In *Shaping Public Theology: Selections from the Writings of Max L. Stackhouse*, edited by Scott R. Paeth et al., 154–67. Grand Rapids: Eerdmans, 2014.

———. "Towards a Theology for the New Social Gospel." In *Shaping Public Theology: Selections from the Writings of Max L. Stackhouse*, edited by Scott R. Paeth et al., 3–20. Grand Rapids: Eerdmans, 2014.

Stiver, Dan R. *Ricoeur and Theology*. Philosophy and Theology. London: T&T Clark, 2012.

———. *Theology After Ricoeur: New Directions in Hermeneutical Theology*. Westminster: John Knox, 2001.

Tanner, Kathryn. *Jesus, Humanity, and the Trinity: A Systematic Theology in Brief*. Minneapolis: Fortress, 2001.

———. *Theories of Culture: A New Agenda for Theology*. Minneapolis: Fortress, 1997.

Taylor, Charles. *A Secular Age*. Cambridge, MA: Belknap, 2007.

Temple, William. *Christianity and Social Order*. Harmondsworth, UK: Penguin, 1942.

———. *Religious Experience*. Cambridge: Clarke & Co, 1987.

Theos, and The Grubb Institute. *Spiritual Capital: The Present and Future of English Cathedrals*. London: Theos and The Grubb Institute, 2012.

Thomson, Heather. "Public Theology and the Politics of Interpretation: A Feminist Reading." In *Public Theology and the Challenge of Feminism*, edited by Anita Monro and Stephen Burns, 35–45. Gender, Theology and Spirituality. London Routledge, 2015.

———. "Stars and Compasses: Hermeneutical Guides for Public Theology." *IJPT* 2 (2008) 258–76.

Tillich, Paul. *Systematic Theology*. 3 vols. London: Clowes and Sons, 1953.

Tombs, David. "Public Theology and Reconciliation." In *A Companion to Public Theology*, edited by Sebastian Kim and Katie Day, 119–49. Companions to Modern Theology 1. Leiden: Brill, 2017.

Tonstad, Linn Marie. *God and Difference: The Trinity, Sexuality, and the Transformation of Finitude*. Gender, Theology and Spirituality. London: Taylor & Francis, 2016.

———. "The Limits of Inclusion: Queer Theology and Its Others." *Theology & Sexuality* (2015) 1–19.

———. *Queer Theology: Beyond Apologetics*. Cascade Companions. Eugene, OR: Cascade, 2018.

Townes, Emilie M. *Womanist Ethics and the Cultural Production of Evil*. Black Religion/Womanist Thought/Social Justice. New York: Palgrave Macmillan, 2006.

Tracy, David. *The Analogical Imagination: Christian Theology and the Culture of Pluralism*. New York: Crossroads, 1981.

———. *Blessed Rage for Order: The New Pluralism in Theology*. New York: Seabury, 1975.

———. "Defending the Public Character of Theology." *Christian Century* 98 (1981) 350–56.

———. "Is There Hope for the Public Realm? Conversation as Interpretation." *Social Research* 65 (1998) 597–609.

———. "Lindbeck's New Program for Theology: A Reflection." *Thomist* 49 (1985) 460–72.

———. *On Naming the Present: Reflections on God, Hermeneutics, and Church*. Concilium. Maryknoll, NY: Orbis, 1994.

———. "Three Kinds of Publicness in Public Theology." *IJPT* (2014) 330–34.

Tripp, Gregory, et al. *Social Capital*. New York: Nova Science, 2009.

Tutu, Desmond. "*God Is Not a Christian" and Other Provocations*. Edited by Allen John. London: Rider, 2011.

Urquidez, Alberto G. "Reply to My Critics: (Re-)Defining Racism: A Philosophical Analysis." *Ethical Theory and Moral Practice* 24 (2021) 679–98.

Van Den Torren, Bennovan. *Christian Apologetics as Cross-Cultural Dialogue*. London: Continuum, 2011.

Van Maanen, John. *Tales of the Field: On Writing Ethnography*. Chicago Guides to Writing, Editing, and Publishing. Chicago: University of Chicago Press, 1988.

Viftrup, Lars, and Dan Grabowski. "The Third Space Between Church and City: Coproduction in a Danish Municipality." *IJPT* 15 (2021) 101–17.

Voce, Antonio. "'Nine Points Up on Europe': Data Shows UK Increase in LGBTQ harassment." *Guardian*, June 26, 2020. https://www.theguardian.com/world/ng-interactive/2020/jun/26/nine-points-up-on-europe-data-shows-uk-increase-in-lgbtq-harassment.

Volf, Miroslav. *Exclusion and Embrace: A Theological Exploration of Identity, Otherness, and Reconciliation*. Nashville: Abingdon, 1996.

———. *A Public Faith: How Followers of Christ Should Serve the Common Good*. Grand Rapids: Brazos, 2011.

———. "Theology, Meaning, and Power." In *The Future of Theology: Essays in Honor of Jürgen Moltmann*, edited by Miroslav Volf et al., 98–113. Grand Rapids: Eerdmans, 1996.

Walford, Geoffrey. "The Practice of Writing Ethnographic Field Notes." *Ethnography and Education* 4 (2009) 117–30.

Walton, Heather. *Writing Methods in Theological Reflection*. London: SCM, 2014.

———. "You Have to Say You Cannot Speak: Feminist Reflections Upon Public Theology." *IJPT* 4 (2010) 21–36.

Ward, Lee. "Rekindling 'Radical Democratic Embers': Rawls and Habermas on Public Reason." *European Legacy, Toward New Paradigms* 24 (2019) 819–39.

Welby, Justin. *Reimagining Britain: Foundations for Hope*. London: Bloomsbury Continuum, 2018.
Wells, Samuel. "Stanley Hauerwas' Theological Ethics in Eschatological Perspective." *SJT* 53 (2000) 431–48.
Wepener, Cas, and Hendrik J. C. Pieterse. "Angry Preaching: A Grounded Theory Analysis from South Africa." *IJPT* 12 (2018) 401–15.
Wijsen, Frans. "New Wine in Old Wineskins? Intercultural Theology Instead of Missiology." In *Towards an Intercultural Theology: Essays in Honour of J. A. B. Jongneel*, edited by Martha Frederiks et al., 39–54. Missiological Classics 9. Zoetermeer, Neth.: Meinema, 2003.
Williams, Hattie. "Church Leaders Join the Voices Against Racism." *Church Times*, June 12, 2020. https://www.churchtimes.co.uk/articles/2020/12-june/news/uk/church-of-england-leaders-join-the-voices-against-racism.
Winkler, Kathrin. "The Provocations of Contact Zones: Spaces for Negotiating Post-Migrant Identities." *IJPT* 16 (2022) 23–38.
Winkler, Tanja. "Super-Sizing Community Development Initiatives: The Case of Hillbrow's Faith Sector." *IJPT* 2 (2008) 47–69.
Woodhead, Linda. "Introduction." In *Religion and Change in Modern Britain*, edited by Linda Woodhead and Rebecca Catto, 1–33. London: Routledge, 2012.
Wright, Jenny Anne. "With Whose Voice and What Language? Public Theology in a Mediated Public." *IJPT* 9 (2015) 156–75.
Yates, Melissa. "Postmetaphysical Thinking." In *Jürgen Habermas*, edited by Barbara Fultner, 35–53. Key Concepts. Durham: Routledge, 2014.
Zabatiero, Júlio Paulo Tavares. "From the Sacristy to the Public Square: The Public Character of Theology." *IJPT* 6 (2012) 56–69.
Zachau, Elga. "Max Stackhouse: A Global Christian." In *Public Theology for a Global Society: Essays in Honor of Max L. Stackhouse*, edited by Deirdre King Hainsworth and Scott R. Paeth, 231–37. Grand Rapids: Eerdmans, 2010.

www.ingramcontent.com/pod-product-compliance
Lightning Source LLC
Chambersburg PA
CBHW070253230426
43664CB00014B/2523